STOP,
IN THE NAME OF
GOD

STOP, IN THE NAME OF GOD

WHY HONORING THE SABBATH WILL TRANSFORM YOUR LIFE

CHARLIE KIRK

STOP, IN THE NAME OF GOD:
WHY HONORING THE SABBATH WILL TRANSFORM YOUR LIFE

Printed in the United States

WINNING TEAM PUBLISHING

ISBN: 979-8-218-77792-0

For more information on this and our other titles, please visit our website:
www.WinningPublishing.com

First edition: December 2025

1 3 5 7 9 10 8 6 4 2

This book is dedicated to Dennis Prager.

Your life's work brought me to honoring the Sabbath.
As a result, I wrote this book.

Thank you, Dennis, for all you have done for humanity.
God bless you.

CONTENTS

FOREWORD BY ERIKA KIRK

When Charlie first spoke of writing a book on the Sabbath, I felt a quiet joy rise within me. Out of all the topics the world might expect from him—politics, culture, or the crises of our day—this was not the obvious choice. And yet, it was the right one. I knew he had been entrusted with a message for weary souls. For beneath the constant hum of urgency and the endless clamor of life, he discerned what so many overlook: the absence of true rest. Not the shallow relief of sleeping late or silencing a phone, but the holy rest that comes only when one surrenders the rush, sits before the Lord, and remembers that He is God.

Charlie's days were full to the brim. He bore a weight of responsibility that few could comprehend. Charlie hosted three hours of live radio each day, traveled more than three hundred days a year, visited college and high school campuses every week, and passionately shared the Gospel at churches around the country. Layered on top of this was the sacred calling of being a husband and a father, roles he never treated lightly. By all appearances, there should have been no margin left. And yet, there was. Charlie understood that human strength alone could never sustain such a life. He anchored himself in the Word of God. He embraced the Sabbath not as an antiquated ritual, but as a bold confession of faith and a declaration that the world is upheld by God's hand, not man's striving.

My husband's conviction was not born in a moment, nor did it appear without root. From the earliest days of our marriage, I watched him earnestly pursue what it meant to walk in obedience to God. He was well acquainted with the lure of busyness and the subtle tyranny of distraction, as we all are, and he understood the quiet devastation they bring to families, to communities, and even to a nation. Honoring the Sabbath became his defiance against that lie. It was his declaration that a man's value is not measured by his output and productivity level, but by his surrender. In keeping the Sabbath, Charlie was saying with his life: "God, You are enough . . . -and because You are enough, I need not carry the weight of a world that was never mine to hold."

This book is the fruit of that conviction. In *Stop, in the Name of God*, you will hear Charlie's voice inviting you to recover what our hurried culture has nearly erased. His desire was for every generation, young and old alike, to rediscover the Sabbath as he did: not as a burden to bear, but as a gift to receive. A sacred rhythm meant to draw us nearer to God, to steady our hearts with His peace, and to restore our strength for the battles to which He has called us.

I knew Charlie so deeply, in a way no one else could. That is why I can say with certainty: these pages are not theory for him, they are testimony. The words you hold in your hands were the convictions he lived that were written on his heart. Week after week, no matter how crowded his calendar or how heavy the demands, he made room on Saturdays to step back. He had an elevated intentionality to be present with our family, to unplug from the world, to open his Bible, and to bow his head in prayer. In full transparency, there were moments when responsibilities pressed in and work could not wait, and he'd switch his Sabbath day to a different day of the week. But perfection was never the aim. His desire was obedience. And in that obedience, he was learning week by week to quiet the clamor of the world and to trust the God who holds it all.

Looking back now, I see this book as one of Charlie's most enduring gifts to the world. He did not know how brief his time on earth would be—none of us did—but the truths written in this book are not bound by time. They will outlive us all, as will the legacy of his faith. In public, Charlie was bold and unflinching in his defense of truth; at home, he was tender and incredibly loving. He fought fiercely for freedom, yet he also shepherded hearts with gentleness. He lived at a relentless pace, but he also knew the sacred value of stillness. And through it all, his gaze was fixed on eternity. More than anything, he longed for others to set their eyes there, too.

There is no doubt in my heart that Charlie left this world doing what he loved most: standing firm for truth, for faith, for family, and for America. The mark he made will not fade; it is etched into countless lives and stories. Though he is no longer beside us, I find deep comfort in knowing his voice still carries on.

Through this book, his podcast, his videos, and every testimony, Charlie continues to speak. He continues to point us back to what matters most. He reminds us that our lives are not our own; they belong wholly to God. And he shows us that the truest freedom is never won by endless striving, but by surrendering our will to the One who holds every plan in His hands.

If you knew Charlie, you know he could never be content to stand on the sidelines. He was a man of action, of courage, of pressing forward no matter the cost. But he also understood something deeper, that action without a firm foundation is hollow. That is why this book is so vital. It reveals the bedrock beneath everything he did: an unshakable faith in the promises of God and a life ordered by the truth of His Word.

As Charlie's widow, I write these words through tears, yet also with a steady hope. My prayer is that you (and one day my two precious children) will not only read these pages but weave them into the fabric of your life. That you will let one of Charlie's final messages quiet your hurried steps and lead you nearer to God. And I ask that you honor his memory in the way he longed for most: not with applause or recognition, but with a life marked by simple, faithful obedience to the Lord.

Thank you for opening these pages, for allowing Charlie's words and convictions to take root in your own life, and for helping to carry forward the legacy of a man who poured himself out for his Savior, his family, and his country.

My prayer is that, through this book, you will discover what Charlie discovered in the Sabbath: a holy rest that steadies the heart, renews the soul, and gives strength for the road that lies ahead.

May God bless you . . . and now go make Heaven crowded.

—Erika Kirk

PROLOGUE

In this book, I intend to persuade you of something that may, at first, seem quaint, old-fashioned, or even unnecessary: that the Sabbath is not merely a helpful tradition or a cultural relic—it is essential to the flourishing of the human soul.

I will define the Sabbath not just in doctrinal terms but in existential ones. We will explore its origin—not in history, but in eternity; not in law, but in creation. I will show you how to incorporate it not as a weekly burden but as a life-giving rhythm that reorders your time, renews your mind, and restores your humanity. And yes, we will address the pressing and often polarizing question among Christians: *Are we still bound to observe the Sabbath?* My answer will not be glib or conveniently theological—it will be drawn from the deep well of Scripture, history, and the lived wisdom of saints and sages across centuries.

Even if you are not (yet) a follower of Jesus Christ, I implore you to read on. This book is not written for the religiously initiated alone. It is written for the exhausted parent, the anxious student, the burned-out executive, the soul-numbed scroller. This is not a suggestion manual or a spiritual upgrade for those with spare time. This is a manifesto against the machine of modern life. It is a call to war against the endless noise and the ceaseless hurry that have slowly robbed you of your joy, your wonder, and your rest. I am not writing to affirm your lifestyle; I am writing to interrupt it. I am writing to cut at the root of some of the deepest wounds in our society—disconnection, anxiety, spiritual fatigue, moral confusion—and to offer you a concrete, ancient, and divine practice that can begin to heal them.

The Sabbath is not merely a religious tradition for observant Jews or pious Christians. It is a spiritual technology woven into the fabric of creation itself. Long before Moses received the Ten Commandments, before Israelites ever wandered the desert, before there was synagogue or church, there was Sabbath. *"And on the seventh day God finished His work that He had done, and He rested"* (Genesis 2:2). The Sabbath is not man made—it is God breathed. It is not legalism—it is liberation. And in rejecting it, we have not just dismissed a day—we have denied a divine pattern, and we are now reaping the consequences. As America has abandoned the Sabbath, we have watched nearly every major marker of health—emotional, spiritual, communal—begin to fail. We are more productive and less peaceful, more connected digitally and more isolated relationally. We are overstimulated, undernourished, distracted, discontent, and desperately lonely. We are, in many ways, a Sabbathless people: wandering, overworked, and longing—without even knowing for what.

I have no qualms about this book. My mission in writing this is very simple:

> **I desire to bring all humanity back to God's design to rest for an entire day. To cease working, to STOP, in the name of GOD.**

This book is an invitation to return. Not to a law, but to a life. Not to a calendar restriction, but to a soul restoration. You were not made to live at the speed of your notifications. You were made to know God, to walk with Him, to delight in the world He made, and to rest in His sufficiency. The Sabbath is not the fringe—it is the frame. It holds life together. Let me show you why.

INTRODUCTION

It was summer 2021. By all objective measures, my life was in perfect order: I had recently married that last May; I was traveling the country with my new, beautiful wife, Erika; I was running Turning Point USA. Life on the outside was as good as it gets.

But, inside, there was a battle brewing. I was fatigued, tired, and spiritually confused. Since spring 2020, I was in nonstop hyperaggressive fight mode. The lockdowns (which I spoke out about from the very beginning) only intensified after Joe Biden became president. I found myself in the trenches in summer 2021 looking for a respite, a lifeline.

I found myself at the Baccarat Hotel in New York City just a few days before the Fourth of July. My mental clarity was dulled, and I was physically exhausted and seeking advice. After a long day of TV interviews and donor meetings, I had a late lunch with a dear friend and Turning Point USA board member, David Engelhardt.

David is a very wise man, pastor of Kings' Church in New York City, and someone I am able to confide in when things get tough.

I told him I was hitting a wall, I had more obligations than time, and I was drinking eight cups of coffee a day just to stay afloat. I went to him looking for a sympathetic ear and more hopefully a piece of advice that could get me out of the rut I was in.

David heard all my concerns and listened intently, internalized it all, and plainly said, "Are you honoring the Sabbath?"

I laughed. I am a close friend and student of Dennis Prager, and for years I heard him brag about how he honors the Sabbath and how it's the best part of his week. At times I found myself almost jealous of Dennis while listening to his *Fireside Chats*. "I am too busy for that!" I would say to myself when Dennis would air his monologues touting the biblical and moral importance of honoring the Sabbath. Over time, I secretly had "Shabbat Envy."

I replied to David, "No, I really don't have time for that. I am running three different companies and have three hundred people on payroll. I have to raise $50 million a year and do three hours of radio a day. I will honor God by working harder, not by resting for a day."

David then paused and rebutted, "I think you need to drop everything for a day. God will honor that. Look at it as a test of your faith."

I continued to argue with him, but deep down I felt a strong conviction of the Holy Spirit. I knew he had struck a chord. I knew he had a special word for me and that it was my flesh resisting it.

"Do you mean just stopping?" I muttered.

"Try it for a month. See what it does for your life. Jesus told us if we love him to follow his commands."

We changed the subject, but looking back many years ago, I couldn't tell you a single other thing we spoke about that night. I went up to my hotel room and started finding every single Bible verse that mentioned the Sabbath. I grew obsessed with the idea of stopping everything for a day and challenging myself to live by it.

The first Saturday was extremely challenging. The Bible is very clear: For six days you shall work, and on the seventh day you shall rest. Six days for work—that is it. Get everything you need in six days, because the seventh day is for God and to rest.

Therefore, right then I decided to begin shutting off my phone on Friday night (why Friday, I will explain later in this book).

The first Saturday I woke up around 7:30 a.m. scrambling to check my text messages, frenetic and worried that I might be missing someone or something critical. "What if President Trump calls me and my phone is off?" "What if my parents need to call me about an emergency?" "What if something of high importance happens at Turning Point and I can't be reached?" These questions started swirling in my head, creating a sense of heightened anxiety and dread. Finally, sundown came, and I sprinted to turn my phone back on—just to see I had only a few texts from people that could easily have waited till Sunday.

The first month was a grind, but eventually I released myself from the death grip that modernity commands you hold over your time. The lessons I have derived from honoring the Sabbath are limitless, the most profound of which started me on this journey to write this book.

The more I started to appreciate the Sabbath, the more I realized the great need to share its wondrous beauty with the world. I hold this belief very clearly: If the Sabbath can change my life, it can change everyone's life.

What I have grown to learn is that the Sabbath is the key that unlocks a civil society and a free people, and it could be the secret answer to restore self-government in America.

In this book I will further explain my personal journey, where the Sabbath came from, whether we are still tied to it as Christians, the transformational importance of Genesis 1:1, why tyrants hate the Sabbath, the beauty of stopping when everyone tells you to keep going, and so much more.

Throughout these pages I frequently appeal to and quote Scripture from the Holy Bible. In my life, I hold the Bible as the ultimate authority, drawing from its wisdom to guide my thoughts and actions. I recognize that not everyone who reads this book shares this belief, and I deeply respect that. However, I invite you to pause and reflect on a question I pose to you personally: *By what moral standard—whether it be a book, creed, song, or philosophy—do you live your life?* Every person lives by some guiding principle, and for me, it is the Bible and the truths it imparts.

The Bible is not merely a collection of ancient writings; it is the most authenticated piece of literature in history. No archaeological discovery has ever contradicted the truths found within its pages. The wisdom contained in the Bible remains as relevant today as it was when it was first written, if not more so. Its history, with its vivid portrayal of past events and its prophecies about the future, has shaped the foundation of Western civilization. Indeed, it is the Bible that has built the West, and it is the Bible that will ultimately guide and restore it. Its message is timeless, offering principles of justice, morality, and grace that transcend cultural and historical boundaries. For those who seek truth, guidance, and purpose, the Bible stands as a beacon—a guide that continues to illuminate the path for those willing to follow it.

The Bible is more than a sacred text; it is a living testament to the divine truth that transcends time and culture. Throughout history, it has withstood countless challenges—from persecutions and translations to skepticism and secularism—yet it remains unchanged in its essence. Its teachings have molded societies, inspired movements, and provided solace to the weary. The Bible's ability to speak to the human condition, with all its struggles and triumphs, is unparalleled. It offers answers to the deepest questions of life: Who are we? Why are we here? What is our purpose?

The moral framework it provides is not bound by the limitations of human ideology or fleeting trends; it is rooted in a higher order of justice, love, and truth, serving as both a mirror to reflect our imperfections and a guide to help us overcome them.

Moreover, the Bible's influence on the Western world cannot be overstated. It has shaped the laws, ethics, and cultural norms that define modern society. Concepts such as individual rights, justice, mercy, and the inherent dignity of all people find their foundations in biblical principles. Even in a world that often turns away from faith, the echoes of biblical wisdom are woven into the very fabric of our legal systems and moral compass. As civilization faces growing challenges, it is not merely political or philosophical ideologies that will save us, but a return to the timeless truths found in the Bible. Its message offers a pathway to renewal, not only for individuals but for entire societies, calling us back to a moral order that can heal the divisions of our age and restore meaning to a world desperately in need of it.

Even if you believe you already know what is contained in the Bible, I encourage you to continue reading. I can guarantee that as you delve deeper into its pages, you will encounter something that causes you to pause, reflect, and walk away with a newfound reverence and respect for those of us who submit to its teachings as the ultimate authority. The Bible is not merely a collection of ancient writings; it is a living, breathing testament to divine truth that offers new insights with every reading. Whether you are familiar with its stories or just beginning your exploration, there is always more to uncover—layers of wisdom, depth, and understanding that are often revealed only through continued study and reflection. For those who live by Scripture, it is not just a guide for moral living but a transformative force that shapes our worldview, strengthens our faith, and grounds us in timeless truth.

One of the core contentions of this book is that all around us we are promised "NEW!" And yet, "NEW" doesn't make us happier, more joyful, closer to God, or more connected. Instead of looking for a NEW cryptocurrency or car to make us happy, maybe we need to look at things that have lasted, that have staying power.

How often do you have something in front of you that is five thousand years old, cherished by those who practice it, God-given free of charge, and has unlimited upsides and virtually ZERO downsides?

We all see and are observing the issues with modernity. The crisis is clear, and the danger is present in front of us. The way forward for us as a people might be to take a long step backward, to creation. In the beginning is where we will begin.

Chapter 1

GENESIS 1:1

"In the beginning, God created the heavens and the earth."

Look around you for a moment. Maybe you see trees intricately woven together, their leaves trembling in the breeze. Perhaps you gaze upward into a vast, blue sky with seemingly limitless expanse. Or maybe your eyes rest on something as ordinary as your own feet. Whatever your vantage point, you are observing an effect—evidence of a cause. And that cause, of course, is creation.

Two dominant theological worldviews currently compete in the West, cutting deeper than denominational differences between Christianity, Islam, Judaism, or other religious traditions. Before we even enter the realm of doctrinal distinctions—before we ask whether the God of the Bible is the one true God—we must first confront what I call the **"Western Binary."** Fundamentally, there are only two possible explanations for our existence:

1. You are created. You are designed. Your life has purpose and intentionality. You are not a mistake—you are a miracle.

2. You are a mistake. You are the product of random mutations and molecular coincidences, a "happy accident." Your consciousness, agency, and emotions are simply the result of neurons firing in just the right pattern over the course of millions of years. You are not a miracle—you are merely the most advanced arrangement of carbon in the room.

These are the two choices facing the modern West. Increasingly, people are choosing the second option as their dominant worldview. Over the past forty years, we've witnessed a sharp rise in secularism and atheism. Their appeal is simple and seductive: If there is no God, then no one has authority over you. If there is no divine order, then there is no moral obligation—no higher law to challenge your desires or instruct your will. In the absence of God, human autonomy becomes the ultimate value, and personal choice reigns supreme.

This trend is not theoretical—it is measurable. According to the Pew Research Center, the percentage of American adults identifying as religiously unaffiliated ("nones") surged from just 5 percent in the 1970s to around 30 percent by 2021. Among younger generations, the numbers are even more stark: Over 40 percent of millennials and Gen Zers claim no religious affiliation at all. In Europe, the picture is more dramatic still. In countries like Sweden and the United Kingdom, belief in God has dropped below 50 percent, and regular religious participation is often in the single digits. A 2018 Gallup survey found that church membership in the United States fell below the majority for the first time in recorded history, dropping to 47 percent—a decline mirrored across virtually every Western democracy.

Why this decline? Part of the reason is trust in science and technology—tools which have, ironically, delivered unprecedented convenience but not contentment. But at a deeper level, the turn toward secularism is about **control**. The very idea that *"there is a God and He wants you to live a certain way"* is now considered offensive—"judgmental" or "harsh." In a culture obsessed with self-acceptance and personal freedom, divine authority is viewed not as liberating, but as oppressive. Our modern gods are autonomy, affirmation, and endless choice.

And yet, if you are among the few in the modern West who still believe we are created—that our existence is not a cosmic fluke, but a divine intention—then your journey begins not in philosophy or politics but in **Genesis 1:1**.

The modern world is afflicted with a growing spiritual disease: a kind of metaphysical emptiness, a **tumor of hopelessness and isolation**. We are materially rich and spiritually impoverished. If you examine nearly every major crisis in contemporary Western culture—depression, anxiety, addiction, loneliness, suicide—the common thread is **disconnection**: from others, from purpose, from rest, and ultimately from God. The further we drift from the Creator, the more fragmented we become. As secularism spreads, the soul shrinks.

Data supports what theology has always known. Data from the US Census Bureau's Household Pulse Survey (January–April 2024) indicates that anxiety and depression rates have stayed at double the pre-COVID levels. Meanwhile, a 2021 Harvard Graduate School of Education report found that **61 percent of young adults aged 18–25** reported feeling "serious loneliness." And prescription rates for antidepressants, antianxiety medication, and sleep aids are at historic highs. Our technological marvels have not quieted our souls; they have only amplified the noise.

But secularism doesn't leave a vacuum—it creates counterfeits. As belief in the God of the Bible has diminished, people have not stopped being spiritual. Instead, they've invented **pseudoreligions**: political ideologies, wellness cults, self-help mysticism, climate absolutism, and digital tribalism. These systems come complete with dogmas, rituals, prophets, and excommunications—but without grace, forgiveness, or redemption. They mimic the shape of religion while denying the source of truth. They offer belonging without transformation, identity without accountability.

Which brings us to the Sabbath.

The Sabbath is the oldest continuous spiritual celebration in human history. Most people, even those raised in religious traditions, do not fully grasp this. And I will emphasize it throughout this book: The Sabbath is not primarily a legal command—it is a *cosmic declaration*. It is a weekly, embodied confession that we are created, not accidental. That there is a Creator, and He is not us.

To keep the Sabbath is to resist the pull of secular chaos. It is to stop, to rest, and to say with your body what your mouth may forget to say: *"I believe in Genesis 1:1."* The Sabbath calls you to lay down your illusion of self-sufficiency and remember that your life is not your own—it is a gift. If you believe that your existence was designed, not random, then the Sabbath becomes more than a rest day—it becomes a weekly act of praise. A ritual rhythm of gratitude. A declaration of allegiance.

Upon a closer reading of Genesis 1:1 and the creation story, we learn six major things about God, his nature, and our relationship to the God of the Bible. All these lessons were instrumental in lay-ing the foundation of the West, and all these truths are celebrated weekly during the Sabbath. At the end of the list, I hope you will pause and internalize just how significant Genesis 1:1 is for you, our world, humanity, and most applicably to this book, how you spend your time.

I've built a career on explaining complex ideas—millions follow me for clarity on the greatest and most pressing issues of our time. And yet, even with all that experience, I find it difficult to fully express the weight and wonder of Genesis 1:1. Those ten words—*"In the beginning, God created the heavens and the earth"*—did not merely begin a book; they launched a worldview. They shattered ancient chaos myths, introduced a rational universe governed by order, and laid the philosophical foundation upon which Western civilization was built. Every assumption we make about meaning, matter, morality, and mind traces back to this verse. It didn't just explain the world—it made understanding the world possible.

Before I go any further on this topic, I must give credit to Dennis Prager for his numerous teachings through the decades that help consolidate this list of things we learn about God and the implications of Genesis 1:1 in this list:

Number One: Everything Came About by God

This is worth emphasizing. The first statement of the Bible is so massive, so theologically and philosophically rich, that it must not be skimmed. *"In the beginning, God created the heavens and the earth."* It means that all that is good—light, beauty, order, reason, life itself—flows from a God who is not partially good or mostly good but who is goodness itself. This foundational truth asserts that behind all existence is a divine will, a moral intelligence, a benevolent Creator. It means, among many other things, that **everything has a purpose.**

The ancient Greeks had a powerful word for this concept: **Telos**. It is where we get the word **telescope**—an instrument for seeing the distant purpose or end. *Telos* means "goal," "end," or "final cause." Aristotle used it to explain that all things move toward some end, some fulfillment of their nature. The Bible not only affirms this, it roots it in the very act of creation. If everything was made by God, then everything has telos—from the stars in the sky to the smallest thoughts you think. You are not a random collection of cells drifting through a cold, meaningless cosmos. Your life has aim. Your story has structure. Your breath is borrowed, but your purpose is eternal.

Let me repeat the point again, precisely because it is so profound: **You are not a mistake.** Every action you take, every question you ask, every moment you live matters. That means your moral choices matter. Your affections matter. Your creativity, your sorrow, your longing—they are not echoes in an empty void. They are responses to a reality that was made by a God who made *you.* Dwell on that for a moment. Let it settle. What a sharp, luminous repudiation this is to the creeping fog of **nihilism** that has blanketed the Western world.

Over the last century, numerous ideological toxins have worked to erode our collective moral code. Of all these poisons, **nihilism** is the most corrosive. It is not simply a rejection of religion—it is a rejection of meaning itself. Nihilism teaches that there is no moral order, no objective truth, no reason for our existence. It says we are accidents and that nothing we do ultimately matters. The fruit of this belief is despair—and we are watching that despair blossom across a generation.

To define it plainly: **Nihilism** is the belief that life is fundamentally meaningless. It denies any higher order, any transcendent moral framework, or any ultimate purpose. It is the ideology of the abyss. Friedrich Nietzsche, one of its most famous and complex advocates, wrote, *"God is dead . . . and we have killed him."* For Nietzsche, the death of God was not cause for celebration—it was a catastrophe. Without God, he predicted, society would descend into moral chaos, and humanity would need to invent its own values in the face of overwhelming meaninglessness. He later warned, *"He who has a why to live can bear almost any how,"* but nihilism leaves no "why"—only the howling winds of randomness and despair.

Jean-Paul Sartre, another key figure in the philosophy of meaninglessness, wrote, *"Man is nothing else but what he makes of himself. . . . There is no human nature, since there is no God to conceive it."* For Sartre, meaning was not found, it was invented—but the burden of self-creation without any foundation leads not to liberation, but to profound anxiety. Without a Creator, you must fabricate your identity, your morality, and your destiny from the dust.

And we are now seeing the psychological and societal consequences of this belief system play out in real time. A 2023 report from the Centers for Disease Control and Prevention (CDC) revealed that over **57 percent of teenage girls** in the United States reported feeling "persistently sad or hopeless," the highest rate ever recorded. Suicide is now the s**econd leading cause of death** for people aged **15–24**, according to the National Institute of Mental Health. And a Harvard Youth Poll from 2022 found that **52 percent of young Americans** think our country's democracy is either "in trouble" or "failing," and nearly half say they feel more fear than hope about the future.

It is one of the great ironies of our age that we are wealthier, more technologically advanced, and more medically capable than any generation in human history—yet our children are sicker in mind and soul than ever before. In a world where material abundance is everywhere—where food is plentiful, information is instant, and comfort is the default setting—we are watching a generation implode under the weight of despair. Suicide rates among teens have surged, anxiety and depression are rampant, and self-harm has become tragically common—not in war-torn or famine-stricken nations, but in the most affluent societies on earth. How can it be that in the age of abundance, our youth feel more worthless than ever? It is because material progress cannot fill a spiritual void. We have given them everything except the one thing they were made for: meaning. When a culture denies its Creator, it also denies its children the ability to know who they are, why they exist, and what they are worth. The result is not liberation—it is devastation.

We have everything to live with but nothing to live for.

This is the cost of believing you are a mistake. This is what happens when Genesis 1:1 is removed from the cultural foundation. The moment you abandon the truth that you are created with intention, you untether everything else. Human dignity collapses. Moral truth disintegrates. Hope becomes sentiment, not substance.

But if you believe—truly believe—that **everything came about by God**, then hope is no longer a mere feeling. It becomes a logical necessity. If you were created by God, then your existence is not a cruel trick of nature but a purposeful act of love. That means your choices have eternal weight. Your suffering is not pointless. Your longing for beauty, truth, and justice is not random—it is a homing instinct for the God who made you. The Bible does not tell you that life is easy; it tells you that life is *going somewhere*. As Paul writes in Romans 8:28, *"And we know that for those who love God all things work together for good, for those who are called according to His purpose."*

Genesis 1:1 is not just an origin story—it is the first step in a divine arc that stretches from creation to consummation. It tells us that the world is not random, that you are not disposable, and that God is not silent. In a world drowning in relativism, Genesis offers a rock. In a generation tempted by despair, it offers **teleological hope**—the belief that your life has an end, a direction, and a destination. And that destination is not the void, but **glory**.

Number Two: God Is Outside of Nature

In the ancient world's religious imagination, the divine was invariably entwined with nature. Across civilizations, gods were understood not as transcendent, but as *immanent*—located within, expressed through, or identical to the material world. The deities of Mesopotamia, Egypt, Greece, and India did not create nature—they *were* nature, or at least embedded within its cycles and phenomena. The Nile was not merely a river, but a manifestation of Hapi; the sun was not simply a celestial body, but the chariot of Ra; fire was personified in Agni, storms in Indra, and war in Huitzilopochtli. In these systems, the divine was dispersed across the natural elements and accessible through ritual appeasement, sacrifice, and omens. Morality, insofar as it existed, was subordinated to appeasing these capricious forces rather than conforming to a coherent moral law.

Into this spiritual landscape comes a singular disruption—the opening line of Scripture: *"In the beginning, God created the heavens and the earth"* (Genesis 1:1). This verse is not a mere statement of chronological order; it is a metaphysical declaration that upends the prevailing cosmologies of the ancient Near East. The God of the Bible does not emerge *from* nature nor is He *contained* by it. He stands outside it, utterly transcendent, existing before time and space, speaking creation into being by the sheer authority of His word. As the prophet Isaiah states, *"For my thoughts are not your thoughts, neither are your ways my ways, declares the Lord. For as the heavens are higher than the earth, so are my ways higher than your ways and my thoughts than your thoughts"* (Isaiah 55:8–9). In this view, God is not part of the created order; He is its architect, its lawgiver, and its sustainer.

This radical theological shift carried profound implications for human understanding. If God is outside of nature, then He is not subject to its whims, and neither are His people. No longer must one tremble before the arbitrary moods of the storm or the capricious "luck" of fertility gods. Instead, a moral structure is introduced—one that is not cyclical, but linear; not chaotic, but ordered; not impersonal, but relational. The God of the Bible is not an anonymous force, but a personal being—*YHWH*, the *I AM*—who speaks, remembers, covenants, and redeems. As such, religion transitions from manipulation of the elements to relationship with a personal Creator. The Psalms echo this intimately: *"The Lord is near to all who call on him, to all who call on him in truth"* (Psalm 145:18).

Nature, for all its grandeur, is impersonal. It evokes awe, but not intimacy. Drive to the Grand Canyon and you may well be overwhelmed by its silent majesty. Sit on its edge, and you might feel peace, perhaps even a vague spiritual resonance. But the canyon will not speak back. It cannot know you. It cannot hear your sorrow or respond to your praise. The God of the Bible, however, introduces a new category altogether—a transcendent yet immanent deity who both inhabits eternity and listens to the cries of His people. As David writes, "*When I look at your heavens, the work of your fingers, the moon and the stars, which you have set in place, what is man that you are mindful of him, and the son of man that you care for him?*" (Psalm 8:3–4). The paradox is staggering: The God who forged the cosmos also bends low to enter covenant with humanity.

This shift—from seeing the divine as nature to seeing the divine as Creator of nature—paved the way not only for monotheism but for moral agency, human dignity, and the concept of progress. When the universe is no longer governed by fickle elemental spirits but by a moral and personal God, ethics can be grounded in absolute truth rather than arbitrary ritual. Humanity is no longer subject to nature's cruelty but entrusted with stewardship over it. As Genesis 1:27–28 affirms, man is made in the image of God, and he is given dominion over creation—not as a tyrant, but as a caretaker under divine commission. This theological foundation ultimately laid the groundwork for Western ideas of law, rights, justice, and the sanctity of the individual. We will cover the idea of being made in the image of God later in the book.

Nature is also a central character in the unfolding story of humanity. At first, we worshipped it—bowing to rivers, trees, stars, and storms. Then, in the age of reason and industry, we ignored it, relegating it to the backdrop of human progress. Later, in our technological arrogance, we began to destroy it—mining, polluting, and exploiting with little thought for consequence. And now, in a kind of spiritual recoil, a growing splinter of modern society seeks to worship it once again. This is the so-called "Green movement," which has made remarkable—and at times troubling—advances across the cultural and political landscape of the West.

At its core, this movement often rejects the moral authority of the God of Scripture. Instead, it offers a kind of resacralized materialism, where divinity is sought not in heaven but in the soil, the forest, the sky. For many within this ideology, salvation does not come through repentance or grace, but through carbon neutrality, ecological harmony, and the denunciation of human exceptionalism. In an observation often attributed to G. K. Chesterton, "When people stop believing in God, they don't believe in nothing; they believe in anything." In this case, the "anything" is the earth itself—a return to the ancient altar, this time rebranded as policy, protest, and planetary piety.

Yet, beneath the surface, the longing is real. The impulse to re-enchant the world reflects a hunger that neither materialism nor activism can satisfy. The tragedy is not that people care for the planet—it is that they mistake the creation for the Creator, the echo for the voice.

At the core of the contemporary Green movement lies a fervor that often transcends scientific concern and enters the realm of sacred devotion. Figures such as Greta Thunberg have emerged not merely as activists, but as symbolic prophets in a new ecological order. Her speeches, laced with urgency and moral absolutes—*"How dare you?"*—resonate not only as political critique, but as prophetic lamentations, echoing the cadence of Old Testament rebuke, though absent its theological center. For many, climate activism has become a surrogate faith: It offers a doctrine (carbon neutrality), sacraments (recycling, plant-based diets), apocalyptic warnings (rising seas, scorched earth), and a priestly class of scientists and influencers whose authority must not be questioned. It is, in structure and tone, a religion without a God—except, of course, the earth itself.

Carbon offsets function as a kind of penance, a way to atone for ecological sins. Recycling, biking, and going vegan are elevated beyond lifestyle choices into moral imperatives, practiced with the seriousness of sacred disciplines. At the center of this eco-liturgical order stands a new priesthood of climate prophets—activists, scientists, and thought leaders whose warnings carry the weight of divine judgment. Greta Thunberg, perhaps the most iconic of these voices, has repeatedly framed climate change in absolute moral terms, declaring before world leaders, "We are in the beginning of a mass extinction, and all you can talk about is money and fairy tales of eternal economic growth." Her rhetoric does not appeal to policy alone—it demands repentance. Similarly, Lynn Margulis, cofounder with James Lovelock of the Gaia hypothesis, once stated that "Gaia is a tough bitch," personifying the Earth as a self-correcting organism whose wrath we have incurred. These ideas echo the structure of ancient myth: a sacred Earth, a fallen humanity, and an urgent call to return to balance. What emerges is not simply environmental concern, but an alternative theology—complete with rituals, prophets, and a gospel of planetary salvation.

This resacralization of the natural world—cloaked in secular vocabulary—mirrors the animistic and pantheistic instincts of prebiblical religion. The ancient Near Eastern cosmologies saw nature as divine, chaotic, and in need of appeasement. In those systems, the divine was not separate from the cosmos, but woven into its fabric. Modern environmentalism, despite its claims to progress and science, often revives these instincts. The planet becomes Gaia, a sentient entity; humanity is cast as the defiler; and redemption is sought through ecological penance. The irony is that while our culture believes it has outgrown myth, it has in fact returned to it—only now dressed in the language of activism and policy.

Biblical theology offers a strikingly different vision. The God of Genesis is not the world, but its Creator; He is distinct from it, yet lovingly involved. Nature is not divine, but it is sacred—sacred because it was made by God and entrusted to human stewardship, not worship. When creation is exalted above the Creator, confusion follows. As Romans 1:25 warns, "*They exchanged the truth about God for a lie and worshiped and served the creature rather than the Creator.*" True environmental care does not require idolatry. It demands responsibility, humility, and a theological framework that honors the earth without bowing to it. In the absence of that framework, the modern Green movement risks becoming not a call to stewardship, but a return to the altars of old.

Philosopher Blaise Pascal once observed, "There is a God-shaped vacuum in the heart of every person which cannot be filled by any created thing, but only by God the Creator." In our secular age, that vacuum has widened into a cultural crisis. People are desperately seeking connection—spiritual, emotional, communal—but are offered only substitutes: consumerism, entertainment, activism, or digital escapism. These may numb the ache for a time, but they cannot heal the wound. They cannot speak back to the soul.

This is precisely where the biblical vision of God as transcendent Creator and personal Redeemer offers something revolutionary. The God who is outside of nature is also the God who enters history—not as a storm or a stone or a vague spiritual force, but as a Person. The incarnation is the ultimate confirmation that transcendence does not preclude intimacy. The God who said, *"Let there be light"* (Genesis 1:3) is the same God who says, *"Come to me, all who labor and are heavy laden, and I will give you rest"* (Matthew 11:28).

The biblical affirmation that God is outside of nature is not a theological abstraction—it is the antidote to a lonely and disenchanted age. It means that the universe has a moral center, that life has meaning, and that you are not alone. It means that the God who made the stars also made you—and calls you by name. As creation itself collapsed under the weight of meaninglessness, the voice of God still calls through the darkness: *"Be still, and know that I am God"* (Psalm 46:10). Not nature, not chaos, not fate. God.

Number Three: God Created Time

There was no "before" in any human sense—no ticking clock, no passage, no beginning or end. Time itself was summoned into existence by divine fiat. In the opening words of Genesis, *"In the beginning, God created the heavens and the earth,"* the phrase *"in the beginning"* is not merely poetic; it is metaphysical. It signals the dawn of chronology, the very first moment where duration entered the cosmos. In the New Testament, the apostle Paul also affirmed the creation of time stating in 1 Corinthians 2:7 that God had destined the coming of Christ *"for our glory before time began"* (NIV). Prior to creation, there was only the eternal, timeless presence of God. From that stillness, He spoke—and with His word came not only matter and light, but sequence, succession, and rhythm.

Out of this divine ordering, God established a framework for existence—not chaos, not randomness, but intentionality and structure. The act of creation unfolds not in a single burst, but across seven distinct intervals, each with its own purpose, culminating in rest. This pattern is not arbitrary. It is a sacred architecture—a divine template for life itself. The seven-day week, as we now observe it, is not a human invention; it is a reflection of God's own work. *"Six days you shall labor, but on the seventh day you shall rest"* (Exodus 34:21 NIV). He commands this balance of labor and rest—not simply as a rule, but as a reenactment of His own rhythm. Humanity was not merely given the gift of life, but the gift of ordered life.

Remarkably, this structure—the seven-day week—has persisted through millennia, across cultures and civilizations, without anchoring itself in astronomy like the day, month, or year. There is no planetary cycle that demands a seven-day rhythm. And yet, it prevails. Why? Because it speaks not to the mechanics of the universe, but to its meaning. It aligns not with the stars, but with the soul. The human spirit, body, and society thrive under this cadence. Work finds purpose when it moves toward rest; rest finds holiness when it reflects the Creator's own pause.

Throughout history, human beings have not only attempted to govern nations and remake economies, but to reorder time itself. Nowhere is this more evident than in the recurring attempts by secular, revolutionary, or totalitarian regimes to erase or reshape the seven-day week—a cycle instituted not by empire or philosophy but by divine ordinance. Genesis 2:2–3 records, *"And on the seventh day God finished his work that he had done, and he rested . . . So God blessed the seventh day and made it holy."* This rhythm of six days of labor followed by one day of rest is not cultural invention, but sacred architecture. Nevertheless, ambitious regimes intoxicated by the idea of progress or control have attempted to overwrite this divine template with man-made systems, believing they could engineer a new kind of society by even reshaping how people count their days. Their experiments have invariably failed.

One of the most dramatic and ideologically driven of these attempts was the French Republican calendar, implemented during the height of the French Revolution. In 1793, in an effort to obliterate the influence of the Catholic Church and Christianity itself, the National Convention introduced a new calendar as part of a sweeping program of de-Christianization. The seven-day week was abolished and replaced with a ten-day cycle, or *décade*, in which only the tenth day was designated as a rest day. The traditional Sunday—long rooted in the Jewish Sabbath and sanctified by Christian observance—was deliberately erased. Revolutionary thinker Gilbert Romme, who led the calendar's development, is attributed with describing it as a way to "emancipate the mind from superstitions born of tyranny and ignorance." The days of the week were replaced with secular designations, and even the names of months were changed to reflect seasonal features—*Brumaire* (fog), *Thermidor* (heat), *Floréal* (flowers)—to align time with nature rather than divine order.

The calendar was implemented with ideological fervor. Churches were shuttered, religious symbols removed, and public festivals renamed to glorify labor, harvests, and "reason." Maximilien Robespierre, architect of the Reign of Terror, promoted a "Cult of the Supreme Being" to supplant Christian worship, and is attributed with declaring that "the idea of the Supreme Being and the soul's immortality is a continual summons to justice." But the practical results were disastrous. Workers, forced to labor for nine days before a break, became fatigued and resentful. Families, disoriented by the unfamiliar cycle, struggled to maintain social bonds. Rural populations resisted, and underground religious gatherings proliferated. Even in Paris, enthusiasm waned. Napoleon Bonaparte, never one to allow ideology to interfere with national cohesion, quietly abolished the Republican Calendar in 1806, restoring the Gregorian calendar and with it the traditional seven-day week.

A century later, the Soviet Union under Joseph Stalin undertook a similarly audacious attempt to erase the biblical rhythm of time. In 1929, the regime introduced the Soviet Revolutionary Calendar, first adopting a five-day workweek known as the *nepreryvka* ("continuous workweek"). Rest days were staggered among the population, meaning that husbands, wives, and children often had different days off, intentionally designed to prevent social and religious gatherings. Stalin's commissars described the reform as necessary to "eliminate religious influence" and maximize industrial output. Sunday worship was criminalized in practice if not in law, and churches, already under attack, lost their temporal anchor. The Communist Party's newspaper, *Pravda*, declared that "we have no need of priests—we have our machines." When the five-day system proved chaotic and inefficient, it was replaced in 1931 by a six-day week, which likewise failed. By 1940, the Soviet Union reluctantly reinstated the traditional seven-day cycle.

The Soviet people were not only exhausted by this calendar experiment—they were spiritually and socially fragmented. Historian E. H. Carr observed that "the attempt to destroy the rhythm of life ended in the disintegration of the labor force itself." Soviet propaganda may have tried to fill the gap with images of tractors, workers, and smokestacks, but it could not replace the human need for shared rest, worship, and rhythm. The machine could not become the sanctuary.

Though Nazi Germany did not formally change the calendar structure, it too sought to sever the spiritual authority of the Sabbath. Sunday rest remained technically legal, but it was quietly repurposed for national service, ideological instruction, and party activities. The Hitler Youth held events on Sundays, and churches were discouraged from asserting any independent claim over the day. Adolf Hitler himself viewed Christianity with thinly veiled disdain, describing it in *Hitler's Table Talk* as "a Jewish invention" and "the first creed in the world to exterminate its adversaries in the name of love." His goal was not necessarily to replace the Sabbath outright, but to co-opt it—transforming it from a holy day into a day of militarized unity and ideological programming. Over time, the Nazi regime hollowed out Sunday of its spiritual significance, using it instead as a tool of the state.

Even in our modern, democratic societies, the Sabbath has not been abolished by decree but slowly eroded by culture. The rise of 24/7 consumer economies, digital technologies, and work-from-anywhere expectations has blurred the boundaries of time. Sunday has become a day for errands, sports, emails, and binge-watching—another cog in the machine of productivity. The idea of sacred rest, of a divinely appointed pause, has been quietly sidelined. Yet, even in the absence of formal policy, the effects mirror those of more overt interventions: burnout, spiritual exhaustion, fractured families, and a profound sense of restlessness.

What all these experiments share—whether revolutionary, totalitarian, or subtly commercial—is their ultimate failure. When societies attempt to reengineer time, to override the divine cadence embedded in creation, they eventually collapse into disarray or quietly return to the old rhythm. The seven-day week, and with it the Sabbath, persists not because of inertia, but because it aligns with something eternal. As Jewish philosopher Abraham Joshua Heschel wrote in *The Sabbath*, "Technical civilization is man's conquest of space. The Sabbath is man's conquest of time." In erasing the Sabbath, societies lose more than a day of rest—they lose a sense of holiness, orientation, and soul.

The divine rhythm laid out in Genesis has survived revolutions, dictatorships, and consumerism because it speaks to a truth greater than political ideology or economic efficiency. It is not merely useful—it is sacred. Those who have challenged God's calendar, whether with guillotines or five-year plans, have faded into history. The Sabbath remains.

Number Four: God Is Monotheistic

Polytheism has been the human norm. Interestingly, atheism is a relatively new phenomenon. Believing in just the five senses and relying on reason is a new Western view within the last one hundred years, and fifty especially. For almost all of human history, from the Egyptians to the Hindus to the Incas, the standard belief system was to pray to MANY gods. As we detailed previously, those gods were typically found in nature or had some natural phenomenon or manifestation.

Growing up, I remember visiting a Hindu family, very gentle and kind people who hired my father to do a major architectural project. In their home was an elaborate shrine with hundreds of different gods. In fact, it is Hindu custom that some families have a series of gods assigned directly to them. Even as a child, I found this to be practically and morally troubling. I had immediate questions, such as,

"What happens when the gods are in conflict?"
"And which God has ultimate authority?"
"What moral code do you live by if you have one hundred deities saying one hundred things?"

I later learned that Hinduism recognizes multiple categories of deities that can manifest in countless forms—an unfathomable amount of power sources to pray to, worship, recite, or even remember!

The God of the Bible is fundamentally different than the prevailing customs and norms of ancient river civilizations. There were not many gods; there is *God*. YHWH, Jehovah, Elohim, El, Adonai are all terms used for the God of the Bible. Here is a helpful, quick summary of what each term means, all of which point to *one God*, a declaration of monotheism.

YHWH (יְהוָה)

YHWH, often rendered as the tetragrammaton (meaning "four letters"), is the most sacred and personal name of God in the Hebrew Bible. It is derived from the Hebrew root *hayah*, meaning "to be," and is closely linked to God's declaration in Exodus 3:14: "*I AM WHO I AM*." This name asserts God's eternal, self-existent nature—He is not created, not dependent, and not part of the material world. In the context of Genesis 1:1, although the name YHWH does not appear until later chapters, its significance as the covenantal name of the one true God anchors biblical monotheism. YHWH is not merely a god among gods; He is the only uncaused cause, transcendent over creation yet intimately involved with it. The reverence for this name was so deep that ancient Jews would not pronounce it aloud, substituting Adonai when reading aloud, thus preserving its sacred mystery.

Jehovah

Jehovah is a latinized transliteration of YHWH, formed by early Christian scholars who inserted the vowels of Adonai into the consonants of YHWH. Though not a biblical word itself, the term became widely used in Christian theology and hymnody to refer to the personal, covenant-keeping God of Israel. The use of "Jehovah" reflects an attempt to vocalize God's name in a way that captures His intimate and revealed nature. Theologically, it helps reinforce the concept that the Creator of Genesis 1:1 is not a distant deity, but one who reveals Himself personally to humanity. While the name appears anachronistically in Genesis 1:1 (which uses Elohim), Jehovah reminds readers that the powerful Creator is also the same God who later binds Himself to humanity through covenant, law, and redemption.

Elohim (אֱלֹהִים)

Elohim is the first name attributed to God in the Bible—"*In the beginning, God [Elohim] created the heavens and the earth*" (Genesis 1:1). The form of the word is grammatically plural, yet it consistently governs singular verbs, suggesting not many gods but a unique and majestic fullness within the one true God. For Christians, this plurality within unity is not a grammatical accident—it foreshadows a truth fully unveiled later in Scripture: the triune nature of God. The Father speaks, the Spirit hovers over the deep (Genesis 1:2), and the Gospel of John later reveals that the Word—

Christ Himself—was active in creation from the beginning (John 1:1–3). Thus, even in the opening verse of the Bible, we see the faint contours of the Trinity: one God, yet richly relational within Himself. Elohim is not a distant deity of abstraction, but the living Creator—self-sufficient, sovereign, and eternally in communion. This name, standing at the head of Scripture, asserts not only that there is one God, but that within the divine unity is eternal fellowship, love, and purpose.

El (אֵל)

El is the singular, more basic form of Elohim, often translated simply as "God." It appears in many compound names for God (e.g., El Shaddai, El Elyon), emphasizing different aspects of His nature. As a root term, El was used in many Semitic cultures to refer to their deities, but in the Hebrew Bible, it is purified and redefined as pointing to the one true God. In Genesis 1:1, though the word used is Elohim, the connection to El reinforces God's identity as singular and supreme. The name El allows for relational and descriptive expansion—He is not just God, but God Almighty, the Everlasting God, the God Who Sees. This redefinition of a common ancient name asserts monotheism by detaching the word El from its pagan roots and aligning it exclusively with the Creator.

Adonai (אֲדֹנָי)

Adonai, meaning "Lord" or "Master," emphasizes God's authority, sovereignty, and ownership over all creation. It is used as a reverent substitution for YHWH, particularly in Jewish worship, to avoid pronouncing the divine name. While not used in Genesis 1:1,

Adonai reinforces the biblical assertion that the God who created the heavens and the earth is not just a distant power, but the rightful ruler of it all. In the context of monotheism, Adonai reminds us that God is not merely the origin of existence—He governs it. He commands, He appoints, He directs. Calling God Adonai expresses submission and reverence; it proclaims that the Creator is also King, and creation itself is subject to His will.

Taken together, these names—YHWH, Jehovah, Elohim, El, and Adonai—do more than describe God; they form a cohesive statement about who God is in relation to the world and to humanity. They emphasize different dimensions of His nature: YHWH reveals His eternal self-existence, Jehovah His covenantal intimacy, Elohim His creative power and unity in complexity, El His supremacy and timeless strength, and Adonai His absolute authority and lordship. None of these names implies multiple gods; rather, each affirms that the God of the Bible is singular in essence, unrivaled in being, and utterly sufficient unto Himself. In a world historically filled with competing deities—storm gods, fertility gods, sun gods—the biblical witness cuts through with a thunderous claim: There is only one God, and He is not like us. The first verse of Genesis is not just the beginning of a story—it is the cornerstone of monotheism, and these names build upon that foundation with clarity, majesty, and theological depth.

Monotheism represents one of the most profound moral revolutions in human history. In the ancient world, polytheism led not only to the worship of many gods, but to the acceptance of many competing moral systems. Each deity had its own temperament, domain, and demands. The result was ethical fragmentation: One god might value war, another fertility, another deceit or cunning. As C. S. Lewis observed in *The Abolition of Man*, "If nothing is self-evident, nothing can be proved. Similarly, if nothing is obligatory for its own sake, nothing is obligatory at all." Polytheism, lacking an ultimate moral source, leaves humanity with a pantheon of preferences rather than a coherent moral law. The God of the Bible, by contrast, is not merely the strongest among gods—He is the one Creator of all things, and therefore the sole foundation for truth, justice, and goodness.

Monotheism was such a profound differentiator that the most repeated and famous prayer is an exaltation and declaration of monotheism. The Shema—named after the first Hebrew word of Deuteronomy 6:4, "Shema Yisrael" ("Hear, O Israel")—is one of the most foundational and sacred declarations in all of Judaism. It affirms the absolute oneness and uniqueness of God: "*The Lord our God, the Lord is one.*" In a world that, both ancient and modern, often bows to many competing powers—whether gods, ideologies, or desires—the Shema proclaims a radical and uncompromising monotheism. This is not just a theological statement, but a call to allegiance: If God is one, then He alone deserves our exclusive worship, love, and obedience. The Shema immediately leads into the next verse (Deuteronomy 6:5), commanding, "*You shall love the Lord your God with all your heart and with all your soul and with all your might.*" Thus, God's unity is inseparable from our call to wholehearted devotion.

In Jewish life and liturgy, the Shema is not a verse to be read in passing—it is a prayer to be lived. Observant Jews recite it twice daily, in the morning (Shacharit) and evening (Ma'ariv) prayers, as commanded in Deuteronomy 6:7: "*You shall teach them diligently to your children . . . when you lie down, and when you rise.*" It is traditionally the first prayer taught to children and the last words spoken before death. Its recitation serves as both a spiritual anchor and a public confession of faith in the one true God. Over centuries of exile, persecution, and diaspora, the Shema has remained the heartbeat of Jewish identity—a whispered reminder that God is near, God is one, and God is faithful.

You can imagine how powerful and countercultural the Shema would have been in the ancient world, where every surrounding tribe and empire worshipped a pantheon of gods—gods of sun and moon, gods of war and harvest, of fertility and death. In a world teeming with idols and competing spiritual forces, Israel was called to stand apart and declare something radically different: *"The Lord our God, the Lord is one."* That single sentence wasn't just theology—it was resistance. It was a daily reminder, spoken morning and night, that their God was not one among many, but the one above all. In a culture where people feared dozens of deities and performed rituals to appease each one, Israel's children grew up hearing that there is one sovereign, almighty, and personal God who created the heavens and the earth—and He alone is worthy of trust, obedience, and love.

This shift from many gods to one God introduced the possibility of a unified moral order—a law grounded not in tribal custom or divine whim but in the nature of a righteous and personal Creator. The Ten Commandments were not merely religious edicts; they were moral declarations that applied to everyone, everywhere, because they came from a universal God. A. W. Tozer, in *The Knowledge of the Holy*, wrote, "The decline of the knowledge of the holy has brought on our troubles. . . . When the concept of God is lost, the sense of moral obligation is also lost." Monotheism bound morality to ontology—what is right is not what the strongest god demands but what reflects the unchanging character of the one true God. This is the great breakthrough of biblical faith:

Moral truth is not negotiated among competing deities, but it is revealed by the Creator who made humanity in His image.

Furthermore, monotheism provides not only a source of morality but the possibility of moral relationship. In polytheism, the gods are powerful but untrustworthy—worship becomes appeasement. However, the God of the Bible is both holy and faithful. His commands are not arbitrary; they are rooted in His goodness and designed for human flourishing. God is not the author of moral laws in the sense that a legislature is the author of the laws of the state. They are not mere judgments of God, but expressions of His own nature. This means that obedience to God is not servility to a cosmic despot but alignment with the moral fabric of reality itself. In monotheism, morality is no longer a tool of fear or survival—it becomes an invitation into covenant, transformation, and communion with the One who is, by nature, good.

In a culture where the lines between good and evil have grown increasingly blurred, a monotheistic worldview provides the necessary anchor for moral clarity. Without belief in a transcendent, unchanging source of goodness, morality becomes little more than social consensus or personal preference—easily reshaped by emotion, peer pressure, or cultural trends. The next generation, growing up amid moral relativism and digital noise, is increasingly untethered from any objective framework that defines what is right, just, or true. Monotheism teaches that goodness is not invented by humans; it is revealed by a God who is Himself the measure of all virtue. As the prophet Micah wrote, *"He has told you, O man, what is good; and what does the Lord require of you but to do justice, and to love kindness, and to walk humbly with your God?"* (Micah 6:8). This vision of goodness is not a floating ideal—it is grounded in the nature of a righteous and personal God.

Absent such grounding, a generation is left to navigate right and wrong with nothing but feelings or hashtags to guide them. When truth is no longer fixed, it becomes politicized, weaponized, or dismissed entirely. A monotheistic worldview resists this drift by asserting that there is such a thing as real good and real evil—not because society says so, but because God, the Creator of all, has revealed it. This foundation is not restrictive; it is liberating. It gives young people something solid to stand on when the world is shifting beneath them. A society without God is not empty—it is flooded with idols, ideologies, and illusions that promise freedom but deliver confusion.

The historical breakthrough of monotheism was not merely a shift in religious belief—it was the birth of a radically new way of understanding reality, morality, and human dignity. When the ancient Hebrews declared, "*The Lord is one*" (Deuteronomy 6:4), they shattered the cyclical fatalism of paganism and introduced the idea that truth is not many, but one—that justice is not tribal, but universal. From this singular vision of God flowed a singular vision of humanity: made in the image of the Creator, and endowed with value, responsibility, and moral agency. The very foundations of the West—its commitment to law, human rights, the dignity of the individual, the value of conscience, and the pursuit of truth—were built on the sturdy framework of biblical monotheism. Strip away that foundation, and the moral architecture begins to crumble. If the West is to endure—not merely economically or politically, but spiritually and morally—it must remember the God who spoke the world into being and called it good, the God who alone defines justice, truth, and what it means to be human. The future depends on whether we still believe what the ancient world once discovered: that there is one God, and He created you, loves you, and wants to rest with you.

Think about what it feels like to walk into a great cathedral—a sacred space like **Chartres** in France, **St. Peter's Basilica** in Rome, or the soaring majesty of Sagrada Família in Barcelona. These are not just buildings; they are theological statements rendered in stone and glass. As you step through their doors, the world's noise begins to fade. Your pace slows. Your eyes are drawn upward by pointed arches, vaulted ceilings, and sun-drenched stained glass. Everything about the architecture conspires to lift your soul heavenward. The verticality of these structures is not accidental—it is intentional, metaphysical. These cathedrals are designed to make you feel small in the presence of something immeasurably great, and in so doing, they orient your heart toward the divine.

In contrast, much of modern architecture is flat, functional, and spiritually mute. It serves utility, not transcendence. Roger Scruton once wrote, "Beauty is vanishing from our world because we live as though it does not matter." Modern buildings, devoid of ornament or aspiration, reflect a society that has lost its reverence for the sacred. They are efficient but not edifying. They ask nothing of the soul. But when you enter a place like **Saint Bernadette Catholic Church in Scottsdale, Arizona**, even if you are not Catholic, something stirs within you. There, the drama of Christ's life is depicted in luminous images above, compelling you to look up—literally and spiritually. It reminds you that there is more to life than what is seen at eye level. You are, for a moment, re-centered. Re-enchanted.

Now imagine the **Sabbath** as a **cathedral in time**. It has no marble columns or flying buttresses, but its structure is just as solid, just as enduring. The Sabbath is not a place, but a sanctuary carved out of time itself. Like those magnificent cathedrals, it demands that you stop. That you look up. That you remember who you are in relation to God, to others, and to eternity. While the rest of the week may feel like a blur of tasks, emails, obligations, and noise, the Sabbath stands still—like a bell tower in a storm. It is scheduled, predictable, and unwavering. It invites you to dwell, not produce; to rest, not rush; to contemplate, not consume.

In a world obsessed with speed and novelty, the Sabbath anchors us in rhythm and ritual. It reorients our days around what is eternal. Just as medieval peasants once entered cathedrals to step into the story of redemption depicted in stone and stained glass, so, too, we enter the Sabbath to step into God's story of creation, liberation, and restoration. It is a weekly act of resistance against the tyranny of the urgent, a recalibration of our humanity toward peace and praise. As Abraham Joshua Heschel so powerfully put it, "The Sabbath is not for the sake of the weekdays; the weekdays are for the sake of the Sabbath. It is not an interlude but the climax of living."

The Sabbath is not merely a day off. It is not simply a lifestyle hack. It is holy architecture for the soul. A cathedral in time, with liturgies of rest and windows of joy. It is not made with human hands, but it is no less beautiful—and perhaps all the more eternal.

Number Five: God Didn't Just Create the World—He Designed It

A Refutation of Atheism

As I travel to more than fifty college campuses a year and engage in hundreds of hours of debates with professors, influencers, and students, one question keeps rising to the surface: the God question.

In our age of technological triumphalism, we like to think of ourselves as profoundly enlightened. "Look at us! We have cross-country travel, vaccines, antibiotics, AI, and smartphones—surely that God stuff must be ancient superstition!" The hubris embedded in this argument is both shocking and chilling. It reveals not only historical ignorance but a dangerous arrogance—one of the reasons, I believe, why the West is collapsing under the weight of its own supposed brilliance.

Growing up, atheism was fashionable. It carried a spirit of rebellion and intellectual elitism. The New Atheists—Dawkins, Hitchens, Harris, and Dennett—weren't content to merely doubt; they attacked. They brought a new militancy to unbelief; one that was hostile, condescending, and frequently dishonest. Inspired by Enlightenment-era skeptics like David Hume, they framed their opposition to theism as a moral and intellectual crusade.

I watched all this unfold in the early 2000s. The church was caught off guard. Atheism had momentum. And as the church faltered, the "dechurching" movement gained serious traction. Only in the last eighteen months have we seen some cultural signs of reversal.

But atheism is not just a denial of God—it's the absence of any coherent alternative. It seeks to deconstruct the foundations of religious belief while offering no meaningful structure in return. In that sense, atheism is not just skeptical—it's parasitic.

Agnosticism at least acknowledges the mystery. Atheism pretends to solve it with a shrug. And that is its first and fatal error: It cannot explain existence. The atheist must confront the question "Why is there something rather than nothing?"—yet has no adequate answer.

Thankfully, atheism is on the decline. Not only is it increasingly difficult to defend scientifically the idea that existence sprang from nothing, but morally it's bankrupt. Look around: Has the West grown stronger, nobler, and happier the less it has believed in God?

We mention God all throughout this book, and I feel it is important that we build out the biological, scientific, and moral case for God.

Chapter 2

NOTHING DOESN'T CREATE SOMETHING

My friend, mentor, and all-around extraordinary thinker Frank Turek wrote a phenomenal book titled *I Don't Have Enough Faith to Be an Atheist.* I strongly recommend it to anyone exploring questions about God and atheism.

In his book, Frank dismantles the core claims of atheism with clarity and precision. He focuses on this: **Space, time, and matter require a spaceless, timeless, immaterial cause.**

Frank Turek's argument begins with the now widely accepted conclusion from modern cosmology: The universe had a beginning. The moment of the Big Bang—roughly 13.8 billion years ago—was not just the start of matter, but of time and space itself. This view is supported by the Borde-Guth-Vilenkin Theorem, which shows that any universe that is expanding (like ours) must have a definite beginning.

Turek argues that anything that begins to exist must have a cause. This is not theological bias—it's the basic law of causality that undergirds all of science. You don't see objects popping into existence uncaused in a laboratory or on a sidewalk. And so, if the universe began, it must have a cause.

But here's the dilemma: If matter, space, and time all began at the Big Bang, then the cause of the universe must transcend all three. It must be:

- **Spaceless** – because it created space.
- **Timeless** – because it created time.
- **Immaterial** – because it created matter.

This cause must also be enormously powerful (to bring the universe into being) and intelligent (given the order and fine-tuning that followed). These attributes—eternality, immateriality, power, intelligence—just happen to match what classical theism has always said about God.

Atheism has no such cause. Nothing in physics can explain its own origin. Nothing inside the universe can be the reason the universe exists. That's circular. And so we are driven outside the system—to a Cause beyond nature. A Supernature.

Turek rightly calls this "not a God of the gaps, but a God of the origin."

Even though I don't claim to be a scholar or theologian, here's how I've come to understand the absurdity of atheism.

When you strip away the rhetorical flair, what atheism proposes is a belief system requiring four enormous leaps—each of which, on its own, is a stretch. Taken together, they form a worldview that defies reason, experience, and probability. These are the four pillars of materialistic atheism, and each one is more fantastical than the last.

1. That the universe came from nothing—

a spontaneous event of unimaginable precision and order, arising from nonbeing.

The atheist must believe that everything—the galaxies, time, space, matter, energy—sprang into existence without a cause, from absolutely nothing. Not a vacuum, not a quantum field, not empty space. Nothing. Philosophers and physicists have long debated whether anything can come from nothing, and the overwhelming consensus from logic and experience is this: It cannot.

Nothing has no properties. It cannot act, cannot cause, cannot initiate. To claim that the universe arose from literal nothingness is not only scientifically unsupported—it's philosophically incoherent. As the Latin maxim says: *Ex nihilo nihil fit*—from nothing, nothing comes.

And yet, the atheist must accept that not only did *something* come from nothing, but that it did so in a way that launched a mathematically precise, finely ordered universe with the constants required for life. That's not science. That's blind faith dressed up in technical language.

2. That this explosion resulted in a planet—Earth—

perfectly suited to sustain intelligent life under finely tuned and stable conditions.

After the alleged accidental beginning of the universe, the atheist must believe that through pure chance, conditions aligned in such a way that one planet—ours—formed with the exact distance from its star, the right tilt of its axis, the correct rotation speed, an atmosphere capable of blocking radiation, and a magnetic field to protect against solar flares.

Earth's position in the so-called "Goldilocks Zone" is not just lucky—it's absurdly fortunate. If we were slightly closer to the sun, we'd burn. A bit farther, and we'd freeze. The presence of water, the role of the moon in stabilizing our axis, the ratios of oxygen and nitrogen, and the timing of tectonic activity all had to converge precisely.

Astronomer Fred Hoyle, once an atheist himself, admitted that "a commonsense interpretation of the facts suggests that a super-intellect has monkeyed with physics, as well as with chemistry and biology, and that there are no blind forces worth speaking about in nature."

In other words, Earth isn't just a random rock. It's a miracle platform, tuned for life.

3. That life somehow emerged from nonliving matter—
against statistical odds so overwhelming they make winning the lottery look inevitable.

The third leap is the most baffling of all: The atheist must believe that inorganic, lifeless matter somehow arranged itself into the first living cell—complete with a boundary membrane, replication system, energy source, and genetic information.

This is the mystery of **abiogenesis**, and it remains completely unsolved. In fact, many scientists now privately admit that we are no closer to understanding how life began than we were fifty years ago. The odds of even a single functional protein forming by chance are astronomical—often cited as 1 in 10^{77}. That's a probability of one out of ten followed by seventy-seven zeros. And a living cell requires hundreds of these, functioning in precise harmony.

To believe this happened without design is to believe a Boeing

747 assembled itself during a windstorm in a junkyard—not once, but in a way that could copy itself, adapt, and improve.

This leap is not based on evidence. It's based on desperation to avoid the implication of design.

4. That life then evolved into intelligent beings—
capable not only of language and reason, but of morality, self-awareness, and spiritual longing.

The final leap may be the most profound: The atheist must believe that from this original accidental cell, evolution alone led not just to diversity of life—but to conscious, rational, moral human beings.

They must believe that blind, directionless processes eventually produced minds that ask questions like "Why are we here?" Evolution may account for physical adaptations, but it cannot explain **consciousness**, **logic**, or **morality**.

Why should a molecule care about justice? Why should atoms-in-motion feel guilt, love, wonder, or awe? Where does beauty come from? Why do humans create music, seek meaning, or believe in eternity?

Even atheists like Thomas Nagel have acknowledged that consciousness is a massive problem for materialism. If we are nothing more than chemical machines, then our beliefs—including belief in atheism—are simply the product of electrochemical reactions, not rational conclusions.

Yet, every day we live as though we are free, conscious beings capable of making moral choices. We assume human rights, objective wrongs, and higher truths. All of these point not to chaos, but to a Creator.

The Grand Absurdity

Any one of these four claims would be hard to swallow. But when stacked together, they form a worldview that is, frankly, more unbelievable than any religious storybook ever written.

To say that

- the universe came from nothing,
- Earth was randomly suited for life,
- life emerged from nonlife,
- and that life produced morality and mind is not the rejection of faith. It is *faith in its most irrational form.*

Atheism claims to be built on reason, but it is a pyramid balanced on four miracles—with no Miracle Maker.

Theism, by contrast, offers one elegant explanation for all four: **God**.

Stephen Meyer and the Return of the God Hypothesis

Dr. Stephen Meyer, a brilliant scientist and philosopher, has done the heavy lifting in making the scientific case for theism in our time. His book *Return of the God Hypothesis* deserves far more attention than it has received. In it, he identifies three major discoveries in modern science that point powerfully to an intelligent cause behind our universe.

1. The Origin of the Universe

Meyer points to the now-undisputed evidence that the universe had a beginning—a moment in which time, space, and matter came into being. This flies in the face of the old belief in a static or eternal universe. The Big Bang theory, though secular in its packaging, implies a very theistic premise: The universe had a definite starting point.

Modern science has brought us to the precipice of one of the most profound truths imaginable: The universe had a beginning. This claim, which would have sounded like theology a century ago, is now a pillar of mainstream cosmology. And that changes everything.

In the early twentieth century, Edwin Hubble's observations of an expanding universe—combined with Einstein's equations—led to the development of the Big Bang theory. This model posits that the universe expanded from an initial singularity, a point of infinite density, where time, space, and matter did not yet exist.

What existed "before" the Big Bang? Nothing. Not empty space. Not ticking time. Literally nothing. That's not just hard to imagine—it's metaphysically impossible to reconcile with materialism. Stephen Meyer explains this with careful detail: If the universe had a beginning, then it cannot be self-existent. Something else must have brought it into being.

Atheists such as Lawrence Krauss have attempted to argue that "nothing" is unstable and can give rise to something. But Krauss's "nothing" turns out to be a quantum vacuum—something, not nothing. In fact, it is governed by physical laws, which already assumes the existence of a space-time background. His nothing is really a "something lite." It dodges, rather than answers, the question of ultimate origins.

Meyer shows that all attempts to skirt the implications of the Big Bang fail. Whether it's oscillating universes (which violate the second law of thermodynamics), multiverse speculation (which cannot be tested), or quantum models (which require pre-existing laws), every escape route collapses under scrutiny.

This brings us to one of the oldest and simplest arguments for God, known as the **Kalam Cosmological Argument**, honed and made renowned in recent decades by philosopher William Lane Craig. Meyer echoes it with scientific rigor:

Premise 1: **Everything that begins to exist has a cause.**
Premise 2: **The universe began to exist.**
Premise 3: **Therefore, the universe has a cause.**

Let's examine each premise in more detail.

Premise One: Causality

This is the very foundation of science. Every observable effect has a cause. Every change is preceded by something that brought it about. Even quantum events—often cited as exceptions—don't come from literal nothing; they arise from pre-existing fields governed by probabilistic laws. So, the idea that the universe popped into being causelessly is not just counterintuitive, it's a rejection of scientific methodology.

Premise Two: The Universe Began to Exist

This premise is now supported by multiple lines of evidence: the redshift of galaxies, the cosmic microwave background radiation, and the second law of thermodynamics (which implies the universe is running down). Most strikingly, the Borde-Guth-Vilenkin Theorem (2003) proves that any universe with a net expansion—no matter how exotic—must have a beginning.

Even if a multiverse existed, it too would require a beginning.

Premise Three: A Cause Beyond Nature

So if the universe began to exist, what could cause it? The cause must transcend time, space, and matter, since all three began at the Big Bang. That rules out any physical process or material explanation.

It also rules out any "brute fact" answer. To say "the universe just is" is no answer at all—it's intellectual surrender. The better explanation is a cause that fits the evidence: a spaceless, timeless, immaterial, powerful, and personal Mind.

Meyer argues that only a personal agent has the ability to freely choose to create. Impersonal forces act by necessity—gravity pulls, electricity flows. But a timeless cause that *chooses* to create must have will and intention. That implies consciousness. And consciousness implies Mind.

This is not a religious leap. It's a rational conclusion, grounded in the best cosmology we have.

Meyer also invokes an older philosophical argument: the argument from contingency. Everything in the universe is contingent—it could have failed to exist. Planets, people, galaxies—none are necessary beings. So why does anything exist at all?

If every contingent thing requires an explanation, then there must ultimately be something that exists *necessarily*—that has the power of being in itself. That is not the universe. It is not a quantum field. It is not time. It is something prior.

The only thing that makes sense as a necessary being is God—a self-existent, eternal Mind.

Even Albert Einstein, though not a theist, recognized the metaphysical weight of the Big Bang. He initially resisted the idea of a beginning because it implied a Creator. "I want to know how God created this world," he once said. "I am not interested in this or that phenomenon, in the spectrum of this or that element. I want to know His thoughts—the rest are details."

That longing—to understand the source—is not just poetic. It's scientific.

2. The Fine-Tuning of the Universe—a Case for God

Stephen Meyer's second line of argument in *Return of the God Hypothesis* is the extraordinary fine-tuning of the universe—a phenomenon that presents one of the most compelling reasons to believe in an intelligent Designer. In simple terms, "fine-tuning" refers to the precise calibration of the constants of nature that allow life to exist. If any of these were even slightly different, the universe would be inhospitable to life.

Let's take just a few examples. The strength of gravity is about 10^{-38} compared to the strong nuclear force. If gravity were just slightly stronger or weaker by one part in 10^{60}, stars couldn't form. If the cosmological constant (which governs the expansion rate of the universe) were off by even one part in 10^{120}, the universe would have either collapsed back on itself or expanded so rapidly that matter would never form. These are not generous margins of error—they are razor thin.

To put this in perspective: Imagine a dartboard the size of

the known universe—some ninety-three billion light-years across. Now imagine throwing a dart from Earth and hitting a single molecule in the middle of that board. That's the level of precision required in just one of these constants. The idea that this happened by accident stretches credulity far past the breaking point.

Meyer argues, convincingly, that the fine-tuning of the universe cries out for explanation. There are only three major options: chance, necessity, or design.

Chance is the most commonly offered explanation by skeptics, but it is mathematically indefensible. The odds against the correct parameters lining up randomly are so vast they exceed the number of subatomic particles in the entire universe. Roger Penrose, the Oxford physicist, calculated that the probability of our universe's low entropy condition existing by chance is 1 in 10 to the 10^{123} power—an unimaginably small number.

Necessity suggests that the laws of nature could not have been otherwise—that they are the only way things could be. But this is not supported by physics. Nothing in theoretical physics demands that the constants be what they are. In fact, they appear arbitrary. They must simply be assumed. There is no "law of laws" requiring gravity to be exactly what it is.

Design is the last explanation. And it is the only one that fits what we know from experience: that finely calibrated systems are always the product of intelligence. A safe that opens only with one precise one hundred–digit combination is not the result of chance—it's the result of intentional design.

Some have invoked the **multiverse** theory to counter this conclusion. The idea is that if there are trillions of universes, each with different physical laws, then ours just happens to be one of the lucky ones that can support life. But this too fails. First, there's no observational evidence of other universes. It's a metaphysical escape hatch, not a scientific discovery. Second, even a multiverse would require fine-tuning of the universe-generating mechanism—what makes that process possible? You're just pushing the question back one step.

Furthermore, the multiverse cannot account for the origin of the laws of logic, mathematics, and moral order. It may address probability, but not meaning. And finally, the multiverse argument contradicts **Occam's Razor**—the principle that we should not multiply entities beyond necessity. Postulating trillions of unobservable universes is far more extravagant than positing a single, intelligent Creator.

The **anthropic principle**—often cited by skeptics—says we shouldn't be surprised the universe supports life because otherwise we wouldn't be here to observe it. But this is not an explanation; it's a tautology. It's like saying, "Of course I won the lottery; otherwise I wouldn't be holding the winning ticket." That doesn't make the odds any less miraculous.

Meyer's argument is not a "God of the gaps." He's not saying, "We can't explain this, so God must have done it." Rather, he's showing that we have evidence FOR design—that the best and most rational explanation for the data is an intelligent Designer. Every experience we have with complex, functional, finely tuned systems—from watches to spacecraft—teaches us that design is real, detectable, and rational to infer.

The fine-tuning of the universe is not just impressive—it's overwhelming. The deeper physicists peer into the laws of nature, the more they encounter harmony, precision, and order. As Nobel laureate Arno Penzias put it,

> "Astronomy leads us to an unique event, a universe which was created out of nothing and delicately balanced to provide exactly the conditions required to support life. In the absence of an absurdly-improbable accident, the observations of modern science seem to suggest an underlying, one might say supernatural, plan."

That's exactly what Stephen Meyer concludes. The fine-tuning of the universe is the fingerprint of a Creator—not a guess, but an **inference to the best explanation**.

3. The Digital Code in DNA

The third line of evidence Stephen Meyer offers in *Return of the God Hypothesis* is the presence of information—specifically, digital code—at the foundation of life. This is perhaps the most devastating argument against atheistic materialism and the clearest pointer to an intelligent Creator.

At the heart of every living cell is **DNA**: a molecular string of nucleotides that stores vast amounts of information. This information is not vague or chaotic—it is functional, specific, and highly ordered. It instructs the cell to produce proteins, and it guides replication, manages repair, and drives the operations of life itself. DNA is, quite literally, a **language**.

Bill Gates famously remarked that "DNA is like a computer program but far, far more advanced than any software ever created." And he's right. Each human cell contains around **three billion base pairs**—a code using four letters: A, T, C, and G. This code is transcribed, translated, and executed by cellular machinery in a process astonishingly similar to reading, editing, and compiling software.

So, here's the question: **Where does this information come from?**

In every other area of human experience, **information comes from minds**. Whether it's words on a page, data in a hard drive, or Morse code, the origin is always intelligence. Random chance may produce patterns, but not meaningful content. Rocks don't write poetry. Ocean waves don't compose symphonies. Chemistry doesn't draft instruction manuals.

Meyer argues that the information in DNA exhibits what he calls **"specified complexity."** It's not just improbable—it's functionally arranged to achieve specific outcomes. That's the signature of a designer.

Naturalistic explanations fail. **Evolution by natural selection** can only operate on systems that already reproduce. It cannot explain the **origin of the first replicating system**—the very genesis of life. **Abiogenesis** (life from nonlife) remains an unsolved, almost untouched problem in science. Leading researchers like **Paul Davies** and **Eugene Koonin** have admitted that current models fail to account for the origin of biological information.

Moreover, appeals to "**self-organization**" or "**emergent complexity**" are not explanations—they are descriptions of the problem. Saying that order "emerges" doesn't tell us *why* or *how* the instructions came to be.

DNA uses a genetic alphabet of four letters (rather than twenty-six), and your genome is a genetic book 3.2 billion letters long. No one believes a book comes into existence by accident. If you found a novel on a beach, you'd never think the wind and waves wrote it. Language implies a writer. Code implies a coder. And DNA is **code**.

Meyer also points out that **information is not reducible to matter**. The same message can be transmitted in ink, sound waves, or electrical signals. The medium changes—the message remains. This shows that information is **immaterial**—it exists above and beyond the matter it's written on. That undermines materialism at the most fundamental level.

DNA is not just a molecule. **It is a message.** A sophisticated, digital, information-rich language written into the fabric of life. And no law of chemistry explains how it came to be. That's not just an argument for God—it's an overwhelming pointer toward Him.

To deny this is to ignore everything we know about how information arises.

And as Meyer puts it: "The best explanation for the origin of information is a mind."

That Mind is God—the Divine Author, the Coder of life, the Logos behind all living systems.

Here are now a few analogies I like that show the mathematical improbability of the universe coming into being from nothing. Atheism, when carefully examined, is one of the greatest intellectual cons in history.

1. A Hurricane Assembling a Boeing 787

Analogy: Believing the universe came into existence by random chance—with all its fine-tuned physical constants, cosmic order, and life-supporting precision—is like believing a hurricane swept through a junkyard and spontaneously assembled a fully functional Boeing 787 Dreamliner, fueled, staffed, and ready for takeoff.

Explanation: A 787 is a marvel of human engineering. It contains millions of precision parts: turbines, avionics, hydraulics, GPS systems, composite wings, pressure seals—all requiring design, purpose, and harmony. Even if every part were already in the junkyard, the odds of them being violently thrown into their correct places and combinations, all at once, are functionally zero. Now imagine this scenario producing not just a plane, but a planet, a DNA code, a biosphere, and human consciousness. The atheist must accept that not just one such miracle occurred—but many.

2. Letters Spilling into Shakespeare

Analogy: Believing life arose from nonlife without intelligent guidance is like dumping a box of alphabet letters onto the floor and having them land in perfect sequence to form all 37 plays and 154 sonnets of William Shakespeare—punctuated, formatted, and footnoted.

Explanation: DNA is a language—a biological code using four letters (A, T, C, G). The average human cell contains roughly **3.2 billion** base pairs, or "letters," that communicate instructions far more sophisticated than any book ever written. This information is both complex and specified—it doesn't just exist, it *means* something. And in our entire experience, meaningful information never comes from random chance. It always comes from intelligence. Just like a sentence or sonnet requires a mind to write it, so does the genetic information that constructs a human being.

3. The Coin Flip of the Universe

Analogy: Imagine flipping a coin and having it land heads-up **ten quintillion** times in a row. That's about how improbable it would be for all the physical constants of the universe to be exactly what they are—by random chance.

Explanation: The cosmological constant, gravitational force, the strength of electromagnetism, and the mass of subatomic particles are all *incredibly* fine-tuned. If any of them were off by even one part in $\mathbf{10^{120}}$, the universe would either collapse in on itself or expand too rapidly for stars or life to form. The odds of all these constants lining up perfectly on their own are so low, it surpasses statistical absurdity. And yet, here we are. Why? Because it was designed that way.

The case for God is not merely sentimental or psychological—it's philosophical, moral, and increasingly scientific. Atheism cannot explain why we are here, what we are for, or how we ought to live. Theism can.

Dozens of physical attributes in our universe—and within our own solar system—are fine-tuned to an astonishing degree. If even one of these values were altered by the smallest margin, life as we know it would be impossible. Consider just one example: If the strength of gravity were increased by a mere 1 part in 10^{34} relative to the strong nuclear force, the universe could not sustain life-bearing planets. What does that number even mean? One part in 10^{34} is a ratio so mind-bendingly small it defies everyday comprehension. So, let's make it visual.

Imagine the entire North American continent—from Central America to Greenland—covered in dimes stacked all the way to the moon. That's 238,000 miles of dimes. Now replicate that feat on one billion more North American continents, each one blanketed with stacks of dimes reaching to the moon. Combine all those dimes into one incomprehensibly massive pile. Then mark one single dime red, mix it in thoroughly, blindfold a friend, and have him choose one dime at random. The odds of him selecting the red one? That's 1 in 10^{34}.

Would you bet your life on him picking the red dime? Of course not. You would need *immense* faith to believe that could happen by chance.

So, what caused the universe to be calibrated with such razor-sharp precision? These values—along with dozens of others—were either designed or they weren't. Those are the only two possibilities. Which makes more sense? That they were intentionally designed. What requires more blind faith? That they weren't.

Even leading atheists have admitted that the fine-tuning of the universe is among the most formidable arguments against a godless cosmos. Because when you really look at the numbers, belief in design isn't blind faith—it's the most rational conclusion.

To believe in God is not to surrender your reason—but to fulfill it.

Number Six: Out of Chaos, God Created

Before there was beauty, there was bedlam.
Before order, there was an abyss.
Before light, there was ***darkness over the face of the deep*** (Genesis 1:2).

Genesis 1 is not a sterile record of creation—it is a war story. A conflict between **chaos and cosmos**, between void and voice, between the meaningless and the meaningful. And it opens not with peace, but with mystery and turbulence.

"The earth was without form and void, and darkness was over the face of the deep. And the Spirit of God was hovering over the face of the waters" (Genesis 1:2).

The Hebrew phrase used here is profound: תֹהוּ וָבֹהוּ (*tohu vavohu*), often translated as "formless and void," but better rendered as *wild and waste, chaotic and empty*, or even *confused and desolate*. It's a poetic pair used elsewhere in Scripture to describe judgment, devastation, and the unraveling of creation itself (cf. Jeremiah 4:23).

This is the raw canvas of God's creativity; not a blank slate, but a swirling, unordered, lifeless deep. **The "deep"** (Hebrew: *tehom*, תְּהוֹם) echoes ancient Near Eastern mythology, where creation myths portrayed the gods battling sea monsters or conquering watery chaos to create the world. But Genesis radically departs from those myths. In the biblical account, **there is no battle**. God does not struggle with chaos—**He hovers over it**. He doesn't war against the darkness—**He speaks** into it.

"Let there be light" (Genesis 1:3).

This is the birth of distinction. The first incision of order into disorder. Light separated from darkness. Structure from shapelessness. Meaning from madness.

And this act is not incidental—it is theological. God's nature is revealed in what He does: He **separates**, He **orders**, He **names**, He **blesses**, and He **fills**. He does not merely *create*; He calms. He does not merely *make*; He **masters**.

The Spirit's hovering (Hebrew: *rachaf*, רָחַף) evokes the image of a bird fluttering protectively over her young (cf. Deuteronomy

32:11). This is not detached power—it is tender authority. Before the world is shaped, the Spirit is present, near, watching. This suggests something astonishing: **God's first response to chaos is not destruction but intimacy.**

The Modern Rejection of Order

Today's cultural revolution seeks to undo this divine ordering. Postmodern thinkers reject the Creator's distinctions and instead return us to *tohu vavohu*. The new gods of the age chant: "There is no male or female," "There is no truth," "There is no right or wrong," "All is fluid," "All is self-created."

But when we blur God's boundaries, we don't liberate—we liquefy. We are not evolving forward; we are devolving backward—**back into Genesis 1:2**, into the unformed void from which we were rescued. The irony is bitter: In the name of progress, we are regressing into precreation chaos.

The Left calls it liberation. Scripture calls it **darkness over the face of the deep**.

Order Is Freedom

Biblically, **freedom is not the absence of structure—it's the presence of the *right* structure**. The universe only flourishes because it is not random. It is designed, distinguished, and disciplined. Every law of physics, every rhythm of the earth, every category of biology points to a mind that makes distinctions.

In Hebrew, the word for *holy*—קָדוֹשׁ (*qadosh*)—means "set apart." To be holy is to *not be chaotic*. It is to be distinct, ordered, beautiful. God is holy because He is not like the formless void. His people are holy because they live in alignment with the structure of reality He made.

The Sabbath is holy because it is **set apart** from the rest of the week. Marriage is holy because it is **set apart** from all other unions. Gender is holy because it reflects a **created distinction**. Life is holy because it is **called into being by God's word**, not human will.

Every Sabbath, we testify to the Creator not only as the maker of all things but as the One who ordered all things. Sabbath is not laziness—it is alignment. It is not merely rest—it is remembrance: that **we are not accidents of chaos**, but recipients of cosmos.

To keep the Sabbath is to proclaim this:

"I will not return to *tohu vavohu*. I will live in the light."
"I will not be ruled by disorder. I will honor the God of boundaries, rhythms, and meaning."
"I will not believe the lies of the serpent, who blurs all lines. I will trust the God who speaks clearly."

Chapter 3

THE HISTORY OF THE SABBATH

I chose the title of this book deliberately: *Stop, in the Name of God*. The phrase is not a poetic flourish—it is a direct theological claim. The Hebrew word for "Sabbath" (*Shabbat*) literally means "to stop" or "to cease." It derives from the root verb *shavat* (שָׁבַת), which connotes a full cessation, a deliberate interruption of action. In ancient Hebrew, it is not merely rest in the passive sense, but a sovereign act of halting. This linguistic foundation reveals the Sabbath not as absence or leisure, but as presence and consecration.

To stop—utterly, decisively, rhythmically—is perhaps the most radical command God ever gave humanity. In a world governed by unrelenting drive, by the mantras of "faster," "harder," and "more," the divine voice says something astonishing: Stop. In His name, cease. Cease striving. Cease earning. Cease proving. Cease buying and selling and producing. This is not a suggestion. It is a divine imperative.

In a culture saturated with advertising and seduced by accumulation, the command to stop stands as both countercultural and salvific. The Sabbath is a sanctified protest against the tyranny of constant motion. As philosopher Abraham Joshua Heschel reflected, "The Sabbaths are our great cathedrals, the Jewish equivalent of sacred architecture." Rather than building monuments in space, the people of God were called to consecrate time. And in doing so, they declared that God—not Pharaoh, not Caesar, not Mammon—governs the hours.

This theme—ceasing in the name of the Creator—underscores the spiritual and cultural depth of the Sabbath as an institution. What follows is an exploration of this singular commandment as it unfolds through history, theology, and civilizational development.

In the ancient world, there was no parallel to the Sabbath. It was not borrowed, synthesized, or assimilated from neighboring cultures. It was revealed. In a milieu where time was cyclical, labor relentless, and gods insatiable, the Sabbath entered history not as a cultural evolution, but as a divine interruption—a revelation that shattered prevailing assumptions about time, the human condition, and sacred order.

In the words of Rabbi Jonathan Sacks, "The Sabbath is the most radical thing in the Torah. It declares the equality of all and the dignity of the human being." The Sabbath represents a spiritual insurgency against tyranny—whether the tyranny of ceaseless toil or the tyranny of empire. It proclaims that time itself is not merely economic, but theological. It testifies that rest is not the cessation of meaning, but the recovery of it.

Unlike fertility cults or solar calendars, which were rooted in natural rhythms, the Sabbath was anchored in divine speech. There was no agrarian necessity that dictated a seven-day week. It is not lunar, nor seasonal, nor economic. As cultural historian Mircea Eliade observed, "The week is not a natural unit of time but a cultic one." That is, it exists because it was commanded—not discovered.

The Sabbath is thus a theological event—revelation encoded into time. This chapter will trace the origins, elevation, and institutionalization of the Sabbath, its adoption and distortion in Christian civilization, and finally, its systematic abandonment in modernity. Yet, even in its decline, the Sabbath continues to echo—like a buried bell whose reverberations stir something dormant in the soul.

1. The Sabbath Before Sinai: A Primeval Benediction

The first reference to the Sabbath is not legal, but liturgical. In Genesis 2:2–3, the narrative concludes with divine rest: "*So God blessed the seventh day and made it holy, because on it God rested from all his work that he had done in creation*" (v. 3). There is a rhythm to creation, and it ends not with more doing, but with cessation—*shavat*, rest.

This rest is due not to fatigue, but to fullness. It is not the withdrawal of power, but the crowning of meaning. It is the divine punctuation mark at the end of the most magnificent sentence ever spoken. It is the declaration that the created world, imbued with divine speech and radiant with order, is not merely functional but good—and that its goodness is worthy of joy.

But why did God rest? Not because He was weary—"*the everlasting God, the Creator of the ends of the earth . . . does not faint or grow weary*" (Isaiah 40:28). Rather, God rested because the work was finished. His rest is the artist's stillness after the final stroke of the masterpiece, not the laborer's collapse from exhaustion. It is the repose of royalty surveying a realm, the contentment of a Father who sees that it is very good.

Here we are faced with a profound mystery: the Infinite stopping. God, who upholds all things by the word of His power, chose to pause. This pause is not passivity, but purpose. It is a divine dwelling with creation, a sabbath-ing with what has been made. Rest is not what happens after creation; it is part of creation. It is the seal.

To rest, in the divine sense, is to enjoy—to bless, to name, to hallow. This is why the text does not merely say that God ceased, but that He "blessed" the seventh day and "made it holy." This Hebrew word for "holy" (*qadosh*) is used here for the first time in Scripture—and not to describe a place or object, but a slice of time. God sanctifies a moment. The seventh day becomes sacred not because of what happens in it, but because of what does not happen. The absence of work becomes the presence of worship.

In this way, the Sabbath is not only God's final act of creation—it is also His first invitation to man. Before man does anything, he enters into rest. The first full day of human existence is not toil, but communion. The Sabbath teaches us, from the very beginning, that we were not created primarily to produce, but to walk with God.

As theologian Jacques Ellul reflects, "God's rest was not withdrawal from the world, but His entering into it in a new way—as the God who delights." The Sabbath is, therefore, a mystery of presence. It is not an intermission in history; it is the moment when history steps into the holy.

The seventh day is unique in the creation narrative. Unlike the first six days, which end with *"and there was evening and there was morning,"* the seventh day has no terminus. It is open ended. In Jewish theology, this is not accidental. The Sabbath transcends the ordinary and becomes an eternal sign: the beginning of sacred time.

Exodus 16, which recounts the miraculous provision of manna in the wilderness, offers profound evidence that the Sabbath was not instituted for the first time at Sinai—it was already known, already observed, already sacred. The people are instructed to gather bread for six days, and on the sixth day to gather double. On the seventh, there would be none. Some ignore the instruction and go out to gather anyway, and Moses rebukes them: *"See! The Lord has given you the Sabbath"* (Exodus 16:29). This is a striking phrase—not "The Lord is giving you," but "has given." It implies prior existence. The Sabbath here is not a new law handed down from heaven, but a divine inheritance rediscovered. It is a gift first, a command second. God gives rest before He requires it.

This quiet moment in the desert reveals something more than a logistical rhythm for food collection. It reveals that God's rest was not just a heavenly concept, but a lived reality for His people even before the codification of the law. And what is more—God makes provision for that rest. He aligns heaven's economy to accommodate sacred time. The people are fed in such a way that they can cease, not by accident, but by design. Sabbath is not man's improvisation in hardship—it is God's intention in the wilderness.

That the Decalogue—the Ten Commandments—begins its Sabbath commandment with *"Remember the Sabbath day"* (Exodus 20:8) only reinforces this ancient thread. The imperative to "remember" is itself a summons to sacred memory—a command not simply to avoid forgetting, but to actively recall, reengage, and reenter into something already known and already loved. In the Hebrew language, the word for "remember" (*zakar*) carries not only the connotation of mental recollection, but of covenantal action. To remember is to reenact, to embody, to affirm through faithful practice. In this light, remembering the Sabbath is not merely nostalgia for Eden—it is a participation in Edenic time.

And significantly, the Sabbath is not a peripheral command. It is one of the Ten Words, inscribed by the finger of God. It appears more than one hundred times in the Hebrew Bible, with profound theological force. No other commandment receives as much detailed commentary in the Pentateuch as the Sabbath. It is reinforced in the narratives, the legal codes, the prophets, and the psalms. It is the only command in the Decalogue that God Himself is explicitly said to observe. It is also the only command given to all of creation—man, woman, child, slave, foreigner, and beast. The frequency of its invocation in Scripture underscores its foundational role in the covenantal imagination of Israel.

Throughout the Torah, the Sabbath is named again and again as a "sign forever," a "delight," a "holy convocation," a "covenant," and a "test." Its consistent reappearance—across Exodus, Leviticus, Numbers, and Deuteronomy—reveals its function as a theological anchor and a moral compass. Even the land itself was commanded to keep Sabbath years (Leviticus 25), extending the principle of rest into the fabric of ecology.

To "remember the Sabbath day" is therefore to return to the foundational logic of creation, to submit time itself to the lordship of Yahweh. As Abraham Joshua Heschel aptly stated, "The Sabbath is not an interlude but the climax of living." It is not an interruption from reality—it is the unveiling of reality's true purpose. In the silence of the seventh day, God speaks again—not in thunder, but in rest. And in remembering that rest, we remember who we are: not slaves, not machines, not commodities, but image-bearers called to be still and know that He is God.

2. The Sabbath as Covenant: From Freedom to Holiness

When the Sabbath enters into covenantal law at Sinai, it does so not merely as an ethic of rest, but as a theology of identity, anchoring the covenantal relationship between God and His people in the fabric of time itself. Sinai—the mountainous setting where God delivers the law to Moses—is arguably the most pivotal moment in Israel's collective memory. It is at Sinai that the divine will is inscribed not only in the hearts of the people but literally on tablets of stone. This moment forms the foundation of biblical law and spiritual order. At its center stands the Decalogue—ten utterances that serve as the moral architecture of the covenant.

The significance of the Sabbath's place in the Decalogue cannot be overstated. It is the longest commandment, the hinge between duties to God and duties to neighbor, and—unlike the prohibitions against murder, theft, and adultery—it is ceremonial in nature. It alone among the ten regulates the use of time. That it would be enshrined alongside laws of moral permanence suggests something staggering: that the sanctification of time is not ancillary to moral life, but essential to it.

Exodus 20:8–11 grounds Sabbath observance in creation: God made the world in six days and rested on the seventh. But Deuteronomy 5:15 roots the command in deliverance: "*You shall remember that you were a slave in the land of Egypt . . . Therefore the*

LORD your God commanded you to keep the Sabbath day." The Sabbath, then, stands at the intersection of creation and redemption. It is both protological and eschatological. It looks backward to Eden and forward to a world where the yoke of Pharaoh is broken and beyond. It is liberation encoded into liturgy. To keep the Sabbath is to bear witness that the cosmos is not owned by an empire and that man is not a beast of burden.

It is a spiritual act of civil disobedience—an embodied rejection of any system that commodifies the human being. On the Sabbath, the Israelite was saying, "I am not a slave, not even to my own ambition." It was a day of holy refusal.

Moreover, the Sabbath is inclusive in a way that shattered the social hierarchies of the ancient world. Servants, foreigners, and even animals are granted rest. The Sabbath democratizes dignity. Historian Tom Holland notes in *Dominion* that "The Sabbath, in its egalitarian insistence on rest for all, including slaves and foreigners, was unprecedented in the ancient world." Its very structure subverted the norms of stratified civilizations and presented a weekly foretaste of justice.

Its theological depth intensifies in Exodus 31:13–17, where God declares the Sabbath a "sign forever" between Himself and Israel: *"It is a sign forever . . . that in six days the Lord made heaven and earth, and on the seventh day he rested and was refreshed"* (v. 17). The Hebrew word translated "refreshed" (*vayinafash*) is rarely used of God and implies a kind of soul-breathing, as if the Creator Himself pauses, not because He is depleted, but because He delights. This anthropomorphic image is the language of intimacy: a God who breathes not only life into man, but also breathes deeply in the joy of His completed work.

Thus, the Sabbath became a defining mark of Jewish identity. It was not the day of production, but the day of sanctification. It was the time in which Jews bore witness to their God not through action, but abstention—not by building, but by ceasing. In a world that demanded productivity as proof of worth, Israel declared something more ancient and more human: that the image of God in man is most clearly seen when he rests in God.

3. The Sabbath Against Empire: Exile and Resistance

In the centuries following the giving of the law, Sabbath observance became central to Jewish fidelity, especially in times of exile and oppression. The prophets repeatedly called the people back to Sabbath faithfulness. Isaiah declares, *"If you turn back your foot from the Sabbath, from doing your pleasure on my holy day, . . . then you shall take delight in the Lord"* (Isaiah 58:13–14). Jeremiah warns that neglecting the Sabbath will lead to the fall of Jerusalem (Jeremiah 17:21–27).

Exile, in the biblical imagination, is not merely a geographic displacement, but a theological catastrophe. It was cultural devastation, national dismemberment, and spiritual trauma. When the First Temple was destroyed by the Babylonians in 586 BCE, it was not just a building reduced to rubble—it was the unthinkable rupture of the meeting place between heaven and earth. The temple had been the dwelling place of God's glory, the heart of Israel's worship, identity, and purpose. Its destruction was like extinguishing the sun at midday.

The book of Lamentations captures the devastation with a sobering poetic intensity: *"How lonely sits the city that was full of people! How like a widow she has become"* (Lamentations 1:1).

Children cried out for food in the streets. Priests were slaughtered, elders mocked, mothers boiled their own children in desperation. Jerusalem, once the joy of the whole earth, became a smoldering ruin.

And yet—astonishingly—within days, perhaps even the very next Sabbath after the exile began, faithful Jews rested. Not because they were comfortable, but because God had told them to. Even as they were marched into Babylonian captivity, the rhythm of the seventh day was not broken. The fires of Jerusalem could not extinguish it. The weeping by the rivers of Babylon did not silence it. The Sabbath was not dependent on the temple because it predated the temple. It was not an artifact of location, but a gift of time.

In this unimaginable dislocation, the Sabbath functioned as a defiant tether to covenant and to identity. Each week that they ceased from labor in a foreign land, the Jewish people bore witness: "Our God still reigns. Our time is not owned by Babylon. We will not forget who we are." The Sabbath was their ark of memory, their sanctuary in exile, their protest against despair. It preserved the soul of a people when their bodies had been scattered; dislocated from the land, the temple, and, symbolically, from divine intimacy. After the destruction of the First Temple in 586 BCE and the forced deportation to Babylon, Israel experienced a profound crisis of identity. The cultic center was gone, the priesthood disrupted, the monarchy dismantled. Yet, amid this loss, the Sabbath endured.

The Sabbath became a portable sanctuary, a cathedral not in stone, but in time. When sacred space was razed, sacred time remained. In Babylon, the people of Israel could not offer sacrifices or ascend to Zion, but they could still cease from labor. They could still keep time according to the rhythm of the Creator. The observance of Sabbath in exile was thus not an act of nostalgia, but one of covenantal defiance. It was a declaration that even in foreign lands, under foreign gods, the people of Israel remained bound to Hashem ("the Name," meaning God). Sabbath became the connective tissue of Jewish identity, threading continuity through rupture.

Later, in the Hellenistic period, the Sabbath emerged as a flash point of resistance. Under Antiochus IV Epiphanes, Jewish practices—including circumcision, Torah study, and Sabbath observance—were banned. Many chose death over desecration. The Maccabean martyrs were among those who refused to fight or flee on the Sabbath, demonstrating an almost unimaginable fidelity to divine rest. Even after that stance was revised for purposes of self-defense, the episode burned itself into the Jewish conscience as a testament to how sacred this day had become.

Writers like Philo of Alexandria and Josephus marveled at the uniqueness of this practice—an entire people who every seventh day abstained from labor. To pagan minds, it was puzzling at best, contemptible at worst. Roman philosopher Seneca derided Jews for "wasting" a seventh of their lives in idleness. But this critique only underscores the strangeness and singularity of the Sabbath. No other culture institutionalized weekly rest. There was no precedent. It was not agricultural or lunar. It was sui generis. Revelation, not evolution.

And therein lies its power. The Sabbath has preserved the Jewish people under the relentless pressure of assimilation, persecution, exile, and dispersion. Empires have come and gone—Babylonian, Persian, Greek, Roman—but the seventh day still arrives, and the faithful still light candles, say blessings, and cease. The Sabbath is more than a day; it is an act of covenantal continuity. It has been the spiritual glue that held the people together when everything else fell apart.

As Heschel observed, "The Sabbath is the presence of eternity in time." For a people denied permanence in land or government, eternity in time became the sacred shelter. Sabbath was the ark in the flood of history. And those who kept it—even while exiled from the temple, deprived of sovereignty, and scattered across the earth—testified with their stillness that the God who created the world in six days and rested on the seventh still reigns, and still remembers His covenant.

This covenantal memory is enacted and renewed every Friday night in the Jewish home. As the sun sets, families gather to welcome the Sabbath as one would welcome a royal guest. The table is set with care. Two braided loaves of challah are placed on a cloth, recalling the double portion of manna God provided in the wilderness. Candles are lit, symbolizing the arrival of sacred light into ordinary time. A woman of the household recites the blessing over the candles, and a hush settles over the home—the week is over, and eternity has entered.

Then comes the kiddush, the sanctification of the day over a cup of wine. The head of the household lifts the cup and chants the ancient blessing, declaring the Sabbath a memorial of creation and exodus, the dual pillars of sacred history. This is not mere ritual; it is a reenactment of covenant. To say kiddush is to stand in continuity with Sinai, with exile, with every generation that has paused, blessed, and sanctified time.

After the kiddush, hands are washed in ceremonial fashion, echoing the temple rites, and the challah is blessed and shared. The meal that follows is festive and unrushed. Psalms are sung.

Stories are told. The peace of Shabbat seeps into the bones. It is a foretaste of the world to come.

On Saturday morning, the family attends synagogue, where the weekly Torah portion is read. The congregation stands when the scroll is lifted, affirming that this Word is the heartbeat of Israel. Prayers are recited—some ancient, some newer—binding together generations in worship.

As the day wanes, a bittersweet ceremony called havdalah marks the Sabbath's departure. Over a candle with multiple wicks, a cup of overflowing wine, and fragrant spices, the family chants blessings that distinguish the holy from the ordinary, light from darkness, Sabbath from the six days of labor. The flame is extinguished, the wine spills over, the scent of spices lingers—and the soul, having tasted eternity, prepares to reenter the world.

This is not mere tradition. It is covenant in motion. It is theology practiced at the table. It is the remembrance of God's creation and deliverance, enacted through bread and wine, light and song. In keeping the Sabbath, the Jewish people do not simply honor history—they inhabit it.

4. Christianity and the Reconstitution of Sacred Time

Jesus honored the Sabbath but reoriented its meaning. His healings and teachings on the Sabbath were not abolitions of the day, but restorations of its purpose. *"It is lawful to do good on the Sabbath,"* He declared (Matthew 12:12). He did not discard the Sabbath, but stripped it of human legalism to recover divine intent.

Yet, the resurrection inaugurated a new order. On the first day of the week, the tomb was empty. The early church began gathering on that day to break bread and worship (Acts 20:7; 1 Corinthians 16:2–3). By the end of the first century, Sunday had emerged as the Lord's Day (Revelation 1:10).

Church fathers such as Ignatius of Antioch exhorted believers to no longer "live according to the Sabbath" but to live in accordance with the Lord's Day. Justin Martyr, writing in the mid-second century, describes Christian worship on Sunday as a remembrance of both creation and resurrection. Tertullian and Origen viewed the Sabbath typologically, as pointing toward eternal rest in Christ.

Sunday became the new day of sacred assembly, though not immediately a day of rest. It was the 321 CE decree of Emperor Constantine I that transformed Sunday into a civil day of rest: "On the venerable Day of the Sun let the magistrates and people residing in cities rest, and let all workshops be closed." This edict—though partly syncretic—set the legal precedent for the sanctification of Sunday across Christendom.

The Council of Laodicea (363–364 CE) forbade Christians from "Judaizing" by resting on Saturday. Sunday was not merely a resurrection remembrance; it was now the civic Sabbath of the Christian empire. The transition was more than doctrinal—it was institutional and imperial. As Sunday observance gained civil enforcement, the character of Sabbath rest began to shift from a Jewish covenantal identity to a Christian imperial norm. The theology behind the shift was not without its tensions; many early Christians wrestled with the balance between continuity with Jewish sacred time and the radical newness of resurrection life.

It's important to note that this chapter introduces, but does not yet fully resolve, the complex relationship between the Sabbath and Christianity. Later chapters in this book will explore in greater theological and historical detail how Christians across time—Catholic, Orthodox, and Protestant—have interpreted the Sabbath commandment. We will also address the debates surrounding the so-called "Lord's Day," the question of continuity with Jewish Sabbath, and the enduring relevance of Sabbath ethics in modern Christian spirituality.

For now, what is clear is that Sunday became, by the fourth century, both a theological symbol and a political reality. Augustine, writing in the fifth century, spoke of the Sabbath as a sign of "future rest," locating its fulfillment in the eternal peace of heaven. Others, like Ambrose of Milan, saw Sunday as the "eighth day," the beginning of a new creation. And so, the Sabbath did not disappear from Christian thought—it was reframed. Rest was no longer tied to the seventh day per se, but to the person and resurrection of Christ.

As we move forward, we will see how this reframing shaped not only theology, but the very rhythm of Western civilization.

5. The Western Inheritance: Sunday as Sacred Time

Throughout the Middle Ages, Sunday observance was woven into the fabric of Christian life. Canon law prohibited servile labor. Mass attendance was obligatory. Feasting and rest were encouraged. While theological justifications varied, the rhythm of six days of labor and one day of sacred rest remained.

The Protestant Reformation complicated the picture. Luther emphasized Christian freedom and downplayed Sabbatarian rigor. Calvin upheld the moral obligation of weekly worship but rejected legalistic constraints. Yet, in the Anglo-American context, especially among Puritans, a robust Sabbatarianism took root.

The Puritan vision of the "Christian Sabbath" regarded Sunday as a continuation of the fourth commandment. The Westminster Confession (1646) codified this view: "This Sabbath is to be kept holy unto the Lord." In New England, blue laws forbade not only labor, but leisure. Sunday was a day for two sermons, Scripture reading, and catechesis.

Historian Daniel Boorstin observed, "In no other civilization has a day of rest been so deeply institutionalized."

Before we trace the Sabbath's unraveling in modernity, we must first deepen our account of its robust institutionalization in the West.

Throughout the Middle Ages, Sunday observance was more than a moral expectation—it was embedded in the legal, cultural, and architectural framework of Christendom. Church bells structured the week. Cathedrals stood as sentinels of sacred time. Canon law prohibited servile labor, and absence from Sunday Mass was considered a grave sin. In many villages and towns, markets were closed, fields left untended, and court proceedings paused. Feasting, rest, and religious devotion turned Sunday into a weekly festival of grace.

Theological justifications varied. Some saw Sunday as the "eighth day," inaugurating a new creation. Others, especially within monastic communities, saw it as a microcosm of eternity. Whatever the nuance, the core remained: six days were for man, but one belonged wholly to God. Sunday was not just a cessation of labor; it was the renewal of the soul.

The Protestant Reformation complicated this landscape. Luther, wary of legalism, emphasized the freedom of the Christian and saw Sabbath-keeping primarily as a matter of worship rather than regulation. "It is not necessary to observe the sabbath or Sunday because of Moses' commandment," he wrote, because "nature also shows and teaches that one must now and then rest a day, so that man and beast may be refreshed." Calvin likewise maintained Sunday as a moral necessity for worship and instruction, but he rejected the notion of its divine perpetuity in Mosaic form.

Yet, among the Reformed, especially in the English-speaking world, a stricter Sabbatarianism began to emerge. The Puritans, drawing deeply from Old Testament precedent, saw Sunday as the rightful heir to the fourth commandment. In their view, the Sabbath had not been abrogated, but transformed—its spirit fulfilled in Christ, but its practice still required. They insisted that the Christian Sabbath should mirror the Jewish one in sanctity, regardless of whether in exact ritual.

The Westminster Confession of Faith (1646) codified this with striking clarity: "This Sabbath is to be kept holy unto the Lord, when men . . . do not only observe an holy rest all the day from their own works, words and thoughts about their worldly employments and recreations; but also are taken up the whole time in the public and private exercises of his worship."

This vision took firm root in New England, where blue laws were instituted to enforce Sabbath observance. These laws forbade not only labor, but leisure—no public games, no shopping, no unnecessary travel. The Sabbath became a day of spiritual rigor and moral formation. Families attended multiple church services. Children recited catechisms. Scripture saturated the home.

Historian Daniel Boorstin observed that in no other civilization had a day of rest been so deeply institutionalized. In Puritan society, Sunday was not a reprieve from the week—it was the week's defining axis. It shaped schedules, informed community life, and framed one's relationship to God. In these cultures, the Sabbath was less a retreat than a re-centering.

These practices, though often viewed today as austere or even oppressive, were rooted in a belief that human beings flourish when time is ordered by something greater than impulse or utility. The Sabbath was not a denial of joy—it was an invitation to deeper joy. In the American colonies and well into the nineteenth and early twentieth centuries, these values were not merely held by isolated religious communities—they were woven into the cultural and legal fabric of a nation that broadly identified as Christian.

Blue laws—statutes enforcing Sunday rest and worship—were not fringe policies, but normative expectations. In predominantly Protestant regions of early America, they reflected a civil consensus that time must be structured around the sacred. Businesses were shuttered, courtrooms were silent, and civic life stilled on the Lord's Day. Even nonobservant citizens came to expect a quiet Sunday, not merely as a tradition, but as a legal rhythm grounded in moral vision.

These laws were not seen merely as religious impositions, but as social goods. They ensured that working-class laborers could attend church. They upheld the sanctity of family gatherings. They reminded the community that there were goods higher than economic productivity. Sunday was not primarily a restriction—it was an offering. It was the collective recognition that a society must pause, must secure itself in something beyond consumption.

As historian Alexis de Tocqueville observed in his travels through nineteenth-century America, "In the United States . . . religion is the first of their political institutions." Blue laws, then, were not an aberration, but the natural outflow of a people who believed that liberty without sacred order was hollow. The nation breathed differently on Sunday—not despite its religious heritage, but because of it.

It is difficult to overstate how deeply this weekly rhythm shaped American civic life. Schools, factories, and courts all deferred to the Sabbath. Even professional sports and entertainment venues routinely shut down. The assumption was not merely that Sunday was different, but that it must be different—for the sake of the soul, for the sake of the nation. In a society increasingly governed by market and machinery, the Sabbath called people back to meaning, covenant, and worship.

6. From Holy Day to Holiday: The Modern Eclipse

The industrial revolution and Enlightenment ushered in profound changes. Time, once structured by bells and liturgies, was now governed by clocks and production quotas. The factory bell replaced the church chime. The Sabbath, once the crown of the week, became an obstacle to efficiency. As modern economies demanded unbroken labor cycles, the theological rhythm of rest clashed with industrial momentum.

By the nineteenth century, labor unions began invoking the language of Sabbath—not to hallow a day, but to humanize the workweek. The campaign for shorter work hours and the five-day week drew moral credibility from the idea that man was not made for unceasing toil. Saturday was added to Sunday, not for reasons of sanctity, but to appease labor unrest. The result was the modern weekend—a secular solution to a sacred loss.

At the same time, Sunday blue laws in the United States proliferated. These laws banned Sunday commerce, alcohol sales, public entertainments, and in some places even fishing, sports, or hanging laundry. They were designed not merely to enforce piety, but to carve out protected time for the soul, the family, and the church. For decades, these statutes enjoyed broad support across denominational and even political lines.

Yet, in the increasingly pluralistic and commercial twentieth century, they began to face legal and cultural resistance. Jewish and Catholic minorities often protested the Protestant basis of Sunday laws, especially when it required business closures on both Saturday (for the Sabbath) and Sunday, effectively harming their livelihood. Secular civil libertarians questioned whether such laws violated the separation of church and state. The Supreme Court upheld blue laws in several key rulings—most notably *McGowan v. Maryland* (1961)—but the cultural tide was turning.

By the 1970s and 1980s, economic interests aligned with civil libertarians to erode what remained. Shopping malls pushed to open on Sundays. Sports leagues scheduled weekend tournaments. Political leaders increasingly saw Sunday restrictions as antiquated obstacles to commerce. By the late twentieth century, most blue laws were repealed or hollowed out.

The disappearance of Sabbath protections marked more than a legal change—it was a cultural shift. Sunday became indistinguishable from Saturday: a day of errands, games, consumption, and digital distraction. Historian James K. A. Smith is credited with noting that "the weekly cathedral of time was quietly rezoned as a shopping plaza."

The effects rippled beyond religion. Families found it harder to gather. Worship became optional. Youth sports leagues filled Sunday mornings once reserved for church. The steady hum of retail and entertainment diminished opportunities for shared stillness. Time was no longer sanctified—it was sold.

The retreat of blue laws was geographically uneven. States like Massachusetts, Connecticut, and Pennsylvania—strongholds of Puritan and Reformed influence—clung longest to strict Sunday restrictions. In Massachusetts, for example, laws forbade most forms of Sunday commerce well into the twentieth century, and only in 1983 was the ban on Sunday retail broadly repealed. Bergen County, New Jersey, still maintains blue laws for certain commercial zones even today, a rare holdout amid widespread deregulation. By contrast, states like Nevada, California, and New York were among the earliest to peel back Sunday restrictions in the name of economic liberty and pluralistic inclusion.

The popularity of blue laws rested on a shared moral ecology: that society needed rhythms rooted in something higher than profit or convenience. Their unraveling mirrored not simply a legal liberalization, but a cultural amnesia. What was once a civic consensus—that the soul needs one day not to strive—gave way to market absolutism. Everything could be open. And so, everything was.

But in opening everything, something closed. We lost our collective hush, our cultural inhale. We lost the idea that the week culminates in consecration, not consumption. In a seven-day economy, every day is the same, which means every day is forgettable.

As Abraham Joshua Heschel is claimed to have remarked, "The modern man has no Sabbath and no festival, only a paycheck and a holiday." The result is not merely busyness, but forgetfulness—a loss of the sacred dimension of time and the covenantal call to stop, remember, and rejoice.

7. The Sabbath Is About Seeing and Remembering

Yet, even in decline, the Sabbath calls. Theological voices like Walter Brueggemann have urged a rediscovery of Sabbath as resistance. "In our own contemporary context," Brueggemann writes, "the celebration of Sabbath is an act of both resistance and alternative." It challenges the endless cycles of achievement and consumption. It invites us to stop, to see, to delight.

Secular culture, too, has begun to sense the void. Movements like "digital detox" or "tech Sabbaths" bear witness to a yearning for rest—even among those who do not know the commandment. Author Judith Shulevitz has called for "a secular Sabbath" to recover community and sanity.

But the original Sabbath was more than a wellness tip. It was the declaration that the world is God's, not ours—that time is not a possession, but a gift.

The Sabbath began not in the synagogue or the church, but in Eden. Before there were empires or economies, before toil had entered the world, there was rest. The Sabbath was not reasoned into existence—it was revealed. It did not arise from human exhaustion, but from divine completion. *"And on the seventh day God finished His work that He had done, and He rested"* (Genesis 2:2). In that sacred pause, time itself was sanctified. The Sabbath was God's signature on creation—a weekly temple in time where man might dwell with his Maker.

Throughout history, this day has not merely marked rest—it has marked remembrance. In the wilderness, Israel was commanded to *"remember the Sabbath day, to keep it holy"* (Exodus 20:8). It was to be a sign between God and His people, a rhythm that declared this to the watching world: We are not slaves to Pharaoh, to productivity, or to profit. We are covenantal beings, set apart by grace, bound to a Lord who gives rest.

But in the modern age, memory has eroded. The liturgies of commerce and consumption have drowned out the call to cease. Blue laws have faded. Church bells ring less often. Even in religious households, the Sabbath is often reduced to a convenience—if not forgotten altogether. The West, having desacralized time, now finds itself disoriented, anxious, and addicted to busyness. The cost of forgetfulness is not only spiritual, but civilizational.

And yet, even now, the Sabbath calls. It echoes in the ache of overstimulated minds and burned-out hearts. It flickers in the rising movements of "digital detox," "slow living," and "mindful rest." It is no coincidence that amid all our technological advancement, millions now long not for speed, but for stillness. Surveys reveal that while only a minority strictly observe the Sabbath, a vast majority of Americans express a desire for one day of uninterrupted rest. This longing, however inarticulate, is not nostalgia. It is a whisper of eternity.

For the Sabbath was never merely about stopping. It was about seeing. Seeing the world not as raw material for exploitation, but as creation imbued with purpose. Seeing others not as competitors, but as fellow image-bearers. Seeing time not as a tyrant, but as a trust. To keep the Sabbath is to remember who God is—and who we are not.

This chapter has followed the Sabbath from Genesis to the modern era—from the divine pattern at creation, to the stone tablets of Sinai, through exile, reformation, and industrial rupture. We have watched it shape Jewish identity, define Christian piety, and structure Western law—only to see it pushed aside by the gods of efficiency and endless labor. And yet, the thread has not been severed.

Because the Sabbath is not a cultural artifact. It is a covenantal gift. It was not man's idea, but God's. It is not rooted in utility, but in revelation. And as long as there are people weary of the world's pace, there will be a remnant who hear its call.

The real question, then, is not whether the Sabbath will survive. It will. The sun will still set on Friday night. The candles will still be lit in faithful homes. Church bells will still ring in quiet towns. The rhythm remains.

The question is whether we will remember.

Whether we will reclaim what was given—not as a rule to restrict us, but as a mercy to restore us. Whether we will trust that our worth is not measured in output, but in being known by God. Whether we will dare to stop—not as an act of laziness, but as an act of rebellion against the cult of ceaseless striving.

To keep the Sabbath in an age of frenzy is to declare this with your body and your time: I am not my own. I am not a machine. I will rest, because God rested. I will remember, because He remembered me.

Let the world race on.

But as for me and my house—we will stop.

Chapter 4

WHAT DO YOU WORSHIP?

Everyone worships something. Whether you know it or acknowledge it, you are worshipping something every day.

At its root, the English word "worship" comes from the Old English *weorþscipe* (pronounced "worth-ship"), meaning "the condition of being worthy" or "worthiness, honor, or respect." Over time, it evolved to mean the act of expressing that reverence.

Every culture, every nation, and every generation has worshipped. Deep within the human spirit is an unshakable sense that there is something greater than ourselves, something grander and beyond the reach of human hands. We instinctively know we were made for more than what we can see or touch. Our purpose, our destiny, our very identity can only be found when we are rightly connected to the One who is above it all—the living God who stands beyond time, beyond nature, and beyond the small ambitions of man.

You can easily tell what you are worshipping based on what you sacrifice to. In the old covenant, many times worship was tied to the offering of animal sacrifices. Whether a lamb, a bull, or a dove, each was brought forth as a visible sign of repentance, thanksgiving, or consecration. These acts were not hollow ceremonies, but profound acknowledgments that sin exacts a price, and that communion with a holy God demands humility, obedience, and the surrender of something precious. As it is written, *"For the life of the flesh is in the blood, and I have given it for you on the altar to make atonement for your souls, for it is the blood that makes atonement by the life"* (Leviticus 17:11). The sacrificial system underscored that life itself must be offered to bridge the chasm between man and his Creator.

Yet, these sacrifices were only shadows of a greater reality to come. Every altar and every spilled drop of blood served as a foreshadowing of the perfect and final offering. Worship under the old covenant taught that reconciliation required more than mere intention; it demanded the surrender of life itself. In Christ, the true and spotless Lamb, the need for endless sacrifices was fulfilled in a single, all-sufficient act of love and obedience (Hebrews 10:1–10). Thus, the old covenant rites, though temporal, pointed beyond themselves to the eternal redemption found in Him.

So, what are you sacrificing to?

I have developed a list of the most common counterfeit substitute religions that people give their lives to. You will definitely recognize some of these and maybe even realize that you yourself are unknowingly prioritizing something artificial and earthly above something eternal and real.

Before diving into this, it is critical to understand the importance of the first commandment, *"You shall have no other gods before me"* (Exodus 20:3), and the context in which it was given.

After three months of wandering in the wilderness following God's deliverance from Egypt, the children of Israel came to the foot of Mount Sinai—weary, fearful, yet called. Amid the barren desert and the trembling earth, God summoned Moses to ascend.

From the heights of Sinai, the Lord spoke, offering a covenant: If Israel would hear His voice and keep His commandments, they would become His treasured possession, a kingdom of priests and a holy nation (Exodus 19:5–6).

Moses ascended Mount Sinai, cloaked in cloud and fire, summoned into the very furnace of the Divine. For forty days and forty nights, he remained in the courts of the Almighty, receiving the law, the pattern of worship, the vision of a people set apart for holiness. Below, the Israelites waited, having seen with their own eyes the smoke, the thunder, the trembling mountain. Moses descended to the people and declared the words of the Almighty, and with one voice they pledged, *"All that the Lord has spoken we will do"* (Exodus 19:8).

But the days stretched long. Impatience festered. Fear set in. Doubt gnawed at their souls. In their restless hearts, the ancient hunger for something visible, tangible, and graspable returned. They turned to Aaron, the very man appointed to aid Moses, and demanded, *"Make us gods who shall go before us. As for this Moses, the man who brought us up out of the land of Egypt, we do not know what has become of him"* (Exodus 32:1).

Aaron, weak and capitulating, commanded them to bring their gold, the treasures they had been given by God's providence when they fled Egypt. From the spoils of divine deliverance, Aaron fashioned a grotesque idol, a golden calf, and lifted it before them. And Israel, scarcely freed from the chains of Pharaoh, willingly knelt and declared, *"These are your gods, O Israel, who brought you up out of the land of Egypt!"* (Exodus 32:4).

While Moses stood in the presence of the living God, the people desecrated themselves with drunken revelry, worshipping the work of their own hands. They did not wait. They could not endure a God who could not be seen. They returned with sickening speed to the tribal idolatries of Egypt, clinging to what was familiar, what was controllable, even as they stood beneath a mountain burning with the presence of the one true God.

God saw it all. His anger blazed. *"Go down,"* He said to Moses, *"for your people, whom you brought up out of the land of Egypt, have corrupted themselves. They have turned aside quickly out of the way that I commanded them"* (Exodus 32:7–8). He threatened to consume them in His wrath and start anew with Moses.

Moses, burning with righteous anger, interceded for them, pleading for mercy, reminding God of His covenant with Abraham, Isaac, and Jacob. God relented, but the reckoning was not delayed.

Moses descended the mountain, carrying in his hands the two tablets of stone, the work of God Himself, inscribed by His own finger. What he saw shattered his heart. There was the calf gleaming in the sun, there were the people dancing and shouting in a frenzy of paganism. In his fury, Moses hurled the tablets from his hands and shattered them at the foot of the mountain, a physical sign of the covenant they had already broken.

He seized the golden calf, burned it with fire, ground it into powder, scattered it on the water, and made the Israelites drink it, forcing them to consume the filth of their own rebellion. Turning to Aaron, his voice cut with incredulity and rage, Moses demanded an explanation. Aaron, spineless, blamed the people and muttered absurd excuses. In fact, in one of the funniest, and yet most tragic, lines in all of Scripture, Aaron essentially claims that he threw the gold into the fire and a calf came out (Exodus 32:24).

His excuse is almost laughable in its absurdity, but it reveals something dark about the human heart. Rather than confessing his sin, Aaron attempts to distance himself from it, as though idolatry were something that simply happened by accident, with no human will behind it. But idolatry is never accidental. Idols are shaped first in the imagination, then with the hands. Aaron's weak attempt at denial captures the reflex of fallen man: to blame circumstances, to deny responsibility, to pretend that the things we bow to somehow emerged without our choosing. It is not merely foolishness; it is a refusal to reckon with the deliberate rebellion of the heart.

We do the same today. We look at the idols in our lives—the career we worship, the image we chase, the comforts we refuse to surrender—and shrug as if they "just happened," as if we are innocent bystanders rather than architects of our own rebellion.

One can only imagine the depth of Moses' disgust. After witnessing the unveiled glory of God on Sinai, after hearing His voice and seeing His majesty, after trembling in the holy darkness, he returned to find the people, and even his own brother, prostituting their souls before a lump of gold. It was an agony almost beyond bearing. He had stood in the fire of God's holiness, only to descend into the stench of man's idolatry.

Here is the tragedy: When left to ourselves, we return again and again to worship the works of our own hands. We crave what we can see, what we can mold, what demands no true surrender of the heart. We build counterfeit gods—wealth, pleasure, power, status—and bow before them. We dress them up with new names and modern veneers, but at their core, they are the same golden calves.

The human soul is not neutral. It was made to worship. If it will not worship the living God, it will worship something else. As the story of the golden calf makes brutally clear, we all indeed worship something whether we realize it or not. Worship is not optional; it is inevitable. The only question is whether we will worship what is true, or what is false.

It is no wonder, then, that the very first commandment thunders forth from the mountain with unshakable primacy: "*You shall have no other gods before me*" (Exodus 20:3). It is the first because it is the foundation. It is the commandment upon which all others stand or fall. To break the first is to break them all. To place anything else—anything visible, anything created—in the place of the Creator is to cut out the heart of true faith. It is to exchange glory for shame, truth for a lie, life for death.

With that foundation laid, now it's time to examine and explore some of the deceptive and sham religions that dominate today. If you are not worshipping God, you are worshipping something else. Let's try to discover what that might be as well as what happens to society when we fail to worship the Lord.

The Creed of Anti-Racism

Anti-racism today is not merely a set of ideas or moral instincts; it has hardened into a fully developed religious structure. It possesses its own creeds, customs, rituals, sacraments, and public ceremonies of penance. The philosopher Herbert Marcuse, one of the key architects of neo-Marxist critical theory, laid much of the groundwork for this new orthodoxy. In "Repressive Tolerance" (1965), Marcuse argued that true liberation required the suppression of all dissenting views—an inversion of classical liberalism—and this idea metastasized into a demand for constant vigilance against "oppression" in every form. Angela Davis, a disciple of Marcuse, carried these ideas into the racial sphere, fusing Marxist class struggle with racial identity politics. To the adherents of this new creed, systemic racism is not an evil to be corrected; it is the fundamental organizing principle of society, a sin written into the fabric of existence.

Marcuse's contempt for the West ran deep. He saw Western civilization not as the triumph of reason, liberty, and faith, but as an oppressive structure built on exploitation and domination. He rejected the biblical idea of inherent human dignity grounded in the *imago Dei*, the image of God, replacing it with a view that saw all relationships through the lens of power dynamics. To Marcuse, Christianity, classical liberalism, and the American experiment were not forces for good, but obstacles to be dismantled. He disdained the transcendent moral order taught by Scripture and sought to erase it from the cultural memory, believing that true liberation could only emerge from the ashes of the old order.

His malevolence lay not only in what he criticized, but in what he proposed: A society where speech would be curtailed in the name of "justice," where traditional morality would be labeled "repressive," and where perpetual revolution would be a permanent state of existence. Marcuse's ideas were not aimed at reforming the West, but at hollowing it out—stripping it of its Christian soul, its reverence for truth, and its love of ordered liberty. His intellectual heirs continue this project today under the banners of anti-racism, social justice, and equity.

Marcuse was a leading figure in the Frankfurt School, a group of Marxist intellectuals who sought to apply critical theory to dismantle the foundations of Western culture. Their project was not merely economic revolution, but cultural subversion. They understood that to truly overthrow a society, one must first destroy its spiritual and moral underpinnings. The Frankfurt School attacked religion, the family, tradition, and objective truth itself, replacing them with a fluid morality grounded in perpetual grievance. Their influence saturated American academia in the postwar years, planting seeds that would blossom into today's obsession with systemic oppression, identity politics, and endless deconstruction. Marcuse's vision was not simply to critique the West, but to gut it from within, leaving a hollow shell ready to be filled with revolutionary ideology.

The explosion of Black Lives Matter (BLM) in 2020 revealed the extent to which this pseudoreligion had captured the moral imagination of the West. BLM was not merely a political movement; it was a liturgical movement. People knelt in the streets, confessed their "white privilege," and engaged in public rituals of humiliation and penance. Foot-washing ceremonies, mass kneeling, and public declarations of guilt became the new sacraments. Corporate executives bowed in submission. Pastors replaced sermons with apologies. Universities issued loyalty oaths to the new moral order.

The parallels to Christianity are deliberate and chilling. In the religion of anti-racism, there is an original sin—whiteness. There is confession, but no forgiveness. There is penance, but no absolution. As Scripture teaches, *"If we confess our sins, he is faithful and just to forgive us our sins and to cleanse us from all unrighteousness"* (1 John 1:9). Anti-racism offers no such promise. Its gospel is guilt without end. Its liturgy is endless apology. Its eschatology is the hope for societal deconstruction, not personal redemption.

This new creed demands complete allegiance. To question its tenets is heresy; to dissent is blasphemy. As Paul wrote, *"There is therefore now no condemnation for those who are in Christ Jesus"* (Romans 8:1). But under the regime of anti-racism, condemnation is total and unrelenting. It is not your actions that make you guilty; it is your very existence.

The demographic center of this new faith is unmistakable. According to a 2020 Pew Research Center survey, white liberals—particularly young, college-educated white women—are among the most fervent believers. A study published in the *American Political Science Review* found that white liberals often express more support for racial grievance narratives than the minority groups themselves. Another poll by the American Perspectives Survey (2021) noted that college-educated white women were the demographic most likely to endorse concepts like "systemic racism" and "white privilege" without qualification.

Why the fervor? Because anti-racism offers what so many rootless moderns crave: a cause to fight for, a hierarchy to climb, a moral drama to inhabit. It fills the vacuum left by the collapse of traditional religion. It provides purpose, belonging, and a sense of righteousness. But it is a cruel and devouring god. It offers no redemption, only endless striving. It demands your repentance but will never allow your restoration.

Anti-racism as practiced today is not about healing or reconciliation. It is about perpetual revolution. It is about dismantling, not building; accusing, not forgiving; shaming, not restoring. It reduces human beings to categories of oppressor and oppressed, replacing the *imago Dei*—the image of God—with the image of grievance. It promises utopia, but delivers only division and despair.

The Scriptures warned us long ago: "*They exchanged the truth about God for a lie and worshiped and served the creature rather than the Creator*" (Romans 1:25). In rejecting God, the modern world has not become secular; it has simply found new gods. Race. Power. Rage. Victimhood.

The human heart is a forge of idols. If it will not worship the living God, it will worship whatever lie offers the nearest counterfeit of transcendence. Anti-racism, in its current form, is a godless gospel. It demands sacrifice but gives no salvation. It demands confession but gives no cleansing. It demands loyalty but offers no love.

You might not adhere to this religion—and given its rapidly

growing unpopularity, you likely do not. According to a May 2025 Pew Research Center study, public support for BLM dropped from a high of 67 percent in mid-2020 to just 52 percent in February 2025, with support among white Americans falling to 45 percent. Confidence in the broader "anti-racist" movement has eroded as its most radical demands—abolish the police, defund institutions, equity by force—have revealed their divisive consequences.

However, you might have a granddaughter or grandson in college who has been captured by it. Or a best friend. Or a neighbor. According to the Foundation for Individual Rights and Expression (FIRE) 2022 Campus Expression Survey, nearly 70 percent of college students reported pressure to conform to woke ideologies on issues of race, with students in humanities and social sciences departments feeling the highest levels of pressure. The next generation is swimming in these currents, often without realizing they have been drafted into a counterfeit religion.

The Pagan Religion of Earth Worship

From the dawn of human civilization, mankind has been tempted to worship the creation rather than the Creator. The elemental forces—the sun, the river, the tree, the mountain—have long seduced the human heart into misplaced awe. Earth worship is not new; it is one of the oldest counterfeit religions on record. And today, under the banners of "climate justice" and "environmental activism," this ancient heresy has found fresh legs, a secular vocabulary, and a growing number of fervent disciples.

The Bible itself was written in a world saturated with earth worship. Ancient cultures across Mesopotamia, Egypt, and Canaan venerated the sun, the moon, the river gods, and fertility deities. Baal, Asherah, and Molech were not distant ideas; they were everyday realities. Temples rose to honor the sun. Groves were planted to commune with fertility spirits. Sacrifices—even of children—were offered to manipulate nature's blessings. Against this backdrop, the opening verse of Scripture stands as a thunderous rejection of all pagan cosmologies: *"In the beginning, God created the heavens and the earth"* (Genesis 1:1). Creation was not to be worshipped, but understood as the handiwork of a transcendent God who alone is worthy of reverence.

Throughout Scripture, we find God warring against this impulse to idolize nature. Israel was repeatedly warned not to *"lift up your eyes to heaven and see the sun and the moon and the stars . . . and be drawn away and worship them"* (Deuteronomy 4:19 NASB 1995). The prophets derided those who *"worship the works of their own hands"* (Jeremiah 1:16 CSB). The Bible is clear: Creation is good, but it is not God.

History shows that when man worships the earth, the results are not benign. Among the Canaanites, fertility cults demanded ritual prostitution and child sacrifice to secure the favor of rain gods. Among the Druids of ancient Britain, human sacrifices were performed in sacred groves to appease the spirits of the land. The Aztecs believed the sun required human blood to rise each morning; thousands were slaughtered to "feed" the heavens. In ancient Greece, Gaia—the personified Earth—was seen as a primal, almost divine force. Time and again, the worship of the elements led to the dehumanization and destruction of those made in God's image.

Why is earth worship so seductive? The human heart craves the tangible. Unlike the invisible, holy, and demanding God of Scripture, nature offers a god you can see, touch, and even manipulate. Earth worship appeals to guilt ("I have wronged the planet"), to fear ("the earth will destroy me"), and to control ("if I do the right rituals, I can appease it"). It is a counterfeit faith that satisfies the religious instinct while avoiding the moral demands of the true God.

In our own time, this ancient seduction has been repackaged as "climate catastrophizing." For decades, environmental prophets have issued apocalyptic warnings. In the 1970s, scientists predicted a coming Ice Age if drastic action was not taken. In the 1980s, fears shifted to acid rain destroying crops and forests. In the 1990s, we were told that entire nations would disappear by 2000 due to rising seas. None of these doomsday predictions materialized. In 2006, Al Gore famously warned that the Arctic could be ice-free by 2013. A decade later, the Arctic remains frozen.

Despite the failed prophecies, the movement's religious fervor has only grown. Climate change activism has morphed into a millenarian movement, complete with saints (Greta Thunberg), sacred texts (the Intergovernmental Panel on Climate Change reports), and apocalyptic visions. Thunberg herself thundered before the United Nations, "You have stolen my dreams and my childhood," echoing the passionate lamentations of an Old Testament prophet, though notably absent was any call to repentance toward God.

Behind the banner of "saving the planet" lurks a more cynical goal: The dismantling of capitalism and the reshaping of society. This is no secret. In 2019, Saikat Chakrabarti, chief of staff to Congresswoman Alexandria Ocasio-Cortez, admitted that the Green New Deal was "not originally a climate thing at all," but rather "a how-do-you-change-the-entire-economy thing." Environmentalism, at its most radical, has become the spear tip for economic revolution.

Yet, most adherents, especially the young, remain blissfully unaware. Their zeal is genuine, but their understanding shallow. They march for "climate justice" without realizing they are advocating for a political and spiritual revolution that would destroy the freedoms and prosperity they take for granted.

The allure is powerful. Earth worship offers a clear villain (humanity), a noble cause (saving the planet), and a simple gospel (reduce your carbon footprint, recycle, and protest). It provides purpose in an otherwise disenchanted world. It offers community. It demands sacrifice. Roger Scruton noted that the loss of religious faith has left a yearning for transcendence, and the earth itself has become the object of a re-sacralized devotion.

The data confirms the trend. A 2021 Pew Research Center survey found that 32 percent of Americans under thirty believe that climate change should be "the top priority" for government policy, eclipsing even health care and education. Among young Europeans, the percentage is even higher. And nearly two-thirds of young Americans (64 percent), aged 16 to 25, believe they are doomed due to climate change, according to a survey published in *The Lancet Planetary Health* in 2024.

Pop culture reflects this spiritual hunger. Films like *Avatar* portray a pantheistic paradise where nature is a living, sacred force. Major corporations embrace "Mother Earth" rhetoric in their branding. Ritualistic practices—like "carbon offset" purchases and "climate strikes"—become moral acts of penance. As one protester's sign at a 2019 climate march put it, "Mother Earth is angry, and we must appease her."

Another telling example is the rise of "climate anxiety" among young people. A 2021 *Lancet* study reported that 59 percent of youth globally are "extremely worried" about climate change, with many reporting feelings of hopelessness, fear, and guilt. This is not scientific concern; it is religious dread. It is the emotional collapse of a generation taught to believe that the earth is their mother, their judge, and their executioner.

But the earth is not merciful. Worshipping it will not save us. Nature is majestic, but it is fallen, groaning under the weight of sin, awaiting its redemption, not demanding ours (Romans 8:19–22). When man worships the earth, he inevitably turns against himself. Humanity is cast as a blight upon the world. Solutions shift from stewardship to self-extinction. Population control, abortion, and euthanasia are justified as acts of planetary piety.

The dead end of earth worship is death itself. It cannot give life. It cannot forgive. It can only accuse, consume, and collapse.

The biblical vision is radically different. God created the earth as good (Genesis 1:31), but not as a god. He gave humanity dominion over it, not to abuse, but to steward (Genesis 1:28). Man is not a curse upon creation, but its caretaker under divine commission. The earth is not our mother; it is our garden. It is not to be feared or worshipped, but to be tended with gratitude, humility, and hope.

The psalmist declares, *"The earth is the Lord's and the fullness thereof, the world and those who dwell therein"* (Psalm 24:1). Creation sings the glory of God (Psalm 19:1), but it is not itself divine. We are called to care for the earth because we worship the One who made it, not because we fear its wrath.

In a world drunk on apocalyptic fear and counterfeit faiths, the church must hold fast to the true gospel. We must reject the false religion of earth worship and proclaim the good news of a Creator who made the earth, who rules over it, and who one day will renew it. Until then, we live as faithful stewards, knowing that our hope is not in the earth below, but in the God above.

The Worship of Self

We live in the age of the selfie. More than ever before in human history, individuals are obsessed with documenting, curating, and promoting their own image. In a world where we have a camera pointing at us, we shouldn't be shocked if that is all we think about. Social media platforms—Instagram, TikTok, Snapchat—have not only normalized self-obsession, they have canonized it. It is no longer enough to live a good life; you must perform a life for the approval of others. This is the worship of self, and it is not merely harmless narcissism—it is a destructive counterfeit religion that draws people further from God and closer to despair.

Jonathan Haidt's work has been crucial in identifying the devastating consequences of this cultural shift. In *The Coddling of the American Mind*, Haidt outlines how the rise of smartphones and social media, particularly around 2012, coincided with a sharp increase in anxiety, depression, and suicide among teenagers.

According to the CDC, suicide rates for Americans aged 10–24 increased by 57 percent between 2007 and 2018. Especially among young girls, the need for social validation—for likes, for approval, for attention—has created a mental health crisis. Haidt points to Instagram in particular, which encourages young users to constantly compare their appearance and popularity. When you think about and talk about yourself all the time, when you are inwardly focused for meaning, truth, and goodness, you don't get more self-improvement. You get an increasing number of suicides left in the wake of the self-esteem movement, a movement that promised empowerment but delivered devastation.

Recent data reinforces Haidt's concern. A study published by *The Journal of Abnormal Psychology* found that between 2009 and

2017, rates of major depressive episodes increased by 69 percent among adolescents aged 16–17 and by 60 percent among those aged 14–15. This spike coincides directly with the mass adoption of smartphones and the explosion of social media use. Another survey conducted by Monitoring the Future in 2019 showed that teens who spent more than three hours a day on electronic devices were 35 percent more likely to have at least one suicide risk factor compared to those who spent less than one hour on them.

The mental health impact is even more pronounced among teenage girls. Between 2010 and 2015, the suicide rate for girls aged 15–19 doubled, and the rate for girls aged 10–14 tripled. Social media, with its endless metrics of likes, comments, and followers, fosters a brutal and constant comparison culture. Teenagers, encouraged by the ideology of self-esteem to fixate on their own image, find themselves trapped in cycles of insecurity and despair. The cult of self-focus breeds not resilience, but fragility.

The roots of this collapse can be traced back to the advent of the self-esteem movement in the 1960s and 1970s. Psychologists like Nathaniel Branden, a disciple of Ayn Rand, popularized the idea that high self-esteem was the key to personal success and societal health. In his book *The Psychology of Self-Esteem*, Branden argued that self-regard was the foundation of all human achievement. His ideas caught fire, and by the 1980s, the state of California even created the Task Force to Promote Self-Esteem and Personal and Social Responsibility, convinced that boosting self-esteem would reduce crime, addiction, and academic failure.

The results? A stunning failure. Studies later showed that artificially inflating self-esteem did not produce better outcomes. Instead, it produced generations more fragile, more narcissistic, and less able to handle failure. Jean Twenge, in *Generation Me*, documented how young people raised with an intense focus on self-esteem became more entitled, less resilient, and more prone to depression when reality collided with their inflated self-image. We primarily teach our children this nonsense—telling them they are perfect just as they are, that their feelings are sovereign, that they are the center of the universe—and it has taught them to look inward for meaning instead of upward for hope, truth, and goodness. In elevating the self, we have cut the cord to any external anchor, and we are watching the ship of culture drift aimlessly toward the rocks.

The ideology of self-esteem has become embedded into nearly every layer of children's education. From elementary school through high school, curricula emphasize "feeling good about yourself" over actual accomplishment or mastery. Participation trophies replace earned awards. Correct answers are less important than "trying your best." Personal expression is elevated above discipline and rigor. Students are taught that their worth is inherent and unassailable, regardless of behavior, effort, or growth. This has created generations of young people who believe they are wonderful—and yet are woefully unprepared to handle the hard truths of real life.

The self-esteem movement has grown like wildfire precisely because it promises an easy path. Who would oppose making children "feel good"? Few had the courage to push back. Critics who warned that resilience, grit, and humility were being sacrificed on the altar of fragile feelings were dismissed as cruel or out of touch. As a result, the false gospel of self-esteem spread unchecked for decades, hollowing out our education system, our work ethic, and even our spiritual formation.

The problem is not merely that self-esteem is misplaced. It is that it short-circuits the necessary engine of growth: dissatisfaction. When we believe we are already wonderful, we lose the drive to improve. Conviction, repentance, ambition—all these require the recognition that we are lacking something. That we need to change. That we must reach higher. The self-esteem movement stole that vital hunger and replaced it with a stagnant, fragile pride.

Worshipping yourself is nothing new. In fact, one of the biggest sins of the Bible is the elevation of self above God. Pride, the original sin of Lucifer, is the temptation to make oneself like the Most High (Isaiah 14:14). Adam and Eve fell for the same lie: *"You will be like God"* (Genesis 3:5). The mirror is the worst place to be focused on. Instead, we must embrace the doctrine of original sin—that we are deeply flawed, desperately in need of grace, and wholly unable to save ourselves. As Paul writes, *"For all have sinned and fall short of the glory of God"* (Romans 3:23). The path to true life begins not with self-exaltation, but with self-denial and surrender to Jesus Christ.

The fake religion of self leads to hypernarcissism, and the data bears this out. Studies from the *American Sociological Review* show that empathy among college students has dropped by 40 percent since 2000. Neighborliness and community involvement have plummeted. Robert Putnam's *Bowling Alone* detailed the collapse of civic engagement long before smartphones became ubiquitous, but the trend has only accelerated. When self is the highest value, the other is devalued. Relationships become transactional. Community dissolves. Love grows cold.

In the West, we are told the self is above all. "Follow your heart." "You do you." "Live your truth." But what has this yielded? Epidemic loneliness. Fractured families. Skyrocketing rates of mental illness. A society that is materially richer than ever and spiritually more impoverished than any in living memory.

People worship themselves today in ways so subtle, they hardly recognize it. Consider the endless curation of online personas—projecting a filtered, idealized self to the world while the true soul withers in isolation. Every carefully staged photo, every caption seeking applause, becomes a small act of devotion at the altar of self. Then there is the cult of emotional sovereignty, where personal feelings become the highest truth. "If I feel it, it must be real" becomes not merely a statement of experience, but a new doctrine of moral authority.

Self-help culture plays its role too. What began as genuine efforts at human flourishing has often been hijacked into an endless cycle of self-obsession. Entire industries now exist to tell people they are perfect as they are—that they must simply "discover" themselves, "accept" themselves, and "believe in" themselves. There is no call to repentance, no need for outside redemption. Only endless, exhausting navel-gazing.

The rejection of any external moral authority—whether Scripture, tradition, or even basic shared human wisdom—is the inevitable result. If the self is ultimate, then anything that contradicts my feelings must be oppressive. Obedience is rebranded as oppression. Sacrifice is recast as self-betrayal.

All of this sounds liberating on the surface. In reality, it is a recipe for collapse. The person who worships themself finds that their god is cruel, demanding constant validation but offering no peace.

The toxicity of self-worship poisons relationships, undermines community, severs the soul from its Creator, and leaves the individual adrift. In the book of James, we are warned: *"God opposes the proud but gives grace to the humble"* (James 4:6).

How do we resist the worship of self?

We must recover the lost art of humility. As C. S. Lewis is attributed with saying, "Humility is not thinking less of yourself, but thinking of yourself less." We must root our identity not in our curated image or our fluctuating emotions, but in Christ, who alone offers a stable, unchanging foundation. *"I have been crucified with Christ, and I no longer live, but Christ lives in me"* (Galatians 2:20 CSB).

We must cultivate gratitude—a heart posture that recognizes every good thing as a gift rather than an entitlement. Gratitude shifts our gaze upward.

We must practice service—pouring out our lives for others, not as an act of virtue signaling, but as a reflection of Christ's love.

And we must immerse ourselves in Scripture—the unchanging Word that reorients our hearts away from self-idolatry and toward the worship of the living God.

Self-worship promises liberation but delivers bondage. It promises happiness but yields despair. It demands attention but gives no peace. It creates a generation obsessed with the mirror but incapable of seeing beyond their own reflection.

Only in dying to self can we truly live. Only in bowing before the throne of God can we find the freedom our souls were made for.

Then Jesus told his disciples, *"If anyone would come after me, let him deny himself and take up his cross and follow me"* (Matthew 16:24).

The world says, "Exalt yourself." Christ says, "Deny yourself."

Choose wisely.

Unfortunately, there are three more false gods of our age clamoring for our worship.

Chapter 5

SCIENCE, STUFF, AND POWER: THE AGE OF COUNTERFEIT WORSHIP

The past few years did not simply expose public health failures or misguided political leadership—they revealed something far deeper and more dangerous: a spiritual sickness gripping the West. Faced with a virus that threatened human fragility, the world did not turn upward to the Creator; it bowed lower before the idol of human expertise. The lockdowns were worse than the virus. And both were man made, born from the same hubristic belief that man can engineer paradise if only he controls enough variables, silences enough dissenters, and manipulates nature itself. What we witnessed was not merely bad policy—it was the full unveiling of a counterfeit religion.

The Cult of Scientism

What emerged was not a rational, cautious trust in genuine science, but a blind, dogmatic faith in "experts," "models," and "authorities" who demanded unquestioning allegiance. "Follow the science" became a mantra, a shield against scrutiny, and a bludgeon against dissent. But beneath that slogan was an unspoken truth: It was never really about following science. It was about trusting scientists—"the right scientists"—who conformed to the narrative blessed by institutional power.

Scientism is not science. Science is the noble pursuit of understanding the natural world, built on humility, curiosity, and the recognition of our limitations. Scientism, by contrast, is the belief that science alone can answer all questions of life, morality, and meaning. It is a totalizing worldview that seeks to replace faith, philosophy, and theology with laboratory reports and press conferences.

Embedded deep within this worldview is a Germanic philosophical contagion stretching back to Hegel. Hegel's thought, later amplified by Marx and Nietzsche, taught that man does not simply observe reality—he must shape it. Nature is not something to understand and respect, but something to dominate and remake according to human will. Man, not God, becomes the central actor of history. The goal is not to conform oneself to an objective moral order, but to forge history anew by the strength of human intellect and desire.

This poisonous seed grew into a monstrous tree, bearing the bitter fruit of Marxist revolutions, Nazi eugenics, and the bloody utopian experiments of the twentieth century. German idealism untethered reason from revelation and gave license to the most horrific atrocities—always under the guise of "progress" and "enlightenment." It replaced divine humility with human arrogance. It cast out repentance and enthroned human ambition. Its intellectual rot has seeped into nearly every institution of the modern West.

The belief that man can engineer utopia has led to the horrors of the twentieth century: the gulags, the death camps, the mass experiments on entire populations. When man enthrones himself over nature, convinced of his perfectible wisdom, he inevitably produces carnage.

The human cost of the lockdowns cannot be overstated. While the virus primarily harmed the elderly and those with preexisting conditions, the lockdowns devastated the young, the poor, and the working class. Global poverty surged. According to the World Bank, over 97 million more people were pushed into extreme poverty in 2020 alone. Small businesses were shuttered by the millions. Mental health disorders exploded. Domestic abuse rose sharply. Children in poor nations lost years of education that they will likely never recover. Suicides, drug overdoses, untreated medical conditions—all collateral damage of a policy regime driven more by fear and the lust for control than by reasoned compassion. The experts insisted they were "saving lives," but in truth, they sacrificed millions on the altar of their own hubris.

Meanwhile, institutions like the World Health Organization (WHO) and the CDC compounded the disaster through a toxic cocktail of incompetence, political bias, and deliberate misinformation. The WHO praised China's early handling of COVID-19 despite obvious evidence of cover-ups, delayed human-to-human transmission warnings, and slavishly repeated false assurances. The CDC issued shifting, contradictory guidelines that seemed driven more by political winds than public health evidence; mask mandates, six-foot distancing rules, and arbitrary shutdowns were enforced despite flimsy or nonexistent scientific backing. Public trust was shattered not because science failed, but because bureaucrats weaponized "science" to advance their own agendas.

The CDC's refusal to release granular data on vaccine effectiveness, the suppression of natural immunity discussions, and the shifting goalposts around herd immunity only reinforced public skepticism. Similarly, the WHO's early denial of the lab-leak theory—despite mounting evidence—exposed their willingness to subordinate truth to political convenience. These were not isolated missteps; they were systemic failures. And the cost was borne by billions around the world who trusted these institutions, only to be misled, manipulated, and abandoned.

The tragedy of medical experimentation—from the ghastly procedures at Dachau to the Tuskegee syphilis study—flowed from this same poisoned spring. The idea that human beings are raw material to be shaped, tested, manipulated, "improved." And this mentality is alive today, thinly veiled by bureaucratic language and institutional prestige.

At its core, the cult of scientism is a refusal to admit a simple, humbling truth: There is a God, and we are not Him. Instead, the high priests of the new order offer salvation not through grace, but through injections, mandates, and social engineering. They do not point upward; they point to themselves.

This became blazingly obvious in the figure of Anthony Fauci. Fauci was positioned as the embodiment of science itself—an infallible oracle whose shifting proclamations must not be questioned. Masks don't work, until they do. Lockdowns are unthinkable, until they are morally mandatory. The lab-leak theory is a conspiracy, until it becomes plausible. Again and again, Fauci's pronouncements changed, yet his authority grew. To criticize him was, in the eyes of his followers, not merely an intellectual disagreement—it was an act of heresy.

What motivates someone to bend the knee at the altar of their ninth booster shot? By what standard does this endless cycle of fear, injection, and moral self-congratulation make any sense?

At a fundamental level, many people WANT science to promise them a salvation it cannot deliver. They want the vaccine not just to protect them, but to make them invincible. They want the experts not just to guide them, but to give them certainty in a chaotic world. They want the system not just to function, but to become their god.

Another insidious temptation is the lust to craft nature in our image. We do not see ourselves as made by God; we see nature as raw material to be remade by us. Modern bioethics debates are soaked with this spirit—the drive to edit genes, to create "designer babies," to "enhance" human life beyond natural limits. Yet, when we reject the *imago Dei*—the belief that man is made in God's image—we inevitably replace it with the lie that nature must be remade in ours. In trying to escape the givenness of creation, we plunge ourselves into chaos.

For some, it is the desperate hope that science will offer life eternal—that with enough boosters, enough technology, enough genetic manipulation, death itself can be postponed indefinitely. But as Christians, we know the truth: Eternal life is not a laboratory achievement. It is the gift of God, won by the resurrection of Jesus Christ. *"I am the resurrection and the life,"* Jesus said. *"Whoever believes in me, though he die, yet shall he live"* (John 11:25).

In 2020, they told us to "follow the science." But science is a method, not a Messiah. What they really meant was "trust the scientists we approve of, obey the authorities we endorse, and silence any dissent." It was not an invitation to critical thinking; it was a command to blind submission.

We saw public health agencies—agencies meant to safeguard lives—become instruments of political and social control. The CDC redefined "vaccine" to fit the evolving failures of their product. The National Institutes of Health (NIH) suppressed alternative treatments not because of evidence, but because of bureaucratic loyalty. The US Food and Drug Administration (FDA) bent its own standards to push experimental solutions onto a terrified population.

The ruin was immense. Children lost years of education and social development. Mental health collapsed. Small businesses were crushed. Families were isolated. Elderly people died alone. And through it all, the cult of scientism marched on, demanding more sacrifices, more obedience, more faith in the system.

Scientism thrives because it promises what the human heart craves: certainty, control, and mastery over death. But it is a false gospel. It cannot deliver on its promises. Its priests are fallible. Its miracles are temporary. Its saviors are corrupt.

Science can tell us how a virus spreads. It cannot tell us how to balance safety and freedom, how to weigh risks and relationships, how to live and die with dignity. Those are moral and spiritual questions—questions that science alone cannot answer.

Romans 1 warns us that when people reject the Creator, they inevitably worship the creation—and that includes the tools and technologies made by human hands. *"They exchanged the truth about God for a lie and worshiped and served the creature rather than the Creator"*(Romans 1:25).

Today, we are witnessing that exchange play out in real time. In laboratories, in policy boards, in television studios. We are being offered a new covenant: Trust the system, obey the experts, and you will be saved.

But we must not bow.

We must remember that science, properly understood, is a tool—a powerful one, but a tool nonetheless. It is a means of understanding God's creation, not a substitute for God Himself. It must be governed by humility, ethics, and a recognition of human fallibility.

When we place our ultimate faith in men, we invite tyranny. When we place our ultimate faith in God, we find freedom.

The cult of scientism is not going away. It has metastasized into climate policy, health care, education, and technology. It demands total compliance and punishes questioning. It seduces with promises of security and progress, but underneath lies the same old lie: "*You will be like God.*"

We must resist it with everything we have. Not by rejecting real science, but by rejecting the worship of science. Not by spurning knowledge, but by submitting all knowledge to the lordship of Christ.

There is a God, and we are not Him.

There is a Savior, and His name is not Fauci.

There is eternal life, but it is found not in a laboratory, but in an empty tomb.

The Adoration of Stuff: Materialism, Flesh, and the Worship of the World

At the beginning of this chapter, you might not have thought you were worshipping anything. But take a moment and ask yourself: What gets me more excited—an afternoon of unhurried time with my children or a new purse? Am I more eager to turn my phone off and dwell quietly with God, or do I reflexively keep it on, tethered to the urgent hum of the world? Do I count my wealth by my bank account balance or by the depth of my intimacy with the living God? Be honest. If you cannot turn off the modern world for a day and honor the Sabbath—if you find every excuse not to—then you are not worshipping the Lord. You are worshipping the love of the world.

Materialism is the quietest and most pervasive religion in the

West. Unlike political ideologies or radical activist movements, it asks for no public creeds, no marches, no slogans. It simply demands your heart. It demands your time. It demands your loyalty. It demands your Sabbath. Worship always requires sacrifice, and millions in the modern West sacrifice their family time, their financial peace, and their spiritual lives at the altar of accumulation. If you are reading this book and have agreed with most of what I have published, this—not scientism or wokeism—is most likely your personal struggle.

We live amid more material abundance than any people in human history. The average American home has tripled in size over the last fifty years, yet still often cannot contain the sheer quantity of possessions. Storage units are now a $40 billion-a-year industry in the United States. According to an *LA Times* article, the average American household contains three hundred thousand items. We buy more, throw away more, and covet more. Online shopping platforms deliver anything we want within twenty-four hours. We have pantries stuffed with food, closets overflowing with clothes, garages packed with things we haven't touched in years. In the West, stuff is not simply owned; it owns us.

Biblically, this is no small issue. Jesus warned plainly, "*Do not lay up for yourselves treasures on earth, where moth and rust destroy and where thieves break in and steal, but lay up for yourselves treasures in heaven*" (Matthew 6:19–20). He spoke these words to an ancient people who lived with far less than we do today—and yet the temptation to idolize possessions was strong even then. How much stronger is it now, when the marketplace beckons us every waking hour, and when every ad whispers, "You are what you buy."

It is not a sin to have things. Abraham, Job, and David were wealthy men. But the danger comes when things have us—when our hearts are tangled in the fleeting comforts of the material world. *"For where your treasure is, there your heart will be also"* (Matthew 6:21).

If you wonder what you worship, look at what you sacrifice for. Many sacrifice their Sabbath—that sacred day of rest and worship commanded by God—for an extra day of work, an extra shopping trip, an extra scroll through endless online sales. Many sacrifice time with their children to chase promotions, bigger homes, and higher status. Many sacrifice their financial peace to purchase things they don't need to impress people they don't even like. Materialism is not content to coexist quietly; it demands blood.

This reality is part of the reason I wrote this book. A true Sabbath—a day set apart, a day of ceasing, a day of reorienting our lives toward God—stands as a bold rebuke to the worship of stuff. It interrupts the machine. It says no to the unrelenting demands of the marketplace. It reminds us that man does not live by bread alone, or smartphones alone, or vacations alone, but by every word that proceeds from the mouth of God.

In the United States, studies show that even among professing Christians, materialism runs rampant. A 2022 Lifeway Research survey found that 62 percent of churchgoers agreed with the statement, "My personal success is defined by the wealth and possessions I accumulate." Only 37 percent said they regularly observed a Sabbath rest in any significant way. The disconnect is staggering—and revealing. For all our verbal allegiance to Christ, the god we trust with our time, our energy, and our anxieties is often Mammon.

We once lived in a country that slowed down, even if imperfectly. Blue laws reflected an understanding that not everything should be available 24/7. Stores closed. Families gathered. There was a rhythm of rest embedded into the civic calendar. Now we are a culture of nonstop consumption. Everything is always open, always on, always beckoning for our attention. We have gained convenience but lost something priceless.

Today, Americans work more hours per year than their counterparts in almost every other developed nation. According to the Organisation for Economic Co-operation and Development (OECD), US workers put in nearly eighteen hundred hours annually—hundreds more than workers in Germany or the Netherlands. We spend more, buy more, and expect more. Yet, surveys show that reported levels of life satisfaction have remained stagnant or even declined. We might have more stuff and more money, but are we wealthier? Truly wealthier?

According to the Global Material Wealth Index, Americans own more personal possessions and consumer goods per capita than any other nation, yet report more stress, anxiety, and dissatisfaction compared to many less materially wealthy countries. Pew Research studies show that Americans rank among the most stressed and least rested people in the developed world, despite outpacing nearly everyone in personal spending. The drive to accumulate has not delivered peace; it has delivered exhaustion.

Meanwhile, church attendance and Sabbath observance have collapsed. Gallup reports that regular church attendance in the US has fallen below 50 percent for the first time in recorded history. This collapse coincides exactly with the rise of 24/7 commercialism—stores, sports, and screens filling every formerly sacred hour. We no longer set aside a day to rest; we fill every day with more striving.

True wealth is measured not by accumulation, but by peace, by joy, by relationship with God and neighbor. The endless pursuit of stuff has left us more anxious, more isolated, and more spiritually impoverished than ever. Even as the Gross Domestic Product

(GDP) rises and malls expand, loneliness, depression, and spiritual numbness grow.

Before you dismiss this as someone else's problem, take an honest look in the mirror. Are you more excited for the next vacation or the next chance to serve someone in need? Does the arrival of a new Amazon package thrill you more than time in prayer? For young men, maybe it's the next gadget, the next truck, the next status upgrade. For young women, maybe it's the new purse, the perfect Instagram post, the perfect body sculpted by endless striving. For older men and women alike, it might be the perfect retirement portfolio, the next remodel, the shiny comforts meant to pad the final decades of life. These are not luxuries; they have become loves. And too often, they have become gods.

Worship is not merely about what we sing on Sundays; it is revealed by what excites our hearts, shapes our calendars, and directs our sacrifices. If you find it harder to fast from a shopping trip than to fast from sin, if you find it easier to spend two hours comparing prices than two minutes bowing in prayer, you are not neutral. You are being shaped. Your loves are being formed. The question is not whether you worship; the question is whether you worship rightly. Christ does not call you to hate good gifts—but He calls you to love Him infinitely more.

The solution is not to embrace asceticism for its own sake. It is to return to the God who gave us life, meaning, and purpose. To remember that we are stewards, not owners. To hold our possessions with open hands. To love people and use things—not the other way around.

Jesus does not call us to poverty for poverty's sake. He calls us to treasure Him above all else. *"But seek first the kingdom of God and his righteousness, and all these things will be added to you"* (Matthew 6:33).

If we seek Him first, the rest falls into its rightful place. If we chase the treasures of this world first, we find only anxiety, exhaustion, and emptiness.

It is worth asking: What is the weight of all your stuff compared to the lightness of walking with Christ? What is the value of endless consumption compared to the pearl of great price?

The Pursuit of Power Above All: The Veneration of the State

At first glance, you might think the worship of power is confined to politicians, CEOs, or the ruthless strivers of Silicon Valley. But look a little closer, and you'll see it is far more widespread—a temptation that lures not just the few, but the many. It lives in corporate boardrooms, yes, but it also lives in school boards, in homeowners' associations, in social media mobs, and even in churches. It is the quiet but deadly desire to dominate, to control, to wield authority over others—not for good, not for service, but for the sheer, intoxicating thrill of supremacy.

The Latin word *dominium* captures this perfectly: ownership, dominion, and rule. It is the same primal urge that fueled the ancient empires, the same spirit that drove kings to conquer and tyrants to oppress. It is no less alive today, merely clothed in modern dress.

George Orwell captured this dark religion with chilling precision through the character of O'Brien in *1984*. In one unforgettable passage, O'Brien declares, "The object of power is power." Power is not a means to an end; it is the end itself. In this worldview, truth is irrelevant, justice is a ruse, and loyalty is disposable. All that matters is domination.

This is a profoundly twisted and dangerous form of idolatry—and though it seems rare, it is a weed that grows quickly if left unchecked.

The pursuit of power for power's sake has deep philosophical roots. Herbert Marcuse, a prominent figure in the Frankfurt School, sowed the seeds of the modern obsession with domination by reducing all human relationships to power dynamics. In Marcuse's view, there are no free individuals, only oppressors and the oppressed. The only moral action is to seize power from your "oppressor" and wield it against them. Power is no longer a stewardship; it is a weapon.

This worldview has metastasized into every corner of American life. In politics, it is obvious—the endless quest for dominance, for control of legislatures and courts, for the ability to dictate terms to one's fellow citizens. But it has crept into corporate America as well, where leadership is too often reduced to naked careerism and influence is treated as a virtue in itself.

It shows up when a manager subtly destroys a promising subordinate out of insecurity. It shows up when activists demand the silencing of dissenting voices, not because they seek truth but because they crave control. It shows up when online mobs swarm to destroy someone's life over a perceived ideological wrong.

This is not leadership. This is not justice. This is raw, unvarnished domination.

The Bible offers a radically different view of power. Recorded in Matthew 20:25–28, Jesus said, "*You know that the rulers of the Gentiles lord it over them, and their great ones exercise authority over them. It shall not be so among you. But whoever would be great among you must be your servant, and whoever would be first among you must be your slave, even as the Son of Man came not to be served but to serve, and to give his life as a ransom for many."*

Christian leadership is not about domination; it is about service. True greatness is measured by how much we pour out, not how much we control.

Yet, in modern America, the hunger for power grows. According to a 2021 Pew Research Center study, trust in government has plummeted to historic lows—yet paradoxically, the size and scope of government continue to expand. Why? Because those who seek power for its own sake are never satisfied. They do not wield authority to protect liberty; they wield it to gratify their own egos.

Similarly, in corporate life, data from the *Harvard Business Review* reveals that among middle and senior managers, the primary cause of burnout and dysfunction is not workload—it is toxic leadership rooted in the abuse of power. When authority is used not to bless but to crush, the human soul shrivels.

The veneration of the state is one outgrowth of this worship of power. Many today look to government—to bureaucratic machinery—as the ultimate source of justice, provision, and salvation. This is a tragic inversion of biblical truth. In Romans 13, we read about Paul teaching that government exists to restrain evil and promote good, but it is not a god. It is a servant.

When the state becomes an idol, it demands absolute loyalty. It demands the sacrifice of conscience, of freedom, of truth. It punishes dissent and rewards flattery. This was true under Caesar; it is true under modern technocratic regimes.

Aleksandr Solzhenitsyn warned of this dynamic in *The Gulag Archipelago*: "Unlimited power in the hands of limited people always leads to cruelty." When power becomes an end in itself, cruelty inevitably follows. Whether it is a petty official abusing their position or a mighty tyrant crushing a nation, the pattern is the same.

And it is growing.

In America, we now see the rise of bureaucratic empires, unelected and unaccountable, who exercise enormous control over daily life. Agencies issue decrees with the force of law. Surveillance expands. Censorship becomes normalized. Freedom shrinks.

All of it justified by the language of necessity. All of it driven by the unspoken conviction that some people must rule, and others must obey.

But this is not the way of Christ.

Power promises what it cannot deliver. It promises security, but breeds fear. It promises greatness, but produces loneliness. It promises victory, but leaves only ruin. Those who worship at the altar of domination discover too late that they have built their kingdoms on sand, and when the winds come, it all collapses.

True greatness, Christ taught, is found in service, not supremacy. True authority flows not from coercion, but from the willingness to carry a cross. It is the meek who will inherit the earth, not the manipulators. It is the pure in heart who will see God, not the power hungry.

The question is not whether power will tempt us. It will. The question is whether we will remember this truth: that we were made to kneel before a throne—but not our own.

There is only one throne worth kneeling before, and it does not belong to any man. It belongs to the Lamb who was slain. Every other throne will crumble.

Bow at His throne, and nowhere else.

The worship of power corrodes everything it touches. It warps the mind, making cruelty seem justified and betrayal seem necessary. It blinds the soul to love, to humility, to mercy. The pursuit of raw domination is a path lined with the broken bodies and broken hearts of those sacrificed along the way.

The person consumed by power sacrifices not only others, but himself. His conscience withers. His capacity for joy diminishes. He becomes a hollow creature—forever seeking, forever clutching, forever afraid of losing what he has stolen.

History bears grim testimony to this truth. Consider Stalin, who ruled through terror, paranoia, and mass murder, sacrificing millions on the altar of his own control. Or Pol Pot, whose thirst for ideological purity led to the deaths of nearly a quarter of his own people. Both were men who worshipped pure domination—and both reaped devastation.

As we move further away from honoring God, the allure of power grows stronger. Without a higher standard to restrain ambition, without the humility that comes from worshipping something greater than ourselves, power fills the vacuum. And history shows again and again—from Pharaoh to Caesar, from Stalin to modern tyrants—that when the worship of power becomes unchecked, ruin follows.

The temptation to dominate seems almost inescapable in the long arc of human history. It is a temptation that must be consciously resisted, again and again, in every generation. Only when power is seen as a stewardship under God's ultimate authority can it be used for good. Otherwise, it remains what it has always been—a devouring fire, consuming all who bow before it.

Chapter 6

THE SABBATH IMPROVES YOUR HEALTH

What if I told you that some of the people who live the longest and are the happiest in the world retreat from the fury and madness of the modern world? Extraordinary evidence now exists that honoring the Sabbath is not just spiritually nourishing, but physically and mentally as well.

I recently spoke at an event on a Friday afternoon held by Seventh-day Adventists in Phoenix, Arizona. They had me come speak about the Sabbath as they were preparing for an all-day worship Sabbath among their congregation. Despite some core theological differences, I was struck by their joy and commitment to unplugging from the modern world. They treated me very well, and I am glad to call some of the people I met my friends to this day. I watched how they interacted with others and how they treated the Sabbath. It was with remarkable reverence, respect, and weight that they approached the seventh day.

For background, Seventh-day Adventists believe that the Sabbath is a sacred, God-ordained day of rest and worship, rooted in the fourth commandment and affirmed throughout Scripture. They observe the Sabbath from Friday sunset to Saturday sunset, following the biblical model established in Genesis 2:2–3 and reinforced in Exodus 20:8–11. For Adventists, the Sabbath is not merely a day off, but a divine appointment—an intentional pause that honors God as Creator and Redeemer. It is a weekly spiritual discipline that calls for cessation from secular labor and worldly distractions, and instead invites worship, fellowship, service, and communion with God. The Sabbath is also viewed as a sign of loyalty to God's law and an expression of their faith in His sustaining power.

According to the official *Seventh-day Adventist Church Manual*, the Sabbath "is a symbol of our redemption in Christ, a sign of our sanctification, a token of our allegiance, and a foretaste of our eternal future in God's kingdom." The Adventist Church teaches that Sabbath observance is both a present blessing and a prophetic marker, pointing forward to the rest and restoration promised at Christ's return. This theological view is deeply holistic—encompassing physical rest, mental peace, social bonding, and spiritual renewal. In the words of their official doctrinal statement, "The gracious Creator, after the six days of Creation, rested on the seventh day and instituted the Sabbath for all people as a memorial of Creation. . . . The Sabbath is God's perpetual sign of His eternal covenant between Him and His people."

As I was preparing to speak at the event, the Adventists worked hard and with much delight to prepare their meals, knowing that they would be leaving the increasingly unjust, cruel, and unfair world for twenty-four hours. They were quietly rejoicing in the fact that God designed an island of worship, a sanctuary of only family, friends, and fellowship.

I left their conference believing that if every Christian community had this same commitment to the Sabbath, there would be virtually zero downsides. Whether you believe you are bound to the Sabbath or not is not the point; it's a self-evident truth that if every church and Christian community turned off from the world for a day, they would arise after twenty-four hours better rested and prepared, and stronger to defend the faith the following week.

At the event, one of the Adventists told me there is profound evidence that people who observe the Sabbath are healthier and happier. I tilted my head in disbelief, never having connected those dots. I, of course, knew it intuitively to be true that the Sabbath was good for you spiritually. But physically? Living longer? I needed more data. So, I went down a deep rabbit-hole hunt of research, and here are some of the shocking discoveries I made.

In a study published in the *American Journal of Public Health*, researchers examined the remarkable health outcomes of the Seventh-day Adventist community in Loma Linda, California—one of the world's five "Blue Zones," regions where people routinely live past one hundred. These Adventists observe a literal Sabbath every Saturday: A full twenty-four-hour period where they cease work, disconnect from the world's demands, and devote time to rest, worship, nature, and family. This weekly rhythm, practiced faithfully for generations, is not incidental—it is central to their identity. According to Dr. Gary Fraser, who has studied over ninety-six thousand Adventists for more than thirty years, the Sabbath isn't just a day off. It's a weekly spiritual retreat that gives its followers a sense of peace and belonging.

Another long-term study published in the journal *Health Psychology* found that Adventists who kept the Sabbath had less inflammation, better sleep, and more resilience to stress-related sickness, even when controlling for diet and exercise. The study's authors concluded that it was the combination of spiritual rest and communal connection that made the biggest difference. As one Adventist put it, "Sabbath is a sanctuary in time. It's where the noise stops and I remember who I am." That's more than a lifestyle—it's a worldview. The very act of stopping, of honoring a day as holy and separate, appears to strengthen not only the spirit, but the immune system, the heart, and the mind.

Loma Linda Adventists also exhibit unique behavioral patterns: They rarely eat out on the Sabbath, instead preparing meals ahead of time; they spend extended time in nature; and they engage in unhurried, device-free fellowship. According to research from the NIH, this intentional withdrawal from the chaos of modern life—done weekly and communally—creates a cumulative buffer against chronic disease and burnout. The study even linked Sabbath-keeping to reduced rates of depression, especially among older adults, who reported that the Sabbath gave them purpose and a sense of being "anchored in something eternal."

Among the most closely studied religious communities on earth, Seventh-day Adventists quietly live lives that defy the trends of the modern West. The 2017–2018 Global Church Member Survey revealed that 88 percent of Adventists around the world describe themselves as happy. This data is staggering when contrasted with Gallup's January 2025 US national survey, which shows that only 44 percent of American adults report being "very satisfied" with their personal life, which is the lowest recorded by Gallup since 2021. In fact, post-2020, the United States recorded its lowest levels of self-reported happiness since tracking began. Yet, within this cultural downturn, Adventists remain a statistical outlier. Their joy is not circumstantial. It is rhythmic, covenantal, and embedded in the sacred structure of time. Their weekly Sabbath is not a lifestyle enhancement—it is a theological declaration: God is in control, and we are not machines.

This joy, crucially, is not disconnected from bodily health. A constellation of peer-reviewed studies shows that Adventists who observe the Sabbath report markedly lower levels of depression, anxiety, and inflammation. One long-term study of pastors who recommitted to Sabbath-keeping found that their mental health and spiritual clarity improved significantly, while those who let go of the practice saw a spike in emotional exhaustion and disorientation. What was being measured here was not placebo piety—it was the tangible consequence of reordering life around rest. A Harvard-affiliated analysis of Adventist behavioral patterns in Loma Linda found that their structured Sabbath routines—preparing meals in advance, avoiding screens, spending time outdoors, and engaging in spiritual community—contribute directly to longer life, better cardiovascular health, and superior stress resilience. Their rest is not passive—it is formative. It shapes their cells, their outlook, and their capacity to endure.

But the deepest truth is this: The Sabbath is not simply a mechanism for recovery—it is a reorientation of meaning. The official Adventist teaching describes it as "foretaste of our eternal future in God's kingdom," a day where heaven breaks into ordinary time. In a culture that measures identity through productivity and assigns worth based on output, the Adventist insists on a different story: that time is sacred, that being is more important than doing, and that silence with God can heal what no therapy, drug, or achievement can touch. Their weekly withdrawal from the world's pace is not escapism—it is resistance. It is prophetic. In stepping back, they recover what many in the modern world have forgotten: how to be present, how to belong, and how to worship. Their happiness, then, is not a fleeting emotion—it is the fruit of living in rhythm with the One who created time itself. And in an anxious, distracted age, that may be the most radical act of all.

None of this is accidental. It is chosen. It is cultivated. The Adventists did not stumble into long life and mental clarity—they built it, brick by sacred brick, upon the practice of Sabbath. Their lives stand as quiet, living arguments against the gospel of productivity and burnout. In an age of speed, distraction, and medical anxiety, their way of life is a kind of resistance, a living parable. When the world says, “Do more,” they say, “Enough.” When the world screams for attention, they retreat to silence. In a century where everyone is trying to squeeze more hours from the day, the Adventists remind us that the most vital hours may be the ones where nothing is “done” at all—except prayer, presence, and peace. Perhaps that is why they live longer: Because they never forgot how to stop.

I decided to not stop my search at Seventh-day Adventists. I wanted to go deeper to see the connection between people who observe some form of a Sabbath day off. Was it true across denominations?

Another large-scale study from the Harvard T. H. Chan School of Public Health tracked over seventy thousand women and found that those who attended weekly religious services—especially within traditions that practiced a structured Sabbath—had a 33 percent lower risk of dying during the study period of over sixteen years. Researchers linked this to stronger social bonds, reduced stress levels, and a greater sense of meaning and belonging. Similar findings were echoed in a 2020 Gallup poll showing that Americans who prioritized weekly worship and intentional rest scored significantly higher in overall life satisfaction, purpose, and emotional stability. The act of honoring the Sabbath—far from being restrictive—appears to be a wellspring of human flourishing.

Stop Scrolling and Start Living

Addiction, especially to technology, has emerged as one of the most pressing and least regulated health crises of our time. The World Health Organization now classifies "gaming disorder" as a medical condition, and researchers are calling for similar recognition of social media and smartphone overuse. In 2023, the analytics firm Data.ai reported that the average American adult now spends over 4.9 hours per day on mobile devices—up from just 3.7 hours in 2019. That amounts to nearly a third of every waking hour devoted to scrolling, tapping, and consuming digital input. These behaviors aren't random; they are carefully engineered. As former Google design ethicist Tristan Harris put it, "Technology is not neutral. It is designed to exploit our weaknesses." Every notification, vibration, and algorithmic feed is built to trigger dopamine release, creating reward loops that mimic the neurological patterns of substance addiction. The result is a populace both overstimulated and undernourished, perpetually online but emotionally depleted.

For young people, the effects are even more pronounced and dangerous. Common Sense Media's 2022 census on media use among children and teens found that teenagers (ages 13–18) now spend an average of 8 hours and 39 minutes per day on screen-based entertainment—excluding school-related use. For tweens (ages 8–12), the number is 5 hours and 33 minutes. These aren't just leisure hours; they are hours of identity formation, emotional development, and worldview shaping—all happening through curated, algorithm-driven platforms that reward outrage, vanity, and conformity. A 2019 study published in *JAMA Pediatrics* reported that excessive screen time was linked to structural changes in children's brains, including reduced integrity in white matter tracts related to language, literacy, and cognitive control. Meanwhile, a 2023 CDC report showed that 42 percent of high school students felt persistently sad or hopeless during the previous year—an all-time high. Among girls, that number jumped to well over 50 percent. Social media, particularly platforms like TikTok and Instagram, was named by respondents as a key source of anxiety, comparison, and sleeplessness.

This comes with remarkable irony—people know their dependence on technology is harmful, and yet they can't seem to stop. This, of course, is the root of addiction that has confounded me for years. I understand people who are addicted but deny it; denial is the shield that makes addiction survivable in the short term. But what is far more perplexing is the individual who *knows* they are addicted, openly admits it, and still takes no meaningful steps toward change. A 2023 Pew Research Center study revealed that over 70 percent of American adults believe they spend too much time on their phones, yet only 31 percent have made any attempt to cut back. This dissonance is not due to ignorance, but entrapment. The awareness is there—the problem is not cognitive; it's spiritual, emotional, even neurological. Like the smoker who inhales with full knowledge of the cancer risk, millions tap and scroll through a glowing vortex, fully conscious of the toll it exacts on their attention, relationships, and peace of mind.

The compulsive nature of tech use among young people is no

accident. Social platforms employ "intermittent variable reward" systems—borrowed from slot machines—to keep users engaged. Likes, notifications, and algorithmic boosts create a digital casino where every swipe holds the promise of a hit. As Dr. Anna Lembke, author of *Dopamine Nation*, notes, "We've transformed the world into a pleasure machine, and the result is a nation of addicts." The adolescent brain, which is still developing executive function and impulse regulation, is especially vulnerable. A 2022 Gallup survey reported that nearly 60 percent of teens say they feel addicted to their phones, with many experiencing withdrawal symptoms—irritability, anxiety, even panic—when separated from their devices. And yet, despite widespread awareness, disengagement is rare. Why? Because the phone is not just a tool—it's an identity portal. It is where friendships are maintained, status is performed, emotions are processed, and boredom is obliterated. It is both mirror and mask, escape and entrapment.

I studied *Dopamine Nation* carefully. I read it intently, pen in hand, underlining paragraph after paragraph, and found it one of the most illuminating books I've encountered on the nature of addiction—especially in the digital age. Dr. Anna Lembke, a psychiatrist at Stanford and one of the nation's foremost experts in addiction medicine, presents a startling thesis: We are not just surrounded by addictive substances and technologies—we are drowning in them. The modern world, she argues, has created a dopamine-rich environment where almost everything is engineered to give us quick, easy pleasure. From sugar to screens, porn to shopping, we are immersed in a culture of compulsive overconsumption. "We've transformed the world into a pleasure factory," Lembke writes, "and the result is a paradoxical epidemic of unhappiness."

What makes Lembke's work especially valuable is her explanation of the dopamine balance. She describes the brain's reward system like a seesaw: Every time we experience pleasure, the brain tips to one side. But the brain always wants to return to equilibrium. If we push the seesaw too often with high-dopamine stimuli—like Instagram, YouTube, TikTok, or video games—the brain compensates by pushing down the other side: pain. This is why people who overindulge in pleasure often feel anxious, numb, or depressed afterward. "We're not able to take joy in more modest rewards . . . our drug of choice doesn't even get us high. It just makes us feel normal," she explains. This isn't just about addiction to substances—it's the biological mechanism behind behavioral addictions, which she warns are now far more common and socially accepted. Smartphones, in this framework, aren't just tools. They are pocket-sized dopamine machines.

Lembke also sheds light on why quitting—or even scaling back—feels so hard. It's not just habit. It's a physiological battle. When we remove high-dopamine behaviors from our lives, our brain enters a withdrawal state. People experience irritability, fatigue, boredom, and emotional discomfort. In the process of resetting our reward pathways, "people will generally feel worse before they get better," according to Lembke. She prescribes a "dopamine fast"—a thirty-day period without the addictive behavior, during which the brain recalibrates its baseline. For people addicted to social media or phone use, this kind of sustained abstinence can feel almost unbearable. But Lembke insists it's necessary. She explains that only after the pain side of the seesaw has had time to reset can we begin to experience real pleasure again—pleasure that's not artificially inflated, but grounded, human, and lasting.

What struck me most while reading *Dopamine Nation* was not

how complicated addiction is—but how simple and ancient the solution might be. Lembke repeatedly emphasizes the need for boundaries, rituals, and discomfort. In other words, what Judaism has built into the rhythm of Shabbat. The Sabbath is a living dopamine fast. No electronics, no shopping, no scrolling. It is a (nearly) twenty-five-hour rejection of the pleasure factory. At first, this can feel difficult, even painful. But then something shifts. As the noise dies down, attention returns. Food tastes better. Conversation deepens. Time slows. In a world engineered for overstimulation, Shabbat is not just restful—it is neurologically reparative. And Lembke's research affirms what Jews have known for thousands of years: Abstaining from pleasure is not punishment. It's the only way to feel it again.

The irony deepens when we consider how powerless most young people feel to resist this pull. A 2023 University of Michigan study found that 78 percent of college students have tried to reduce their screen time, but only 12 percent were able to sustain a change for more than a month. The researchers described this as a form of "behavioral learned helplessness"—a condition in which users, despite wanting change, become resigned to their compulsions. Young people care about changing, but they've tried and failed. They then give up and internalize their dependency. This addiction is not just a private struggle; it's a collective disorder. School performance is declining. Attention spans are shrinking. Physical activity is plummeting. And young people, instead of developing resilience and self-mastery, are being raised inside devices that train them to chase novelty, avoid silence, and outsource worth to strangers' approval.

This is not an exaggeration—it's a growing body of data. A 2021 study published in *Nature Human Behaviour* tracked more than

5,000 adolescents across three years and found that increased time on social media was significantly correlated with a decline in mental well-being, with the effects most pronounced in 14- to 17-year-olds. Girls, in particular, showed strong associations between social media use and increased self-harm behaviors and depressive symptoms. Researchers pointed out that the constant feedback loop of likes, comments, and comparisons amplified insecurities and eroded emotional regulation. "These platforms are not neutral," the authors wrote. "They are immersive environments designed to reward compulsive behavior."

In a 2022 study from the University of North Carolina, researchers found that adolescents who check their phones compulsively show substantial changes in the development of their prefrontal cortex—a region responsible for decision-making and impulse control. MRI scans revealed a stunted maturation curve in frequent phone users, suggesting that constant digital distraction may be impairing the very faculties required to resist it. The study's lead neuroscientist, Dr. Eva Telzer, warned that early introduction to addictive technologies is shaping the architecture of the brain in ways we're only beginning to understand. That shaping isn't just physical—it's behavioral. When distraction becomes the default, focus becomes foreign.

Meanwhile, the American Psychological Association's 2023 report on adolescent mental health found that teens who use screens for more than seven hours a day—now a common threshold—are more than twice as likely to be diagnosed with anxiety or depression compared to their peers who use screens for under two hours. In other words, the dose makes the poison. And for most young people today, the dose is constant. Jean Twenge, a psychologist and author of *iGen*, summarized it bluntly by emphasizing that the massive, sudden change in how teens spend their time is having a clear impact on their mental health. She says we are conducting "an uncontrolled experiment on a generation."

Addiction to devices, especially in the young, is not about pleasure anymore—it's about compulsion. What begins as entertainment morphs into dependency. The feedback mechanisms of apps exploit biological pathways honed for survival—dopamine bursts, social validation, reward anticipation—but twist them into loops of endless craving. The tragedy is not only in the struggle, but in the resignation. Teens know something is wrong. They feel the fatigue, the anxiety, the emptiness. But with nothing to replace the feed, they keep scrolling into a "hollowed-out version of life."

This resignation is perhaps the most haunting part of the modern digital crisis: Young people don't just suffer from screen addiction—they've grown to accept it as inevitable. The implications are not just academic. They are tragic. Around 2012, when smartphones and social media apps like Instagram became widely adopted by teenagers, youth mental health data began to shift in alarming ways. According to the CDC, between 2009 and 2019, the rate of high school students reporting persistent feelings of sadness and hopelessness rose from 26 percent to 37 percent. Among girls, it rose even faster. But more disturbingly, the suicide rate among teenagers—after decades of decline—**began to surge** around this same time. The CDC reports that the suicide rate for youth aged 10–24 increased **by 57 percent between 2007 and 2018**. This sudden reversal aligns almost precisely with the widespread adoption of smartphones, especially in middle and high school students.

Research published in *Clinical Psychological Science* by Dr. Jean Twenge found strong correlations between increased screen time and deteriorating adolescent mental health—particularly around the 2012 inflection point. Her study showed that "teens who spend five or more hours a day on electronic devices are 71 percent more likely to have at least one risk factor for suicide compared to teens who spend less than an hour a day." Twenge concludes: "The sweet spot seems to be less than an hour . . . of use a day" and "three hours of use and beyond per day [is] linked to considerably higher risk of depression and other mental health issues." What was once anecdotal or parental concern is now solidly backed by peer-reviewed data: The arrival of the smartphone, especially when paired with social media, has had a devastating impact on the emotional well-being of America's youth.

Even suicide attempts have become alarmingly common. A 2021 study in *JAMA Network Open* analyzed emergency room visits for suspected suicide attempts among adolescents. For girls aged 12–17, the rate of ER visits **jumped by nearly 51 percent in early 2021** compared to the same period in 2019. While many factors were in play, researchers cited social isolation, online harassment, and compulsive internet use as key contributors. Dr. Lisa Damour, a clinical psychologist and best-selling author on adolescent development, has warned that digital culture is creating a "constant psychological thrum of judgment, comparison, and exposure that previous generations never had to navigate in real time." Young people are now not only living their lives—they are constantly *performing* them for invisible audiences, and being measured in likes and shares at every turn.

A significant factor in this trend is the erosion of boundaries between private self and public performance. Platforms like Instagram and TikTok collapse solitude and magnify comparison. Adolescents, whose identities are still forming, are left with little interior space. Everything becomes content. As social psychologist Sherry Turkle, author of *Reclaiming Conversation*, notes in a lecture, "We're lonely but we're afraid of intimacy. . . We're designing technologies that give us the illusion of companionship without the demands of friendship. We turn to technology to help us feel connected in ways we can comfortably control." For teenagers, whose developing brains are wired for social learning and peer approval, this illusion is particularly harmful. Their attention is no longer free. It is monetized. Their sense of worth becomes entangled in metrics. And their emotional states rise and fall with the tides of digital affirmation—or the absence of it.

This is no longer about individual discipline or better parenting. It is a systemic failure. Children and teens are growing up in an ecosystem that exploits their psychology for profit. A 2021 internal Facebook report leaked by *The Wall Street Journal* revealed that Instagram exacerbated body image issues in **1 in 3 teenage girls**, and that Facebook executives were aware of this fact. One internal slide presentation stated plainly: "We make body image issues worse for one in three teen girls." Another noted: "Teens blame Instagram for increases in the rate of anxiety and depression." These weren't outside critics—they were Facebook's own researchers. And yet, the platform continued operating as designed. The engine kept running. Attention kept selling. And millions of young users continued to sink deeper into comparison, self-doubt, and despair.

At this point, the pattern is undeniable. Smartphone adoption coincides with mental health decline. Social media use predicts depressive symptoms. Prolonged screen time rewires the adolescent brain. And young people, in record numbers, are expressing not just dissatisfaction—but desperation. They are not simply overstimulated; they are overwhelmed, disoriented, and losing their grip on interior stability. Their cries are not subtle. They are coming in the form of anxiety, self-harm, eating disorders, and suicidal ideation. And the most damning truth is that they know it. They scroll, compare, post, and panic—and still, they return to the device. Not because it brings them joy, but because it has become the air they breathe.

What's needed now is not more apps promising "mindful tech" or more parental screen reports. It's a structural reinvention of time, community, and meaning. And that is exactly what the Sabbath provides. For twenty-five hours each week (just before Friday sunset and just after Saturday nightfall), it declares, "enough." Enough scrolling, enough comparing, enough consuming. It creates sacred interruption. It reinstates face-to-face relationships, real rest, and identity rooted in something other than the algorithm's verdict. In an age where young people are losing themselves to screens, Shabbat offers not escape, but recovery. Not silence as emptiness, but silence as a return to self. And that may be the most urgent gift we can offer the next generation.

There is no simple fix. But the scale of the crisis demands something greater than screen-time tracking or mindfulness apps. What's needed is a cultural reset—a sacred structure that mandates disconnection, reinstates silence, and teaches young people how to be *bored*, how to be *present*, and how to live *unplugged* for sustained periods of time. This is why the Jewish Sabbath is so profound in our age: It does not merely recommend rest—it requires it. For twenty-five hours each week, observant Jews live as if the digital world doesn't exist. No phones, no texts, no feeds, no alerts. And in that space, the soul breathes, attention heals, and families sit face-to-face. In a world where most people can't make it through a meal without checking their device, this ancient practice has never looked more radical—or more necessary.

When Work Never Ends

In terms of psychological resilience, the *Journal of Religion and Health* found that regular Sabbath-keeping was associated with reduced markers of burnout, lower cortisol levels, and greater family unity. Sabbath observers reported feeling more emotionally connected, more patient, and more grounded. Among those with high-stress careers, the practice of weekly rest became a lifeline. One of the most striking findings was that Sabbath keepers reported a higher threshold for handling difficulty. In other words, they didn't just rest better—they lived better, loved better, and endured hardship with more grace.

Americans today are more burned out than at any other point in modern history. According to a 2023 report from the American Psychological Association, over 77 percent of US adults report experiencing chronic stress that negatively affects their physical health, mental well-being, and sleep. The World Health Organization has officially classified burnout as an "occupational phenomenon," driven by unmanaged work stress and digital overload. Employees across industries now face blurred boundaries between home and work, with remote technologies extending the workday well past traditional limits. This relentless pace has led to widespread exhaustion, declining productivity, and a sharp increase in anxiety, depression, and sleep disorders. In younger generations, the picture is even more stark: A 2023 Gallup poll found that over 60 percent of Gen Z workers experience frequent feelings of anxiety and detachment at work, with many describing their lives as "numb" or "overstimulated."

The biology of burnout is now better understood than ever before. Recent research from Stanford University found that chronic stress reconfigures the brain's amygdala and prefrontal cortex—making individuals more reactive, less rational, and less capable of regulating emotion. Simultaneously, stress elevates cortisol and inflammatory markers, weakening the immune system and increasing risk for cardiovascular disease, autoimmune disorders, and even cancer. A groundbreaking 2022 study published in *Cell* found that stress can accelerate biological aging by shortening telomeres—protective caps on DNA that degrade over time. In other words, unchecked stress doesn't just make people feel older—it makes them biologically older. Another study from the University of California, Irvine, found that people exposed to continual stress without meaningful breaks were twice as likely to experience long-term cognitive decline in midlife, even when controlling for sleep and diet. Chronic stress, in this model, becomes a slow and silent neurotoxin.

In response, the medical and psychological communities are increasingly emphasizing not just the need for rest, but the pattern of rest. Sleep aids, mindfulness apps, and corporate wellness programs often offer fragmented relief without addressing the core problem: the human need for deep, rhythmic restoration. Scientists at Harvard's Division of Sleep Medicine now argue that scheduled "recovery windows" must be inviolable and sacred—protected from interruption and deeply embedded into life's structure. Dr. Charles Czeisler, one of the world's foremost experts on circadian biology, warns that irregular schedules and "work creep" (the encroachment of work into all hours) disrupt hormonal balance, impair immune defense, and destabilize mood regulation. A 2021 meta-analysis published in *The Lancet Psychiatry* found that people who lack a weekly rhythm of rest—particularly one with social and spiritual dimensions—are at considerably higher risk for major depressive disorder, insomnia, and generalized anxiety.

Put simply, Americans are not just tired—they are untethered. They have access to infinite stimulation but little true peace. They endlessly scroll but rarely stop. They rest without restoring. And despite all the wellness technology, something essential is missing: a weekly architecture of time that commands the soul and body to pause. This is where modern science, after decades of chasing the latest productivity hacks and biohacks, is beginning to return to an ancient truth: The human being needs sacred time. Not merely a break from work, but a covenant with rest. Ritualized, predictable, and honored. In this light, the Jewish Sabbath is not just a cultural tradition—it is a health blueprint designed thousands of years before we had words like burnout or cortisol.

Michael Easter, in his best-selling book *The Comfort Crisis*, dives headlong into this cultural exhaustion and pinpoints one of its root causes: constant digital stimulation. He argues that the modern environment, saturated by screens, convenience, and comfort, has created a physiological and psychological mismatch between how we live and what our bodies and minds actually need. "Western laziness [is] cramming our lives with compulsive activity, so that there is no time at all to confront the real issues," he writes. "Going on as we do . . . can become an end in itself and a pointless distraction." Easter's work highlights the toll this has on cognitive function, emotional regulation, and attention span.

In one striking experiment cited in his book, Easter spent thirty-three days off the grid in the Alaskan wilderness, completely disconnected from technology and immersed in discomfort, nature, and silence. The result was more than psychological insight—it was cellular and visceral reset. He was able to think clearly again, the kind of deep, uninterrupted thought he hadn't experienced in years. He began to realize that the constant checking, scrolling, and reacting is more than just a waste of time; it's a form of dependency. Like any addiction, it wears away who you are.

Easter's insights add weight to the growing scientific consensus: Regular time away from technology isn't a luxury—it's essential for health. Neuroscientists now know that even short breaks from screens restore parts of the prefrontal cortex involved in decision-making and self-control. The Sabbath, in this light, functions as a weekly detox from digital dependence. By halting screen use entirely for twenty-five hours, observant Jews are not just keeping a commandment—they are giving their nervous systems space to breathe, their brains time to regenerate, and their souls room to return.

And increasingly, it's not just the religious or the traditional who are waking up to this truth. A 2023 Pew Research Center survey revealed that nearly 70 percent of Americans aged 18–35 said they wished they could unplug from digital life for at least one day a week. More than half reported feeling anxious, exhausted, or emotionally scattered from constant device exposure and nonstop social media use. These young adults aren't rebelling against rest—they're aching for it. In a culture addicted to productivity and distraction, the longing to exit the frenetic pace of modern life is growing. What many desire is not a new app or mindfulness hack, but something older—something structured and sacred. The Sabbath, once dismissed as a relic, is now emerging as a quiet revolution. It is a reset for the soul, a protest against burnout, and perhaps the most radical thing one can do in a world that refuses to stop.

To Embrace Sabbath Is to Say No to Pharaoh

In Exodus 5, we read that Pharaoh rages when Moses asks for rest: *"You make them rest from their burdens!"* (Exodus 5:5). The Hebrew word used here for "rest"—*shabbat*—is the same word that "Sabbath"—*shâbbath*—is derived from. Pharaoh's empire was built on ceaseless labor, on brick quotas that knew no grace, no rest, no end. And in many ways, that same spirit animates the modern economy. We live in a society governed by invisible Pharaohs—algorithms, deadlines, notifications, and ever-expanding expectations. They whisper: *More. Faster. Always on.*

But the Sabbath is a divine refusal. It is the command to rest—not as reward, but as rhythm. As God Himself did: *"And on the seventh day God finished his work that he had done, and he rested on the seventh day"* (Genesis 2:2). God didn't rest because He was tired. He rested because the work was complete. He rested to bless creation with a pattern: a world not run by endless striving, but by trust. *You can stop, and it will be enough.*

This is deeply countercultural. In a society where identity is increasingly tethered to output—where your worth is measured by how busy you are—the Sabbath invites you to stop, and still be loved. Still be human. It rehumanizes us in a dehumanizing world.

And It Heals

Harvard Medical School research has confirmed what Scripture long taught: that weekly rhythms of worship and rest correlate with lower cortisol levels, improved heart health, and longer life expectancy. One study found that those who attend weekly religious services live, on average, seven to fourteen years longer than those who don't. The act of pausing, of anchoring your week not in anxiety, but in awe, recalibrates the nervous system. It restores balance. *"Return, O my soul, to your rest; for the Lord has dealt bountifully with you"* (Psalm 116:7).

In both versions of the Ten Commandments—Exodus 20 and Deuteronomy 5—the command to keep the Sabbath is nearly identical. Six days you shall labor and do all your work. The seventh is a Sabbath to the Lord your God. You shall not work, nor shall your son, your daughter, your servants, your animals, or the sojourner within your gates. But there's one stunning difference in the rationale.

In Exodus 20, the Sabbath is grounded in *creation. "For in six days the Lord made heaven and earth, the sea, and all that is in them, and rested on the seventh day. Therefore the Lord blessed the Sabbath day and made it holy"* (v. 11). The logic is clear: You rest because God rested. The Sabbath imitates the divine pattern. It is a rhythm embedded into the fabric of creation itself—a sacred cycle of work and rest that declares the world is not held together by endless productivity, but by divine wisdom, order, and blessing. Sabbath, in this light, is cosmic—it reminds us of who God is as Creator, and who we are as creatures.

But recorded in Deuteronomy 5, when Moses repeats the commandments forty years later to a new generation about to enter the promised land, he changes the reason. Here the Sabbath is not grounded in creation, but in *liberation. "You shall remember that you were a slave in the land of Egypt, and the Lord your God brought you out from there with a mighty hand and an outstretched arm. Therefore the Lord your God commanded you to keep the Sabbath day"* (v. 15).

That's the only change between the two texts—and it's monumental. In Exodus, you Sabbath because God made the world. In Deuteronomy, you Sabbath because God set you free.

What's the implication? **Slaves don't rest. Only the free do.**

This isn't a theological footnote. This is the heart of the Sabbath. In Egypt, Israel labored without end. Pharaoh gave them no margin, no mercy, and no Sabbath. They were reduced to units of output—brick quotas, production demands, ceaseless toil. Their worth was tied to their work, their value to their volume. Egypt was an empire of endless striving. It was the prototype of every modern economy that confuses human dignity with performance. And in that world, rest is not permitted. Rest is rebellion.

So when God delivers Israel and gives them the Sabbath, He isn't just instituting a religious holiday. He is declaring a new identity. *You are no longer slaves. You are mine.* And because you are mine, you don't live like the nations. You don't grind seven days a week. You don't build your life on anxiety and exhaustion. You stop. You breathe. You remember. And in remembering, you resist.

The Sabbath, then, is a *political act*. It is a weekly declaration of allegiance—not to Pharaoh, not to empire, not to the machine, but to Yahweh. You cannot serve two masters. You cannot simultaneously live by grace and by quotas. The Sabbath draws a line: It divides those who are free from those still in chains.

And Moses, in Deuteronomy, wants the new generation to understand this deeply. He is speaking to those who never knew Egypt firsthand. These were wilderness-born children. They hadn't felt the sting of the lash. But Moses insists: Remember. Don't forget what it was to be a slave. Don't forget how God rescued you. Because the moment you forget, you'll start to live like slaves again. Or worse, you'll begin to act like Pharaoh.

That's why the Sabbath isn't just personal—it's communal and ethical. It includes your son, your daughter, your servant, your livestock, the foreigner within your gates. It levels the field. It doesn't just command that *you* rest—it insists that *everyone under your influence* rests, too. In a world where the powerful rest and the weak labor, the Sabbath stands as divine protest. God says, *Not in My kingdom.*

In that way, the Sabbath becomes a litmus test for justice. It reveals whether we are reproducing Egypt or building something new. Are we granting rest only to ourselves, or extending it to others? Are we perpetuating systems of exhaustion, or dismantling them with grace?

This has urgent implications for us today.

Because the spirit of Pharaoh is alive and well. It lives in the hustle culture that never lets up. In the algorithms that feed addiction. In the jobs that demand constant availability. In the anxiety that tells you you're falling behind if you take a break. It lives in every lie that says your worth is what you produce, and your value is what you achieve.

And it lives in us when we impose the same on others—when we demand more from those who serve us, when we build our success on the backs of others' exhaustion, when we don't let our systems breathe.

The Sabbath slices through all of that.

It says this, with unwavering clarity: *You are not a slave.* You don't have to earn your rest. You were rescued to receive it. And more than that: You are not allowed to be a Pharaoh to anyone else. Not in your home. Not in your company. Not in your culture.

This is why the Sabbath command in Deuteronomy is so powerful. It doesn't just tell us to stop working—it tells us *why*. It roots rest in the very memory of freedom. It teaches us that rest is not a luxury for the privileged, but a birthright of the liberated. It turns the simple act of stopping into a testimony, a sermon, a song of deliverance.

When we Sabbath, we remember who God is: not a taskmaster, but the Redeemer. We remember who we are: not commodities, but covenant people. We remember where we came from: a land of slavery. And we remember where we are going: a land of promise, where all things are made new.

That is why Sabbath matters. That is why it is not optional. And that is why Moses made this one change—so that the people of God would never forget the cost of their freedom, nor forsake the gift of their rest.

Because only slaves work all seven days. The free do not.

You were set free—so you can *rest.*

The Sabbath Also Reorients Desire

But here's the turn that brings it all together: This is not just about theology or politics. The God who delivered His people and commanded their rest also designed them. He knows the limits of the body and the longings of the soul. The Sabbath isn't just a spiritual gift—it is a *physical mercy.*

Modern science is catching up to ancient wisdom. Study after study confirms what Scripture has whispered for millennia: Those who keep the Sabbath—who regularly rest, unplug, worship, and refrain from commerce—are not only more spiritually rooted, but physically healthier. Lower rates of heart disease. Lower cortisol levels. Stronger immune systems. Greater emotional resilience. Higher life satisfaction. Longer lives.

Modern life breeds discontentment. We scroll, we compare, we chase. But Sabbath slows the scroll. It tells us: You already have enough. *"Better is a handful of quietness than two hands full of toil and a striving after wind"* (Ecclesiastes 4:6). Sabbath teaches contentment. It forms gratitude. It creates space for joy that isn't earned, only received.

Sabbath is also communal. It's not an isolated self-care day—it's meant to be shared. In Jewish tradition, the Sabbath table becomes a miniature altar. Songs are sung. Candles are lit. Bread is broken. There's laughter, storytelling, intergenerational presence. You're reminded you're not alone. You're part of a people. And in a time of rising loneliness—where even secular thinkers describe an epidemic of isolation—the Sabbath's gift of presence may be its most healing power.

As Jesus said, *"The Sabbath was made for man, not man for the Sabbath"* (Mark 2:27). It is not a burden; it is a blessing. A gift. A weekly glimpse of the kingdom to come.

Chapter 7

THE SABBATH IMPROVES YOUR SLEEP

I want to share a little secret with you. I hesitate to call it a superpower—because that sounds grandiose—but it's true. It's incredibly powerful and available to each and every one of us.

In our hyperhustle culture, we venerate the sleepless. I began noticing this in high school, where the best students seemed to operate on little sleep, caffeinating themselves through the day. It became a badge of honor to say you "pulled an all-nighter," proudly walking through the halls with a Starbucks coffee—a luxury item where I grew up.

This didn't change as I got older. As I engaged with prospective donors and funders for Turning Point USA, I noticed that many highly ambitious individuals were sleepless zombies, chugging espressos and energy drinks. I was always bothered by this because I've been a sleeper my whole life. I love sleep, and I don't function well without it. If needed, I can do a week on little sleep, but I feel it—I notice my mental acuity slipping day by day.

How did we get here? Sleep is obviously good for us, yet it's viewed as a sign of weakness or laziness. As my career grew and my need to impress others waned, I began proudly proclaiming to those curious about my success, "Yes, I sleep nine to ten hours a day and take a nap. Don't you?"

It's not easy getting that much sleep. You have to actively cut out distractions. For me, that means rarely going out unless I'm speaking, abstaining from alcohol and desserts, and limiting TV—unless it's a good college football game or the Bears. I prioritize sleep; it's the glue that holds my life together. I notice that the more I sleep, the better my memory recall, the sharper my speaking, and the happier I am. This isn't just my personal story; the data is overwhelming.

In our increasingly sleepless nation, the statistics are alarming. A study by the American Psychological Association found that improving sleep led to significant improvements in mental health, including reductions in depression, anxiety, and stress.

What Happens When You Don't Sleep

Sleep deprivation affects virtually every system in the body. In the short term, missing even a few hours of sleep leads to these:

- Decreased attention span
- Impaired judgment
- Slower reaction times
- Emotional volatility
- Higher cortisol levels

In the long term, chronic sleep loss is linked to these:

- Obesity
- Type 2 diabetes
- Cardiovascular disease
- Depression and anxiety
- Memory loss
- Immune suppression
- Higher mortality rates

A study published by the NIH National Library of Medicine (2006) found that just one night of four hours of sleep results in measurable damage to the brain's synaptic activity, impairing neural communication and attention.

Performance Declines Without Sleep

In the workplace and classroom, sleep loss is productivity poison. The RAND Corporation published a study estimating that the US loses over $411 billion per year in productivity due to insufficient sleep.

A 2003 study published in the journal *Sleep* by researchers from the University of Pennsylvania discovered that individuals who slept only six hours per night for two weeks performed as poorly on cognitive tasks as those who went without sleep for forty-eight hours straight.

That means if you're sleeping six hours a night thinking you're getting by—you're actually functioning like someone who pulled two consecutive all-nighters. And the worst part? You won't notice your own impairment.

Sleep and Weight Gain

Numerous studies now link short sleep duration to increased risk of obesity. When you don't sleep enough, your body disrupts the hormonal balance between ghrelin (which stimulates hunger) and leptin (which signals fullness).

A 2004 study published in *PLOS Medicine* found that individuals who slept less than five hours per night had a 15 percent higher risk of becoming obese compared to those sleeping seven or more hours.

Lack of sleep also elevates cortisol, the stress hormone, which promotes fat storage—especially in the abdominal region. Your body literally clings to calories when you don't rest.

Sleep and Mental Health

Sleep is the bedrock of emotional stability. The NIH has linked chronic insomnia and short sleep duration to increased rates of these:

- Depression (two times more likely)
- Generalized anxiety
- Bipolar episodes
- Suicidal ideation

A 2021 study in *JAMA Psychiatry* found that older adults with insomnia who improved their sleep through cognitive behavioral therapy experienced more than a 50 percent reduction in depressive symptoms compared to those receiving standard care.

Dr. Matthew Walker, author of *Why We Sleep*, puts it bluntly: "The shorter your sleep, the shorter your life."

What Happens During Sleep (Biologically)

Sleep is not passive—it's a period of intense biological work and restoration.

Stage 1: Light Sleep (N1) – Transition phase, lasting a few minutes. Muscles relax, heart rate slows.

Stage 2: Deeper Light Sleep (N2) – Brain waves slow. This stage makes up about 50 percent of your total sleep.

Stage 3: Deep Sleep (N3 or Slow-Wave Sleep) – This is the restorative phase. Your body releases growth hormone, repairs tissues, strengthens the immune system, and consolidates physical memory (muscle memory, athletic skills).

Stage 4: REM Sleep (Rapid Eye Movement) – Critical for emotional regulation, creative problem solving, and memory integration. During REM, your brain is highly active—your body paralyzed to prevent acting out dreams.

Each night, you cycle through these stages four to six times. If you're cutting your sleep short, you're robbing yourself of full cycles—and the neurological and physiological benefits they bring.

The Caffeine Trap

One major reason Americans don't sleep is the normalized overuse of caffeine. Caffeine blocks adenosine, a naturally accumulating chemical that signals sleep pressure. It doesn't give you energy—it masks your fatigue.

The half-life of caffeine is about five to seven hours, meaning that even your 2 p.m. coffee can reduce sleep quality that night. A 2015 study co-led by Kenneth Wright, Jr., PhD, from the University of Colorado Boulder, and John O'Neill, PhD, from the Medical Research Council's Laboratory of Molecular Biology in Cambridge, England, published in *Science Translational Medicine*, found that consuming caffeine equivalent to a double espresso three hours before bedtime can delay the body's internal circadian clock by about 40 minutes, pushing back the onset of melatonin and REM sleep.

Caffeine is not a performance enhancer—it's a loan shark. It robs from tomorrow to pay for today.

Hydration, Energy, and Mental Clarity

While caffeine stimulates, hydration sustains. Even mild dehydration (1–2 percent loss of body weight) can impair these:

- Short-term memory
- Mood
- Focus
- Reaction time

A 2013 study in *The Journal of Nutrition* found that young women who were mildly dehydrated had significantly higher fatigue, tension, and difficulty concentrating—even without any physical exertion.

Hydration also plays a role in thermoregulation—a key function that helps initiate sleep. Drinking water throughout the day improves sleep onset, especially when caffeine and alcohol are avoided.

Sleep is not just restorative—it's defensive. During deep sleep, your body releases cytokines, proteins that fight infection and inflammation. Studies from the University of Tübingen in Germany found that sleep actually increases the efficiency of T cells, your body's infection-fighting warriors.

When you're sleep-deprived, your body produces fewer antibodies after vaccination. A 2023 study published in UCLA Health showed that participants who slept fewer than six hours per night were significantly less likely to develop protective immunity after receiving the flu vaccine.

Alzheimer's researchers have long suspected a link between poor sleep and dementia. In 2017, scientists at the NIH discovered that deep sleep plays a critical role in flushing out beta-amyloid, a sticky brain plaque associated with Alzheimer's disease.

Without enough slow-wave sleep, the brain's glymphatic system—its "trash disposal" network—fails to clear these toxins. This is why chronic sleep deprivation is increasingly seen as a modifiable risk factor for cognitive decline.

Our culture equates sleep with laziness. We idolize the grind, the hustle, the 5 a.m. start-up founder. But as leading sleep expert and neuroscientist Dr. Matthew Walker says, "Sleep is not optional. It is biologically required. We have not evolved out of needing it."

One of the most famous and disturbing studies on sleep deprivation was conducted by Dr. Allan Rechtschaffen at the University of Chicago in the 1980s. This groundbreaking experiment demonstrated the life-threatening consequences of prolonged sleep loss. In the study, lab rats were placed on a rotating platform above water. Whenever the rats fell asleep, the platform moved, forcing them to wake up or risk falling into the water. After just a couple of weeks of this enforced wakefulness, the results were devastating.

Despite having constant access to food, the rats lost weight, developed sores, and experienced organ failure. Eventually, all the sleep-deprived rats died. The most remarkable finding was that they didn't die from starvation or dehydration, but from total systemic breakdown—suggesting that sleep is not just restorative, but essential for the basic functioning of the body. This study was one of the first to make it undeniably clear that sleep is biologically vital.

In humans, studies like the one conducted at the University of Pennsylvania in 2003 echoed these findings on a smaller scale. Volunteers restricted to six hours of sleep per night for two weeks performed as poorly on cognitive tests as those who had been entirely sleep-deprived for forty-eight hours. Yet, most participants were unaware of their performance decline—illustrating how dangerously deceptive sleep deprivation can be.

Together, these studies show that sleep loss isn't just a minor inconvenience—it's a threat to physical and mental health. It impairs memory, weakens immunity, and can even lead to death in extreme cases. While modern culture may celebrate "grinding" and burning the midnight oil, science reminds us: Sleep isn't a luxury. It's a biological necessity.

Two other landmark studies—one conducted by the University of California, Berkeley, and another by Harvard Medical School—have illuminated the profound effects of sleep deprivation on brain function, emotional regulation, and overall health. These studies stand as powerful testaments to the body's desperate need for rest and the dangers of denying it.

1. The Berkeley Study on Emotional Brain Function (2007)

Dr. Matthew Walker and his team at UC Berkeley conducted a study using functional MRI (fMRI) brain imaging to observe how sleep deprivation alters emotional processing. Participants were shown emotionally charged images—such as snarling animals or burn victims—after a full night's rest and again after twenty-four hours of sleep deprivation. The results were astonishing.

Sleep-deprived participants exhibited a 60 percent increase in activity in the amygdala, the brain's fear center. In essence, without sleep, the brain becomes hyperreactive and emotionally unstable. At the same time, there was a dramatic drop in activity in the prefrontal cortex—the rational part of the brain responsible for impulse control and decision-making. This study provided direct neurological evidence of what many have long suspected: Lack of sleep doesn't just make us tired; it makes us irrational, moody, and emotionally erratic.

The implications are sobering. Chronic sleep deprivation may not only fuel anxiety and depression, but also impair our ability to manage relationships, make wise decisions, or maintain emotional balance.

2. Harvard Medical School's Sleep and Memory Study (2004)

Another influential study, conducted by Dr. Robert Stickgold at Harvard Medical School, focused on the role of sleep in memory consolidation. Participants were taught a complex finger-tapping motor task, akin to learning a new piano sequence. Some were allowed to sleep, while others were kept awake. When tested twenty-four hours later, those who had slept performed significantly better, demonstrating not only better recall but actual improvement in speed and accuracy.

The study found that memory consolidation happens most efficiently during deep, non-REM sleep—a stage often shortened or skipped altogether when people cut their sleep short. Without adequate sleep, the brain simply fails to absorb and organize new information.

What's more, follow-up studies revealed that even a single night of poor sleep can damage the brain's ability to form long-term memories. For students, professionals, and anyone in a learning-intensive environment, this research underscores a critical truth: You can't out-study, out-caffeinate, or outwork bad sleep.

Despite overwhelming evidence that sleep is essential for physical health, mental clarity, and emotional well-being, many Americans continue to undervalue it. This disregard for sleep is deeply cultural, rooted in historical attitudes toward productivity, modern work demands, and pervasive myths about success and self-discipline.

In the American psyche, sleep has long been seen as a sign of weakness or laziness. The industrial revolution glorified long work hours, and the twentieth-century ideal of the "self-made man" reinforced the belief that success comes through relentless hustle. Today, this ethos lives on in slogans like "I'll sleep when I'm dead" and "rise and grind," which celebrate sleep deprivation as a badge of honor. In this cultural framework, rest is framed as optional—or even indulgent—while sleeplessness is a symbol of ambition and toughness.

Technology has only made this worse. The smartphone has turned every hour into a potential work hour. Endless notifications, late-night emails, and the blue light of screens have eroded natural sleep cues. Many people stay up scrolling, gaming, or binge-watching—trading rest for short-term entertainment or the illusion of staying "caught up."

When asked why they don't sleep more, Americans commonly cite a range of reasons: stress and anxiety, long work hours, family responsibilities, and lack of time. In a 2022 Sleep Foundation survey, over 35 percent of adults reported that stress kept them from sleeping at night, while others blamed an "overactive mind." Many parents cite the demands of childcare, while professionals say they simply "can't turn off."

Another factor is a widespread misunderstanding of sleep's value. Many people think they can "catch up" on sleep over the weekend or function fine on five or six hours. But science shows this is a dangerous myth. Sleep isn't a luxury—it's a foundational pillar of health, as essential as diet and exercise. Until that mindset shifts, the sleep crisis will only deepen.

As we consider the Sabbath, we must deeply understand that sleep should be something we value—not just one day a week, but all seven. Imagine how much earlier you might get to bed if you turned off your phone, didn't watch TV, and shifted your mindset from "I ought to get to bed by 8:30 p.m." to "I need to get to bed by 8:30 p.m." That simple change in language can lead to significant behavioral changes.

In Scripture, we see the importance of rest:

- **Psalm 127:2:** *"It is in vain that you rise up early and go late to rest, eating the bread of anxious toil; for he gives to his beloved sleep."*
- **Mark 4:38:** *"But he was in the stern, asleep on the cushion. And they woke him and said to him, 'Teacher, do you not care that we are perishing?' "*

- **Genesis 2:2:** *"And on the seventh day God finished his work that he had done, and he rested on the seventh day from all his work that he had done."*

These verses remind us that rest is not only beneficial, but divinely ordained. On a true Sabbath, we should embrace sleep and rest. Closing our eyes and entering REM sleep can be a form of worship, honoring the rhythm God established from the beginning.

Two additional biblical moments stand as towering witnesses to the spiritual importance of sleep: Jesus sleeping during the storm, and Elijah collapsing beneath a broom tree. One occurs in chaos, the other in collapse. Yet, both unveil a profound truth: God values rest—and He meets us in it.

The Savior Slept

Mark 4:35–41 tells the famous story of Jesus asleep in a boat while His disciples fight for their lives in a raging storm. Waves are crashing, the boat is filling with water, and experienced fishermen—no strangers to rough seas—are terrified. And Jesus? *"He is asleep on the cushion"* (v. 38).

Pause for a moment. Jesus, the Son of God, God in flesh, is sleeping. He is not praying. He is not preaching. He is not calming the sea—yet. Now, He is resting.

This moment is not accidental. It is theological. Jesus is revealing something far deeper than mere fatigue. He is modeling perfect trust in the Father. The storm rages, but the Lord of creation is at peace. His body is still because His soul is anchored.

We often think of sleep as the enemy of urgency. But here, in the middle of crisis, Jesus shows that sleep can be the truest act of faith. It is a surrender, a relinquishing of control. The disciples cry out, accusing Jesus of indifference: *"Do you not care that we are perishing?"* But their panic reveals their unbelief. Jesus rebukes the wind, calms the waves, and turns to His disciples: *"Why are you so afraid? Have you still no faith?"* (v. 40).

This is a Sabbath parable. The storm represents the chaos of our modern, frantic lives—emails, deadlines, expectations, demands. And sleep is the quiet rebellion against the tyranny of the urgent. When we sleep on the Sabbath, we echo Jesus' posture in the storm. We say, with our bodies and breath, "God is in control. I am not. I can rest."

Elijah Slept Too

Turn now to 1 Kings 19. Elijah has just won a dramatic showdown against the prophets of Baal on Mount Carmel. Fire from heaven, the vindication of Yahweh, a miraculous display of divine power. Yet, immediately afterward, he plunges into despair. Jezebel threatens his life, and the prophet runs. Alone, afraid, and exhausted, he collapses under a broom tree and begs God to take his life. *"It is enough; now, O Lord, take away my life"* (v. 4).

What does God do? Does He lecture Elijah about being ungrateful? Does He demand more spiritual stamina? No. He lets him sleep.

> *"And he lay down and slept under a broom tree. And behold, an angel touched him and said to him, 'Arise and eat.' And he looked, and behold, there was at his head a cake baked on hot*

stones and a jar of water. And he ate and drank and lay down again" (vv. 5–6).

Sleep. Eat. Sleep again. This is God's prescription for burnout. Before God gives Elijah new direction, He gives him rest. Before the whisper on the mountain, there is divine sleep under the tree.

In Elijah's story, we see that sleep is not weakness—it is wisdom. It is restoration. *"The Sabbath was made for man,"* Jesus says, *"not man for the Sabbath"* (Mark 2:27). It is God's gift, not His burden. He remembers that we are dust. And He does not demand unbroken toil—He commands rest.

Sabbath as Sacred Sleep

When God instituted the Sabbath, He wove rest into the fabric of creation. *"And on the seventh day God finished his work that he had done, and he rested on the seventh day from all his work that he had done"* (Genesis 2:2). God did not rest because He was tired—He rested because He was satisfied. And He invites us to do the same.

In Exodus and Deuteronomy, the Sabbath command is repeated with different emphasis—once rooted in creation, once in liberation. We rest because God rested (Exodus 20:11), and we rest because we are no longer slaves (Deuteronomy 5:15). Sabbath sleep, then, is both an imitation of God and a rejection of Pharaoh.

Modern life, with its screens and schedules, has reintroduced a new kind of slavery: the endless scrolling, the dopamine drip, the pressure to optimize every moment. But the Sabbath says no. The Sabbath calls us to stop, to unplug, to sleep. Not just a nap between meetings, but real, deep, unhurried rest.

Jesus slept in the storm. Elijah slept in despair. We are invited to sleep in peace. Not because everything is finished—but because God is enough.

To sleep on the Sabbath is to entrust your life to God. It is to say, "Even if I don't finish the work, the world will not fall apart." It is to renounce the illusion of self-sufficiency. The psalmist writes, *"It is in vain that you rise up early and go late to rest, eating the bread of anxious toil; for he gives to his beloved sleep"* (Psalm 127:2).

Sleep is a gift. And sleep on the Sabbath is a double blessing: the renewal of body and the renewal of soul.

We do not earn our righteousness by productivity. We are not justified by output. Jesus' sleep in the boat teaches us that rest is not neglect, but faith. And Elijah's story teaches us that rest precedes revelation. You cannot hear the still, small voice of God when you are running on fumes.

This is the great irony: Never has the world had more technology to aid rest—memory foam mattresses, sleep apps, white-noise machines—yet never have we been more exhausted. We are surrounded by the machinery of rest, but we've lost the theology behind it.

Sabbath is the answer. Not merely a day off, but a sacred rhythm. A return to Eden. A protest against Egypt. A recalibration of our humanity. And at the center of this day must be not just silence or prayer, but sleep—true, trusting sleep that declares, "My life is in His hands."

We sleep not because our work is done, but because God's work is finished. Jesus, on the cross, cried out: *"It is finished"* (John 19:30). And then He gave up His spirit—and rested in the tomb on the Sabbath. Even in death, Jesus observed the sacred rest. And from that Sabbath rest came resurrection.

So, we sleep now, on the Sabbath, not in fear or guilt, but in hope. Because resurrection is on the other side of Sabbath rest. Restoration. New life.

Maybe your life feels like the boat in the storm. Maybe you're running like Elijah, depleted and despairing. Hear this invitation: Lie down. Rest. Sleep. You are not God. You do not need to be.

Sabbath sleep is not laziness—it is liturgical trust. It is how we enact our faith with our flesh. It is how we declare, week after week, "God is enough. His grace is sufficient. I can rest."

Jesus Slept. Elijah Slept. So Can You.

So, start tonight. Close the laptop. Power down the phone. Let the dishes wait. Pull the shades, dim the lights, and give your body permission to do what it was created to do—rest. Let your bed become an altar of trust. As your head touches the pillow, whisper to God, "I release it all to You." You don't need to check one more email. You don't need to prove anything. You don't need to carry the weight of the world—it already has a Savior, and it's not you.

Sleep is not a distraction from your purpose; it is part of your purpose. It is a sacred rhythm that restores your mind, heals your body, and quiets your soul. The Sabbath is your weekly reminder that you are not a machine. You are a beloved child. And children sleep well when they know their Father is near.

So go ahead—embrace the gift. Make your Sabbath a day not just of rest, but of sleep. Deep, joyful, replenishing sleep. You're allowed. More than that—you're invited. Rest isn't weakness. It's worship. And tomorrow will be better because you trusted God enough to rest today.

Chapter 8

MELACHAH, EVED, AND YOUR DOG

Remember the Sabbath day, to keep it holy.
Six days you shall labor, and do all your work,
but the seventh day is a Sabbath to the Lord your God.
On it you shall not do any work, you, or your son, or your daughter,
your male servant, or your female servant,
or your livestock, or the sojourner who is within your gates.
For in six days the Lord made the heavens and the earth, the sea, and all that is in them,
and rested on the seventh day.
Therefore the Lord blessed the Sabbath day and made it holy.

—Exodus 20:8–11

Read that passage carefully. Don't skim it. Internalize it. Let it speak to you. What you just read—the fourth commandment—is the longest commandment in the entire Decalogue. That's not incidental. It stands not merely as a call to rest, but as a rich, multilayered moral vision. While I could devote volumes to exploring the moral and civilizational revolution the Ten Commandments introduced—how they laid the very ethical and legal foundations of the Western world—this book is focused on just one of them: the Sabbath.

Yet, even within that focus, we must resist the temptation to reduce the Sabbath merely to a command to rest. To do so is to miss the radical beauty of the full instruction. The commandment is not simply about ceasing from labor. It is about ordering one's entire life around the rhythm of creation, justice, humility, and reverence. Embedded within its words are three moral imperatives that I believe are too often neglected in modern readings—and yet they are astonishingly relevant for our fractured and restless age.

1. It commands you to work.

The commandment begins not with rest, but with labor: *"Six days you shall labor, and do all your work."* This is not optional. Work is not a consequence of sin, nor is it to be despised. It is dignified, God ordained, and essential to the moral order. The Sabbath is not an escape from responsibility, but a sanctified boundary for it. The rhythm is not just rest, but *rest following work*. This is a rebuke to both laziness and to idolatrous overwork. The command affirms that humans are created to be productive, to steward the world, to build, to create—but also to stop. It affirms both human agency and human limits. In our current culture, where some burn themselves out and others drift aimlessly, the command to labor six days and rest one is a balanced, God-given framework for a meaningful life.

2. It reveals that God cares about animals—and so should we.

Tucked into the heart of the command is a small but powerful clause: *"Your livestock"* must also rest. This is no throwaway line. It reveals a divine concern for the nonhuman world, for creatures who cannot speak but who, like us, are made by God. Long before modern conversations about animal welfare emerged, God was writing concern for creatures into the fabric of His moral law. The Sabbath testifies that rest is not just a human right, but a creation-wide principle. This should inform how we think about dominion, stewardship, and compassion. To treat animals as mere tools or machines is to ignore the gentle command of the Creator who made space for their renewal too.

3. It affirms the dignity of all people—especially the lowly and oppressed.

The Sabbath is not just for landowners, prophets, and kings. It is for *"your male servant, [and] your female servant . . . the sojourner who is within your gates."* In a world where hierarchy, exploitation, and dehumanization were the norm, this was a radical, even revolutionary statement. God demands that the Sabbath be extended to the most vulnerable members of society. The command upends social stratification by declaring that every human being, regardless of status, deserves dignity, rest, and space to breathe. That includes laborers, migrants, and yes—even slaves. For ancient Israel, this was a moral leap forward. For us today, it's a sobering reminder that justice begins not in lofty theories, but in small acts of mercy, rest, and equality.

These three insights—often overlooked—are embedded directly in the commandment itself. Yes, much of this book is centered on the need to cease striving, to stop the frantic activity that defines modern life. That is the heart of the Sabbath and the primary lens of this work. But the fullness of the fourth commandment carries deeper moral weight than simple rest. It demands a whole-life reordering: how we work, how we treat the vulnerable, how we care for creation. The command is not merely spiritual—it is economic, social, and ecological. And though there are even more truths contained within this single passage, I will spend the remainder of this chapter exploring these three foundational themes. They are not side notes to the Sabbath. They are the very soul of it.

God Requires You to Work

The fourth commandment is not only a call to rest—but it is also a command to work. *"Remember the Sabbath"* and *"six days you shall labor"* both in the same commandment. This is not a lifestyle suggestion. It is a declaration of moral order. God's design for humanity includes both purposeful labor and sacred rest. He does not call us to drift passively through time, nor to grind ourselves into dust. He calls us to live in rhythm: six days of creative action, one day of holy stillness.

Work is not a curse. It was given before the fall. In Genesis 2:15, we read, *"The Lord God took the man and put him in the garden of Eden to work it and keep it."* Labor, in Scripture, is portrayed not as punishment, but as stewardship. Paul echoes this principle in the New Testament: *"If anyone is not willing to work, let him not eat"* (2 Thessalonians 3:10). And again in Colossians 3:23, *"Whatever you do, work heartily, as for the Lord and not for men."*

The Hebrew word for work—*melachah* (מְלָאכָה)—is profound. Unlike more generic words for toil or drudgery, *melachah* refers to purposeful, creative labor. It's the kind of work associated with artistry, design, and building. The first time it appears in Scripture is in the creation story: *"By the seventh day God had finished the melachah he had been doing"* (Genesis 2:2 NIV). The very nature of God's creative labor becomes the blueprint for ours.

This word appears again in the fourth commandment itself: *"Six days you shall labor and do all your melachah, but the seventh day is a sabbath to the Lord your God. On it you shall not do any melachah"* (Exodus 20:9–10 NIV). Rabbinic tradition identifies thirty-nine categories of *melachah*, all derived from the types of labor used to build the tabernacle. This wasn't mindless effort—it was sacred construction. *Melachah* represents the kind of work that reflects divine intention, structure, and beauty.

But we live in a generation dangerously disconnected from this vision. On one end of the spectrum, millions of people have abandoned work altogether. According to the US Census Bureau, over **70 million Americans** currently receive some form of government welfare. The Bureau of Labor Statistics reports that around **7 million working-age men** (ages 25–54) are not in the labor force. **Nearly 50 percent of young men ages 18 to 34 live with their parents**, according to Pew Research. Meanwhile, Nielsen data shows that young men in their twenties spend an average of **three hours per day playing video games**, and **one in five prime-age men** uses prescription pain medication daily, often to numb a deeper spiritual malaise.

Laziness is often dismissed as a personality quirk or a harmless habit. But Scripture treats it as something far more serious: a corrosive force that slowly degrades the soul. In the traditional Christian moral framework, sloth—also known as acedia—is not mere inactivity. It is the willful refusal to do what one ought, the quiet surrender of one's responsibilities, vocations, and calling. It is spiritual boredom with what is good. The book of Proverbs warns, *"The soul of the sluggard craves and gets nothing, while the soul of the diligent is richly supplied"* (Proverbs 13:4). Sloth leaves a person wanting—not because nothing is available, but because they lack the will to pursue what is good. This kind of stagnation doesn't just impoverish the body—it hollows out the inner life.

Among the seven deadly sins, sloth is perhaps the most ignored in modern Christianity. Lust, pride, and greed are still preached against with some frequency. But sloth? It is rarely named from the pulpit, even though its consequences are everywhere. Proverbs 21:25 tells us, *"The desire of the sluggard kills him, for his hands refuse to labor."* Sloth isn't just a lifestyle issue—it's a death spiral. It strangles the will, dims the intellect, and dries up the spirit. Left unchecked, it breeds cynicism, despair, and addiction. Thomas Aquinas described acedia not just as laziness, but as "sadness in the face of divine good"—a spiritual apathy that recoils from God's call to action. Sloth numbs us to the joy of fulfilling our purpose and blinds us to the needs of others. It turns life into mere survival.

Biblically, laziness is not just unwise—it is offensive to God's design for human flourishing. Ecclesiastes 10:18 warns, *"Through sloth the roof sinks in, and through indolence the house leaks."* Laziness is not neutral. It destroys. It neglects what must be tended, whether it's a home, a relationship, a church, or a soul. We read in Matthew 25 about Jesus telling the parable of the talents. The servant who buries his gift in the ground is not excused—he is condemned as "wicked and slothful." His failure was not that he did evil, but that he failed to do good. The message is sobering: Inactivity, when born of fear or apathy, is not morally neutral. It is rebellion against a God who made us to move, serve, create, and build. The lazy heart isn't just inefficient—it's disobedient.

We are witnessing a crisis—not of jobs, but of purpose. What happens to a culture when men stop building, stop protecting, stop leading? When instead of planting gardens or shaping the world, they retreat into virtual realities and chemical sedation? The Bible doesn't describe that as rest—it calls it sloth. And sloth isn't just laziness. It's a refusal to become what God made you to be.

It is no coincidence that as belief in meaningful work has declined, rates of depression, anxiety, and suicide have surged. In our increasingly secular and fragmented culture, many people no longer see their daily labor as a calling, but as a chore. According to a 2022 Gallup study on workplace engagement, only 32 percent of American workers reported feeling "engaged" in their work, while 18 percent said they were "actively disengaged." The disengaged were nearly twice as likely to experience daily sadness and worry. They also reported higher levels of stress, apathy, and a general sense of purposelessness. The CDC has corroborated these trends, noting that men in lower-income blue-collar jobs—especially those marked by instability—face suicide rates that significantly exceed the national average. These are not just economic metrics. They are spiritual distress signals. The human heart, made in the image of a purposeful God, cannot bear the weight of a life without purpose.

In contrast, those who describe their work as meaningful are dramatically more resilient. According to multiple studies, they experience lower rates of anxiety and depression, have stronger relationships, and exhibit higher levels of motivation, personal responsibility, and life satisfaction. One landmark review published in the *Journal of Occupational Health Psychology* found that employees who perceive their work as meaningful experience fewer symptoms of burnout and depression and report significantly higher levels of overall well-being. The authors concluded that meaning in work serves as a psychological anchor—a source of internal stability especially vital during times of suffering, uncertainty, or societal collapse.

This truth was central to the life and work of **Viktor Frankl,** the Austrian neurologist, psychiatrist, and Holocaust survivor. He also authored an extraordinary book, *Man's Search for Meaning.* Frankl said, "Life is never made unbearable by circumstances, but only by lack of meaning and purpose." Frankl endured unimaginable horror in Nazi concentration camps. He lost his wife, his parents, his home, and his profession. But what he discovered in the midst of that torment was that those who survived were not always the strongest physically—they were those who had something to live for.

Frankl's entire psychological framework, which he called **logotherapy**, was built on this insight: Human beings are not primarily driven by pleasure (as Freud argued), or by power (as Adler believed), but by the pursuit of meaning. When a person's life feels devoid of meaning, suffering becomes unbearable and despair becomes logical. But when suffering is integrated into a larger narrative—when it is connected to something transcendent—it can be transformed.

He illustrated this with stories from the camps: Prisoners who gave up hope quickly withered, while those who mentally projected themselves into a future role—surviving to see their children, to rebuild society, to share what they learned—had a reason to endure. Frankl's point was not that suffering is good in itself, but that it is endurable *only* when it has a telos—a goal. He called despair "suffering without meaning."

In light of Frankl's insights, the biblical vision of work comes into even sharper focus. Scripture consistently affirms that meaningful labor is tied to human dignity and flourishing. In Proverbs 12:11 we read, *"Whoever works his land will have plenty of bread, but he who follows worthless pursuits lacks sense."* This is not merely an economic observation—it's a moral one. Work provides sustenance, structure, and sanity. Likewise, Proverbs 14:23 declares, *"In all toil there is profit, but mere talk tends only to poverty."* These verses echo the Bible's broader teaching: Work is not punishment; it is participation in divine order. God is not idle, and those made in His image are not meant to be either. Labor is a way of mirroring the creativity and faithfulness of the Creator, and when we detach from it, we not only weaken ourselves materially, but unravel something essential in our souls.

When this is lost—when work is stripped of purpose and dignity—societies collapse inward. When people view their jobs as meaningless or their labor as expendable, the soul begins to shrivel. We become detached not just from the economy, but from ourselves. We fall into numbness, distraction, and despair. And in that void, dark ideologies take root: that life is pointless, that humans are burdens, that death is escape.

On the other end of the spectrum lies a different pathology: the cult of overwork. Our society celebrates burnout as a badge of honor. We glorify hustle, even as it devours families, weakens churches, and empties souls. We work endlessly, frantically, and without boundary—not because we love the work, but because we're afraid to stop. And so, we swing wildly between apathy and addiction, idleness and idolatry.

The Sabbath command cuts through both extremes. It affirms the goodness of labor, but also its limits. It insists that we work—not as slaves, but as image-bearers. And then, it calls us to stop—not in exhaustion, but in reverence.

This is not optional. It is not cultural. It is creational.

God wants you to work. We are the only species that builds. While God alone can *bara*—create out of nothing—we are called to build, shape, design, and produce. In the Torah, animals never build. Only humans are given this divine vocation. That's not biology—it's theology.

Personally, I thank God every day for the work I've been given. I leap out of bed without caffeine, energized not by adrenaline, but by gratitude. I get to speak truth. I get to reach people. I get to labor in a cause that matters. I know not everyone feels this way about their job. I know some people wake up to dread. But even in the most thankless tasks, there's a sacred opportunity—to honor God through perseverance, excellence, and integrity.

Work is not a filler of time or a mechanism to make money. It is a calling. A form of worship. A chance to participate in God's ongoing mission to order the world and bless others. As Ecclesiastes 9:10 says, "*Whatever your hand finds to do, do it with all your might*" (NIV).

This is why the socialist worldview—so pervasive in modern education and media—is so dangerous. It teaches that work is inherently oppressive, that labor is a tool of exploitation, and that the highest goal is leisure, dependency, and redistribution. But the Bible teaches the opposite: that work is honorable, beneficial, and godly. The apostle Paul wrote, "*Let the thief no longer steal, but rather let him labor, doing honest work with his own hands*" (Ephesians 4:28).

As Christians, we must reject the lie that working is dehumanizing. The truth is, refusing to work is dehumanizing. We were made to build. We were made to give. We were made to reflect the image of the Builder.

The brilliant scholar Vishal Mangalwadi captures this transformative truth with rare clarity in his remarkable book *The Book That Made Your World*. With penetrating insight and historical rigor, Mangalwadi traces how the biblical worldview did not merely contribute to the rise of Western civilization—it redefined the very meaning of civilization itself, and at the heart of that redefinition was a radical theology of work. In the classical Greco-Roman world, labor was considered degrading. Manual toil was relegated to the slave class, while the elites reserved themselves for leisure and philosophical speculation. Productivity was seen as a necessity for the poor, not a calling for the noble. But the Scriptures inverted that hierarchy. From Genesis to Revelation, the Bible proclaimed that work was not shameful—it was sacred.

Mangalwadi observes that the biblical worldview turned slaves into sons and servants into stewards. This shift was not simply ethical, it was ontological. It reoriented human self-understanding away from passivity and hierarchy, and toward creative participation in God's world. In Genesis, Adam is not cursed with work—he is entrusted with it: "*work [the garden] and keep it*" (Genesis 2:15). Labor is framed not as punishment, but as participation in God's ongoing creation. Jesus, the incarnate Logos, was not born into privilege or priesthood, but into carpentry. Paul, the intellectual and theologian, worked as a tentmaker. The gospel did not emerge from palaces, but from workshops. That is not incidental. It is theological.

Mangalwadi contends that this biblical vision of vocation—

this idea that all work is holy when done unto the Lord—unleashed a cultural revolution. Mangalwadi writes, "The Bible taught the West to value work as a calling, not a curse. The milk-maid and the magistrate, the mason and the musician—all were seen as co-laborers with God in the world He was redeeming." The Protestant Reformation crystallized this conviction. Martin Luther declared that even the most menial task, when offered in faith, was more pleasing to God than the highest ritual if performed in vanity. John Calvin infused the concept of *vocatio* with theological depth, insisting that every Christian has a God-given role to fulfill, and that diligence in one's vocation was a mark of spiritual maturity.

This theology of work, according to Mangalwadi, laid the moral and metaphysical foundation for Western flourishing. It fueled the rise of the scientific revolution, not merely because the Bible spoke of order in creation, but because it taught that exploring creation was a *duty*. It launched the modern university, not simply to transmit knowledge, but to cultivate wisdom for service. It led to the birth of capitalism—not as an unchecked lust for profit, but as an application of stewardship and thrift, rooted in moral responsibility. It catalyzed movements for charity, hospitals, education, and industry—not as random outbursts of human kindness, but as coherent extensions of a biblical understanding of human purpose.

Contrast this with civilizations that lacked a biblical foundation. In India, as Mangalwadi often notes, his own Hindu culture viewed manual labor as spiritually polluting. The caste system institutionalized the idea that some were born only to serve, and others to think. The result was a civilization rich in reflection, but stagnant in action. Likewise, in pagan antiquity, work was seen as beneath the free man. But where the Bible was believed and lived, labor was baptized with meaning. To work was to imitate God. To create, to cultivate, to build, to manage—all were acts of worship.

Mangalwadi writes:

> "What the Bible gave to the West was not just a story, but a structure—a framework in which the dignity of man, the necessity of virtue, and the sacredness of work could all harmonize."

He argues that this structure made the West intellectually curious, economically dynamic, and morally resilient. It was not imperialism, nor geography, nor race, that elevated the West—but a sacred book that taught people they were made in the image of a Creator who worked and called them to do the same. Work became not just an economic act, but a moral one. The cobbler mending shoes, the farmer planting seed, the scholar writing by candlelight—each became a vessel of grace.

In the modern West, however, that sacred view of work is eroding. As secularism severs labor from meaning, work is once again being seen as either exploitation or futility. One class burns out in pursuit of achievement; another withdraws altogether in apathy. We are regressing, not technologically, but anthropologically. We no longer know who we are, because we have forgotten why we work.

This is why the biblical Sabbath matters so profoundly. It reminds us not only to rest—but why we labor in the first place. It places a divine exclamation mark on six days of faithful striving. It declares that rest is only holy when work has been dignified. Without the biblical vision of vocation, Sabbath becomes mere leisure. But with it, Sabbath becomes a window into eternity: a reminder that our labor has worth, because our lives have meaning.

As Mangalwadi so rightly insists, the Bible built the world we now enjoy—not through domination, but through transformation. It took something the world despised—work—and made it sacred. It took people the world discarded—the laborers—and called them priests. And it took cultures trapped in fatalism, and taught them to hope, to build, and to bless.

And that's why the Sabbath matters. It doesn't diminish work—it dignifies it by setting its limits. It says, "Work hard. But remember: You are not God." It anchors our ambition in humility. It sanctifies our sweat with grace.

Work, at its best, is not just how we earn—it's how we build. It gives structure to our days and meaning to our efforts. A civilization that forgets how to work inevitably forgets how to flourish. But equally dangerous is a culture that forgets how to rest. God's command was not only to labor, but to labor with rhythm—six days of striving, followed by one day of sacred stillness. That divine design is not a constraint; it is a gift. Rest is not the opposite of work—it's what makes work sustainable. The Sabbath reminds us we are not machines, and certainly not gods. We were made to work—but we were also made to stop.

I know this firsthand. I lead an organization with over a thousand full-time employees. That means nonstop motion—sleepless nights, red-eye flights, campus talks, debates, daily live broadcasts, all while raising children and managing the relentless weight of leadership. There are constant decisions, constant crises, and an unending demand to show up, speak up, and stay sharp. I carry it all gladly, because the work matters. But even good burdens will break a man if they are never laid down. That's why every week, I feel the glimmering light of the Sabbath coming toward me like a finish line. By Thursday night, I can see it: my pause, my permission to stop. I don't collapse out of burnout—I collapse in reverence. I rest not because I'm tired of the work, but because I'm tethered to something deeper.

The Sabbath gives my work its meaning—and my work, in turn, gives the Sabbath its gravity. They are married together in a purpose-fused harmony. The labor sharpens the sweetness of the rest; the rest clarifies the dignity of the labor. I don't resent the grind because I know the stillness is coming. I can pour myself out completely because I know there is a sacred space where I will be refilled. It is there, in the quiet, that I remember I am not holding the world together. God is. It's in the rest that my pride is checked, my energy is renewed, and my perspective is restored. That rhythm—six days of building, one day of breathing—isn't a lifestyle preference. It's a lifeline.

In a world obsessed with doing everything, and obsessed with doing nothing, the Sabbath is God's ancient, enduring answer. He calls us to work with excellence and integrity—and then to stop with trust and humility. I push hard because the work matters. I rest deeply because He matters more. And in that rhythm—sacred labor and sacred rest—I find my life not fragmented, but whole. Not exhausted, but aligned. Not burned out, but blessed. That is the gift of the Sabbath. And that is why I guard it—not as a rule, but as a rescue.

God Cares About How We Treat Animals

Growing up, we had the best dog in the world—Winston. He was a German Shorthaired Pointer, and loyal, beautiful, and unshakably devoted. Winston was always there for me—after a hard basketball game, or in the early, uncertain years of Turning Point USA, when the odds of scaling our mission seemed slim to none. He had a presence that brought both comfort and protection. When he passed away in fall 2019, it was one of the toughest nights of my life. Winston was a fixture in our home: stalwart, playful, gentle with those he loved, and fiercely protective of our family. I know many of you reading this have had dogs who occupied a sacred space in your heart—and that bond is real, and it matters.

Now, the Bible is clear: Animals are not humans. They are not made in the image of God (*imago Dei*) and should not be elevated to the level of people. Unfortunately, that error has become increasingly common. In places like Scottsdale—where it's not unusual to meet thirty-year-old childless women who treat their dogs as surrogate children—we see a cultural confusion about the role and value of animals. But at the same time, we must be just as clear that it is *because* of the Bible, and not in spite of it, that we do not treat animals as worthless or disposable. While animals are not equal to humans, they are *created by God*—and therefore deserve a measure of dignity, protection, and compassion.

This idea was absolutely radical in the ancient world. In surrounding pagan cultures, animals were either deified (as in Egypt) or brutalized. The notion that animals should be granted rest or humane treatment would have seemed absurd. And yet, the fourth commandment specifically says, *"On it [the Sabbath] you shall not do any work, you, or your son . . . or your livestock"* (Exodus 20:10). God mandated rest not just for man, but for animals. This alone would have been shocking to surrounding nations. And the Bible's regard for animal welfare goes far beyond the Decalogue. In Deuteronomy 25:4, we read, *"You shall not muzzle an ox when it is treading out the grain,"* a command both practical and compassionate. Proverbs 12:10 declares, "*Whoever is righteous has regard for the life of his beast, but the mercy of the wicked is cruel.*" Even in the laws of warfare, God commands restraint: "*When you besiege a city . . . you shall not destroy its trees . . . You may eat from them, but you shall not cut them down*" (Deuteronomy 20:19). These weren't environmental slogans—they were God-ordained limits designed to foster respect for life.

On campuses, I occasionally run into vegans, and while I strongly disagree with much of their ethical framework—especially the idea that snails, cows, or chickens are morally equal to human beings—I do think they're tapping into something worth acknowledging. Many modern industrial farming practices, particularly those involving animal cruelty, are inconsistent with biblical values. The Bible gives us permission to eat meat—"*Every moving thing that lives shall be food for you*" (Genesis 9:3)—but it also calls us to steward creation with wisdom and mercy. God instituted animal sacrifices, Jesus ate fish and lamb, and Paul instructs believers not to judge one another over dietary preferences (Romans 14:2–3). So yes, it is entirely biblical to eat meat—but it is also biblical to do so with thankfulness and an awareness that these creatures are not our equals, but neither are they meaningless.

All of this brings us to an important and often overlooked truth: If your atheistic, animal-loving friend or relative tells you that religion—especially Christianity—has nothing to do with compassion toward animals, they are simply mistaken. It is not secular humanism, nor paganism, nor Eastern philosophy that gave rise to a society in which the ethical treatment of animals is a shared moral concern. It is the Judeo-Christian worldview that laid that foundation. From Genesis to Revelation, Scripture consistently affirms that while animals are not equal to humans, they are part of God's creation—subject to His sovereignty and deserving of mercy.

In Islamic societies, dogs are frequently regarded as impure. Hadith traditions warn against contact with them, and in many Islamic countries, dogs are banned from homes or left to roam the streets, neglected and feared. In Hindu-majority India, cows are idolized in religious ritual, but stray dogs often live in agonizing squalor—malnourished, diseased, and ignored. In neither system is there a holistic theology of compassionate stewardship for all animals. By contrast, the rise of animal shelters, anti-cruelty legislation, veterinary ethics, and humane societies all took root in the Christianized West—precisely because of a biblical understanding of dominion, compassion, and moral responsibility.

In fact, many of the pioneers of the modern animal welfare movement were devout Christians. William Wilberforce, known primarily for his tireless crusade to abolish the British slave trade, was also one of the founding members of the Royal Society for the Prevention of Cruelty to Animals (RSPCA) in 1824. He viewed the humane treatment of animals as an extension of Christian charity and moral responsibility. Arthur Broome, an Anglican clergyman, also helped found the RSPCA and served as its first secretary. Their conviction was clear: Cruelty toward animals is incompatible with Christian virtue. These leaders weren't driven by pantheism or evolutionary sentimentalism. They were driven by Scripture. They believed that *"the righteous care for the needs of their animals"* (Proverbs 12:10 NIV), and they put that belief into public policy and social reform.

This legacy endures. Whether it's animal protection laws, humane slaughter practices, or the existence of veterinary medicine as an ethical profession, these institutions arose from a worldview that said animals are not divine, but they are not disposable either. They are creatures made by a loving God, entrusted to the care of image-bearers. The idea that a donkey should not be overworked (Exodus 23:12), that an ox should not be muzzled while it treads grain (Deuteronomy 25:4), or that a bird's nest should be spared (Deuteronomy 22:6–7)—these were radical commands in the ancient world. They remain radical today in many parts of the globe.

So the next time someone scoffs at religion as being primitive or cruel, remind them gently but firmly: It was from Mount Sinai, not the Enlightenment, that the world first heard that even animals deserve rest. It was through Christian thinkers and reformers—not secular activists—that the West built its compassion for the voiceless. The cross didn't just elevate man—it ennobled how man treats the world beneath him. When you love your dog, your horse, your cat, or your cow, you are not practicing some vague emotionalism—you are echoing a moral revolution begun by a God who *"saw everything that he had made, and behold, it was very good"* (Genesis 1:31).

"All Men Are Created Equal"

As Americans, we know that phrase well. It is the moral bedrock of our national identity and the seed of universal dignity that blossomed into the most stable, free, and enduring political system in history—the United States Constitution. But what many forget is that this concept did not emerge from thin air. It was not the product of Enlightenment rationalism alone. It was born from the soil of Scripture. Hidden and tucked away within the fourth commandment—almost quietly—is a profound affirmation of human equality. "*You shall not do any work, you, or your son, or your daughter, your male servant, or your female servant, or your livestock, or the sojourner who is within your gates*" (Exodus 20:10). In this ancient command to cease from labor, God levels the playing field. The master and the slave, the citizen and the foreigner, the employer and the worker—all are called to rest. All are seen. All are dignified.

This divine declaration was revolutionary. In an age when kings were gods, slaves were property, and women were afterthoughts, the God of Israel declared that *everyone*—regardless of status—was entitled to rest. That idea, though seemingly simple, was radical in its time. And it became the theological seed from which the Western understanding of rights and equality would grow. The Sabbath was not just about rest—it was a reordering of society under a just and merciful God. It reminded Israel that they too had been slaves in Egypt, and that power must never be divorced from empathy. This moral foundation—laid in the wilderness at Sinai—would echo centuries later in the words of our founders. When Jefferson wrote that all men are created equal, he was tapping into a truth much older than 1776.

Human equality is not a natural conclusion of evolutionary biology or materialist philosophy. If the world is nothing more than matter in motion, then there is no reason to treat one person as more valuable than another—nor any reason not to enslave the weak. Equality requires a transcendent standard. It requires a Creator. The West flourished because it embraced that truth. Its greatest achievements—liberty, the rule of law, representative government, the abolition of slavery, the dignity of labor, and the elevation of women—all sprang from the conviction that every human being bears the image of God and is therefore worthy of protection, justice, and freedom. That conviction was not inevitable. It was revealed.

So when we read the fourth commandment, we should not read it narrowly. We should see it as the moral architecture of a free society. It's not just about taking a break. It's about remembering who we are. It's about acknowledging that no matter our job, our title, or our background, we stand equal before the Lord of the Sabbath. That is the seed of equality. That is the foundation of the West. And that is why the Ten Commandments are not simply ancient law—they are the charter of human dignity.

One of the reasons I wanted to address this part of the fourth commandment is a repeated self-righteous question I get on campus more and more frequently. Mind you, this question is not from Christians but from deconstructionists who wish to delegitimize Christianity with their own pompous nineteen-year-old know-it-all attitude.

The question goes like "Charlie, if you believe in the Bible, why did it allow slavery?"

Given the format in which that question is asked, it's very hard to substantively answer that question during a "prove me wrong" event in front of three thousand people. Such an answer would require more time and thought; therefore, I wanted to address that and make the case that the Bible was the sole reason we ever decided to reject slavery altogether.

This charge, often made with little historical or textual nuance, is intended to undermine the moral credibility of Scripture. But to understand what the Bible actually says—and does not say—about slavery, we need to look carefully at its context, content, and trajectory.

Slavery in the ancient world bore little resemblance to the race-based, chattel slavery of the transatlantic slave trade. In biblical times, what was called "slavery" often referred to indentured servitude—an economic arrangement used to repay debt or survive poverty. It could also result from wartime captivity. But unlike the permanent, dehumanizing institution of later centuries, biblical servitude was often temporary, regulated, and even voluntary. *"If you buy a Hebrew servant, he shall serve six years; and in the seventh he shall go out free and pay nothing"* (Exodus 21:2). This system, while still flawed, stands in sharp contrast to the brutal slave systems of the eighteenth and nineteenth centuries.

Much of the confusion surrounding slavery in the Bible stems from a lack of understanding of the original Hebrew language and cultural context. The Hebrew word most often translated as "slave" in English Bibles is *eved* (עֶבֶד). But *eved* does not carry the same connotations as the word "slave" in modern English, which evokes images of the race-based, hereditary, dehumanizing bondage of the Atlantic slave trade. Rather, *eved* is a flexible term that can mean servant, worker, bondman, or subordinate, depending on the context. For example, Moses is repeatedly called the *eved* of the Lord—a term of honor and devotion, not degradation. Kings referred to their most trusted advisors as *avadim* (*eved*, plural). In many biblical contexts, *eved* implies covenantal loyalty, duty, and even familial connection rather than abject ownership or abuse.

Even in cases where *eved* refers to a person in service to another due to poverty or indebtedness, the status was highly regulated under biblical law. A Hebrew *eved* was to be treated not as property, but as a hired worker or guest (Leviticus 25:39–40). The employer was to provide for them, protect them, and release them after six years with a generous gift of livestock and resources (Deuteronomy 15:13–14).

Importantly, many Israelites voluntarily became *avadim* to repay debt or escape poverty, entering into structured and time-limited agreements. The fact that such service was even subject to time caps and mandated liberation shows just how distinct the biblical form of servitude was from the brutal systems of slavery practiced elsewhere in the ancient world.

Understanding the term *eved* helps us see how the biblical vision was never static—it was always pointing forward. God was not endorsing oppression, but managing it in a fallen world, injecting dignity and justice into systems that had long existed without them. In that light, the fourth commandment becomes even more profound. To command that the *eved*, along with the master, was to rest every seventh day was to announce a radical moral equality. The same God who allowed for economic servitude also demanded spiritual equality—everyone was to rest, everyone was to remember, and everyone was to be treated with dignity under His rule.

In the ancient world, the idea of giving slaves rest was utterly foreign. In Egypt, Babylon, and Rome, slaves existed solely for the benefit of their masters—they worked until they died, with no legal rights and no expectation of mercy. They were property, not persons. But in ancient Israel, something remarkable happened: God commanded that even servants and laborers must stop and rest on the Sabbath. *"You shall not do any work, you, or your son, or your daughter, your male servant, or your female servant"* (Exodus 20:10). This was not a footnote—it was a moral earthquake. The very act of granting a servant rest was a statement that they, too, were seen by God, included in His covenant rhythms, and worthy of dignity. It was a weekly declaration that no human being, no matter how lowly their status, existed merely for the exploitation of another.

In fact, owning a servant in ancient Israel came with significant responsibilities and legal obligations. According to the Babylonian Talmud Tractate Kiddushin, "Whoever acquires a servant acquires a master." That was not sarcasm; it was moral clarity. If you took in a servant, you were required to treat him with compassion, fairness, and generosity. You had to provide rest, protection, eventual release, and even material goods upon his departure (Deuteronomy 15:13–14). If you injured him, you had to free him. If he ran away, you couldn't pursue him. The system was structured not to benefit the master, but to protect the vulnerable in a fallen world. In that light, the Sabbath was not merely a day of worship—it was a rebuke of tyranny. It told every Israelite: You are not God, and no one else is your beast of burden.

The biblical witness does not ignore the reality of sin and exploitation—it confronts it, contains it, and then, in Christ, defeats it. From the covenantal servant in ancient Israel to the spiritual brotherhood proclaimed in the New Testament, the arc of Scripture is clear: Slavery, while regulated in a fallen world, is not a biblical ideal. The Bible's message was never to preserve the status quo, but to transform it—one heart, one home, one institution at a time. And the dignity extended to the *eved* on the Sabbath was not an anomaly. It was a foreshadowing of the freedom that Christ would one day offer to all, slave and free alike.

The Old Testament does not morally endorse slavery—it regulates it. God gave laws to ancient Israel within a fallen world, just as He regulated polygamy and divorce without declaring them ideal. These laws restrained abuse, elevated the status of the servant, and pointed toward a more humane ethic. Consider the requirement not to return a runaway slave to his master: "*You shall not give up to his master a slave who has escaped from his master to you. He shall dwell with you . . . You shall not wrong him*" (Deuteronomy 23:15–16). Or the stipulation that if a master injured his servant, even by damaging an eye or a tooth, the servant was to be released (Exodus 21:26–27). These protections were unheard of in the surrounding nations and reveal a God who is both just and merciful.

Scripture often permits certain institutions not because they are ideal, but because they are embedded in the reality of human sin. As Jesus said about divorce, "*Because of your hardness of heart Moses allowed you to divorce your wives, but from the beginning it was not so*" (Matthew 19:8). The same is true for servitude. God worked within historical realities while planting moral seeds that would ultimately flourish into the ideals of freedom and equality.

When we arrive at the New Testament, we see the ethical center of gravity shift even more dramatically. The gospel doesn't launch a political revolution against slavery—it launches a spiritual revolution that would, over time, upend the very foundations of servitude. Paul writes in Galatians 3:28, "*There is neither Jew nor Greek, there is neither slave nor free, there is no male and female, for you are all one in Christ Jesus.*" This wasn't a metaphor. It was a radical redefinition of personhood in a society deeply stratified by status, ethnicity, and power.

One of the most powerful examples of this ethic is found in Paul's letter to Philemon. In a deeply personal appeal, Paul asks Philemon to receive his runaway slave Onesimus not as property, but as "*a beloved brother*" (Philemon v. 16). This wasn't just a kind suggestion—it was a theological declaration. In Christ, social hierarchies collapse. The slave is not only a fellow human, but a spiritual equal. Within the context of Roman law, Onesimus had no legal standing. But within the kingdom of God, he had full dignity.

Importantly, the Bible never says slavery is good. There is no command to own slaves, no moral defense of slavery as an ideal, no elevation of the institution as virtuous. What the Bible does, again and again, is take a flawed structure and point it toward redemption. The arc of Scripture bends toward liberation, restoration, and equality—not in spite of the Old Testament law, but because of its ethical direction.

This is precisely why the abolitionist movement was not secular in origin—it was overwhelmingly Christian. William Wilberforce, the British parliamentarian who led the decades-long battle to end the transatlantic slave trade, did so not out of philosophical abstraction or Enlightenment theory, but out of unshakable biblical conviction. Wilberforce viewed the slave trade as a moral abomination unharmonious with the gospel of Jesus Christ. He famously declared, "God Almighty has set before me two great objects: the suppression of the slave trade and the reformation of manners." His campaign was powered by long hours of prayer, profound theological reflection, and a profound belief that every human being was made in the image of God. He endured public scorn, political sabotage, and personal illness, but after nearly fifty years of work—often against overwhelming odds—he saw the passage of the Slavery Abolition Act in 1833. He died just three days later, having witnessed the triumph of Christian perseverance over generational evil.

In the United States, this same biblical fire animated the great abolitionists of the nineteenth century. Harriet Tubman, an escaped slave and underground railroad conductor, described herself as "the Moses of her people." She credited her escape and rescue missions not to luck, but to divine guidance, often claiming to hear God's voice directing her steps. She carried a pistol in one hand and a Bible in the other, combining courage with faith in a way that defied the institutional brutality of her time. Likewise, Thaddeus Stevens, one of the most influential figures in the US Congress during and after the Civil War, drew on both constitutional logic and moral certitude, forged in the fires of Scripture. He was unrelenting in his opposition to slavery and racial injustice, pushing not only for emancipation, but for full citizenship and legal equality for freed slaves. Stevens believed that a just society must reflect God's impartiality: "There can be no peace in this Republic, until the black man has full equality before the law."

And then there was Frederick Douglass, too often miscast by secular historians as a mere rationalist. Douglass was a devout reader of Scripture, and it was the contrast between biblical Christianity and the hypocrisy of American slavery that sharpened his prophetic edge. In his famous narrative, he writes, "I love the pure, peaceable, and impartial Christianity of Christ: I therefore hate the corrupt, slaveholding, women-whipping, cradle-plundering, partial and hypocritical Christianity of this land." He was not rejecting the Bible—he was calling America to return to it.

A belief in human equality is the exception, not the norm. For most of history, across nearly every culture and empire, people were not considered equal—they were sorted by class, caste, race, tribe, or strength. The weak existed to serve the strong. From Pharaohs to Caesars, rulers were often viewed as divine while peasants were treated as expendable. Ancient philosophers like Aristotle believed that some people were born to be slaves by nature. The assumption that every human being possesses equal value and inherent dignity would have sounded absurd—if not dangerous—in most of the ancient world. And yet, in the West, we now regard this belief as obvious, even intuitive. But it is not. It is not natural, and it is certainly not rational in the sense of being logically deduced from nature alone. It is theological. It came from one place and one place only: the Bible.

It was the opening page of Scripture that made this shocking claim: "*God created man in his own image . . . male and female he created them*" (Genesis 1:27). That verse, quietly nestled in the creation account, launched a moral revolution. It meant that dignity did not come from wealth, ancestry, or power—it came from being human. Not just kings, but commoners. Not just men, but women. Not just insiders, but foreigners. This single doctrine—*imago Dei*—laid the foundation for everything the West would later celebrate: human rights, civil liberty, equality before the law. It is the cornerstone of our moral universe. Strip it away, and the edifice collapses. The Sabbath, too, participates in this radical moral shift. In Exodus 20, God commands that everyone—*sons, daughters, male servants, female servants, even livestock*—must rest. In one command, He levels every social hierarchy. The employer and the worker stop together. The powerful and the powerless alike are reminded that they are creatures, not gods.

That's why you cannot reason your way to equality. At best, you can mimic its language while denying its source. The secular Enlightenment tried, and for a brief moment, it succeeded—borrowing the fruit of the Christian tree while denying the root. But eventually, that denial bore bitter fruit: the guillotine, the gulag, the gas chamber. In the absence of a transcendent Creator, human value becomes negotiable. Utility replaces dignity. The unborn become expendable, the elderly burdensome, and the disabled invisible. Reason alone cannot sanctify life. It can categorize, optimize, and exploit—but it cannot hallow. Only revelation can do that. Only a word from outside the system can declare, definitively and eternally, that all men are created equal.

This is the West's secret weapon—but it is not self-sustaining. Our institutions of law, education, science, and freedom were built upon biblical foundations. But foundations, once buried and ignored, begin to crack. If we forget the source of our equality, we will soon lose the substance of it. The same secular West that abolished slavery because of Christian conviction now teeters on the edge of dehumanization once again. We divide people by race, by class, by usefulness. We tolerate child exploitation in foreign supply chains and euphemize away the slaughter of the unborn at home. We no longer know what a human is, let alone why one matters. Why? Because we have forgotten God.

And that brings us back to the Sabbath. The Sabbath was never just about rest—it was about recognition. It was a weekly act of rebellion against pride, oppression, and forgetfulness. It reminded the Israelite farmer that his servant had worth. It reminded the businessman that his wealth could wait. It reminded the mother, the foreigner, the outcast, and the weary that their lives mattered—not because of what they produced, but because of who made them. It was God's divine pause button, His sacred protest against a world that devalues the soul. And that rhythm, when honored, restores the moral architecture we are so desperately trying to rebuild with secular bricks.

So, let us say it clearly and without apology: Human equality did not begin in Paris, Geneva, or Washington—it began at Sinai. It began with a God who commands justice, a Christ who suffered for the least of these, and a church that, when faithful, has turned the world upside down. The Sabbath command is not peripheral to justice; it is its heartbeat. It taught a weary world to stop and see—not just God, but one another. And that is why we rest: to remember. To remember who we are, who our neighbor is, and who made us both. The gospel doesn't just save souls—it restores civilizations. And the command to rest may be the most radical—and most needed—revolution of all.

Chapter 9

ARE CHRISTIANS BOUND TO THE SABBATH?

This chapter may not apply to everyone reading this book. My purpose in writing is to urge the world—people of all faiths and backgrounds—to stop for one day. To pause. To reflect. To step away from the noise, the demands, the screens, and the constant striving, and to be still with God. Not everyone reading this is a follower of Jesus, though it is my sincere hope and prayer that each person eventually comes to know Him.

This chapter is written primarily for Christians. It is a focused exploration, a stand-alone theological essay drawn from years of study, personal reflection, and prayer on one important question: Are Christians still bound to keep the Sabbath?

If that question doesn't feel relevant to you, you're welcome to skip to the next chapter. But if you are a believer who has ever wondered whether Sabbath observance is still required, overlooked, or fulfilled in Christ, then this chapter is for you. The following is the result of years of obsessive research, work, and prayer. I pray it impacts you as much as it did me.

I have personally struggled with the idea of whether or not Christians are bound to the Sabbath. The reason I find this so difficult is that it is clear that God Himself rested upon creation. The Sabbath was taken so seriously by ancient Israel that disobedience to it would result in capital punishment. If the Sabbath is so good for us, why aren't Christians bound to it? Yet, when I visit churches, pastors are insistent—pointing out verses that show we are no longer bound to the festivals, feast days, or Sabbaths. I wrestle with this greatly, and after my study, I think I have come to a clearer understanding of how Christians should proceed.

This isn't just a theological footnote for me. It's personal. I've spent years asking these questions with my Bible open and my heart burdened, trying to reconcile what feels like a glaring tension in Scripture. There's something deeply raw in confronting the reality that the same God who thundered commandments from Sinai—who etched the Sabbath into stone with His own finger—is now, according to many in the church, somehow content for that command to be obsolete. That feels jarring. At times, almost irreverent.

The gravity of the Sabbath in ancient Israel is hard to overstate. Recorded in Exodus 31:14, God declares, *"Everyone who profanes it shall be put to death."* To violate the Sabbath wasn't a casual mistake—it was a capital crime. This wasn't just about taking a break; it was about allegiance, about covenant, about who ruled time itself. That same sacred day was also woven into the very rhythm of creation. Genesis 2:2–3 tells us that God Himself rested, blessed the seventh day, and made it holy. That's before there was a Sinai, before there were tribes, before there was sin. The Sabbath is primordial.

For extremely observant Jews—especially within Haredi and

Hasidic communities—the Sabbath, or Shabbat, is not merely a day of rest. It is the beating heart of their week. From just before sundown on Friday to just after nightfall on Saturday, time itself changes. The world becomes quieter, holier, and slower. Everything about life—speech, dress, movement, ritual—is transformed into an offering. In this sacred twenty-five-hour window, the secular world fades, and eternity steps forward.

Shabbat is not simply about stopping labor. It is about entering a different dimension of existence—what Jewish mystics call a "foretaste of the world to come." It is a rehearsal for redemption, a sanctuary in time. To understand how observant Jews keep Shabbat, one must understand that it is not about legalism or restriction. It is about reverence, and a longing to imitate the God who created the heavens and the earth—and then stopped.

The Sabbath begins with light. Precisely eighteen minutes before sunset on Friday evening, candles are lit—usually by the woman of the house, often with her daughters. This moment marks the transition from the mundane to the sacred. It is an act of separation, sanctification, and welcome. The Sabbath is personified in Jewish tradition as a bride or a queen, and the home is readied to receive her.

Observant families prepare all week for this moment. Meals are cooked in advance. Homes are cleaned. Clothes are laid out. Lights are placed on timers. Special warming plates are arranged so that food can be enjoyed without violating the prohibition against cooking. Everything is intentional. There is a palpable sense of anticipation, as though a long-awaited guest were coming to stay.

At the core of Shabbat observance is the cessation of thirty-nine categories of *melachah*—creative or constructive acts derived from the types of labor used to build the tabernacle in the wilderness. These include lighting a fire (and by extension, using electricity), writing, carrying objects outside the home, cooking, washing clothes, planting, harvesting, and more. The laws are detailed, intricate, and exhaustive.

No phones are used. No computers. No cars are driven. No elevators are pushed. No money is handled. All modern technology is suspended. Not because these things are evil—but because they tether the soul to a world that never stops. On Shabbat, the goal is not productivity. It is presence. The Jew ceases from shaping the world so he can remember *who* shaped him.

Time itself is measured with precision. Shabbat begins and ends not by feeling, but by law. When three stars appear in the sky on Saturday night, Shabbat ends with a brief but beautiful ritual called havdalah. Over a cup of wine, sweet-smelling spices, and a braided candle, the family marks the division between the holy and the ordinary. It is a farewell to the sacred guest, and often an emotional one. Many feel a pang of sadness as Shabbat departs—because something eternal has passed through time and gone again.

On Shabbat, observant Jews refrain not only from action, but from certain kinds of speech. Conversations about business, politics, and financial concerns are avoided. The very topics of the week are left behind. Instead, families talk about Torah, share stories, sing songs, and speak words of encouragement. The home becomes a sanctuary. The table becomes an altar.

Meals are at the heart of Shabbat. Jews eat three festive meals: one on Friday night, one on Saturday afternoon, and a lighter one before sunset. Each begins with "Shalom Aleichem," a song welcoming the Shabbat, then the father and children sing "Eshet

Chayil" (A Woman of Virtue) taken from Proverbs 31:10–31 to the mother of the house, then kiddush is recited (a sanctification over wine), followed by the blessing over two loaves of challah, symbolizing the double portion of manna that fell in the desert on Fridays. The meals are long and unrushed. Multiple courses are served, often correlating to the ethnic backgrounds of each family, each with their passed-down recipes: fish, soup, meat, kugel, salads, desserts. *Zmirot*—traditional Shabbat songs—are sung. *Divrei Torah*—words of Scripture and reflection—are shared. Children recite what they've learned. Fathers bless their sons and daughters.

This is not dinner. It is liturgy. Eating becomes an act of worship. Hospitality becomes a mitzvah. The table becomes a place where body and soul are fed in harmony. The best dishes are used. The finest clothing is worn. Time slows. Conversation deepens. The soul exhales.

In the synagogue, Shabbat is celebrated with even greater intensity. Men attend prayer services Friday night, Saturday morning, and Saturday afternoon. The Friday night service includes *Kabbalat Shabbat*, a mystical liturgy that welcomes the Sabbath bride with psalms and songs. The Saturday morning service includes the public reading of the weekly Torah portion—one of fifty-four sections that complete the Five Books of Moses each year. The atmosphere is reverent, yet joyful. The melodies are ancient, the prayers lengthy, and the participation wholehearted.

Not all Shabbat observance is solemn. Children play freely in the streets, especially in tight-knit communities where no cars drive on Shabbat. Parents walk with strollers. Neighbors greet one another with "Shabbat shalom." It feels like another world—not stuck in the past, but rooted in something deeper than modernity. A world where time is ruled not by urgency, but by grace.

For women, the Sabbath rhythm may be different but no less sacred. While many men spend hours in the synagogue, women often manage the home, preparing meals, caring for children, and creating an atmosphere of peace and beauty. The woman's role in welcoming Shabbat is foundational; she lights the candles and, in a sense, lights the entire experience. In many Hasidic teachings, the feminine presence is central to the soul of Shabbat.

The prohibitions may seem overwhelming to outsiders. No writing, no turning lights on or off, no adjusting thermostats, no using electronics, no carrying objects outside unless within an erub (a symbolic boundary). And yet, these boundaries are not experienced as burdens. They are cherished as protection. They guard the sanctity of the day. They create the quiet necessary to hear the divine whisper.

Halacha—Jewish law—does not see these limitations as arbitrary. Rather, they are scaffolding for a sacred life. Just as a museum protects its masterpieces with glass and alarms, Shabbat is protected by precise guidelines. These rules create space for joy to flourish undisturbed. They make room for God.

And behind it all is theology. The Sabbath is not just one of the Ten Commandments—it is the *only* one described as a "sign" of the covenant. In Exodus 31, God says the Sabbath is a sign "forever" between Him and Israel, a testimony that He created the world in six days and rested on the seventh. To keep Shabbat is to testify that creation has a Creator, and that history has a goal.

But there's more. In Jewish thought, Shabbat is not only a remembrance of creation—it is a taste of redemption. The Talmud says, "Shabbat is a taste of the world to come." It is a glimpse of the Messianic future, when work and war will cease, and peace will reign. On Shabbat, the Jew lives as if the world were already whole.

That's why the preparations are so extensive. That's why the details are so exacting. That's why the songs are so joyful. Because Shabbat is not merely a duty—it is a homecoming.

And when it ends, there is often a longing. As the braided candle of havdalah is extinguished in wine, the aroma of cloves lingers—a sensory memory of what was just lived. People feel elevated, softened, more human. They return to the workweek not depleted, but renewed.

For extremely observant Jews, Shabbat is the most important day of the week—not because of what they avoid, but because of what they embrace. It is the day when the soul catches up with the body. When heaven touches earth. When time bows to eternity.

In an age of relentless speed, digital noise, and spiritual exhaustion, Shabbat stands like a mountain of light. It says to the human soul: *You are not a machine. You are not alone. You are not in charge. You are loved. You are free.*

And that, in the end, is why the most observant Jews give Shabbat everything they have. Because in return, it gives them back everything they are.

As Christians, we watch the beauty of Shabbat unfold in the Jewish tradition with deep respect and admiration. We can learn much from the reverence, intentionality, and sacred rhythm that our Jewish brothers and sisters uphold each week. Yet, we must also acknowledge that we live under the new covenant, established through the death and resurrection of Jesus Christ. The law was fulfilled in Him, and so the question naturally arises: *Are we still bound to keep the Sabbath?* Is the fourth commandment a moral obligation for Christians today, or has it been transformed, fulfilled, or even set aside in light of Christ's finished work? In the following section, we will explore this question with theological care, biblical depth, and historical awareness—examining both sides of the argument to better understand what Sabbath means for the Christian in a new covenant age.

When I began exploring modern Christianity—especially in the evangelical, nondenominational world—I noticed a marked shift. Pastors would reference Colossians 2:16 or Romans 14:5 as proof texts to explain that the Sabbath is no longer binding. And they weren't wrong to do so. Those verses are in the Bible. They must be reckoned with. But I couldn't shake the feeling that the explanation felt too easy, too dismissive of something God clearly set apart. There was no wrestling. Just doctrinal declarations. And I needed more than that. I needed clarity that came through the fire of grappling.

As someone who now observes a Saturday Sabbath, I want to be clear: I don't think the specific day—Saturday or Sunday—is of primary importance. Paul himself says, *"One person esteems one day as better than another, while another esteems all days alike"* (Romans 14:5). I grant that. The heart behind the day matters more than the day itself. The legalism that traps many Sabbatarians can be as spiritually deadening as the apathy that leads others to neglect rest altogether. This is not about ticking a box on a calendar—it's about stepping into a rhythm that God designed for our good.

And still, the debate remains enormous. Few Christians today believe the Sabbath is on Saturday. Fewer still believe that it's binding in any form. Most Christians see Sunday as the Lord's Day and consider it a commemoration of the resurrection, not a Sabbath.

And many others see no single day as sacred at all. They claim the Sabbath is fulfilled in Christ, that our entire lives are now to be lived in a state of spiritual rest, not tied to a specific date. I understand that position. I even sympathize with parts of it.

But then I think of the church fathers. Not all were in agreement, but some voices, like Ignatius of Antioch, began shifting Christian worship to Sunday very early on. Justin Martyr, in the second century, also noted that Christians gathered on Sunday because it was the day Jesus rose. This is the seed of what would later grow into the institutionalized "Lord's Day." Yet, it's also clear that early Jewish believers continued Sabbath observance, sometimes alongside Sunday gatherings. There was tension then, too. And it wasn't easily solved.

Others have suggested that the Sabbath is no longer external at all—that it now lives "in the heart." That in Christ, the believer carries a spiritual rest that transcends days. There's poetic beauty in this. Hebrews 4 speaks of entering God's rest through faith. And yet, it doesn't dismiss the command. It leaves open a tension: *"There remains a Sabbath rest for the people of God"* (Hebrews 4:9). Not just metaphorically, but in some mysterious, enduring way.

So, here I am—still a bit raw. Still tender about it. I honor Saturday as my day of rest, not because I believe it earns me righteousness, but because it reminds me I'm not God. I'm not limitless. I'm not defined by my labor. It teaches my children that God's world runs on trust, not hustle. It lets my body breathe. It lets my mind heal. And it gives my soul a rhythm of remembering.

I don't keep the Sabbath because I must. I keep it because I can. Because it was made for me. Because it's a gift.

And in this journey of wrestling, reading, failing, and returning, I've come to a place of peace—not with every detail, but with the direction. The following pages are not written from a mountaintop of certainty, but from a well-worn path of seeking. I've come to believe that the Sabbath matters. That God's rhythm is good. That rest is resistance in a world addicted to noise. And that Jesus, the Lord of the Sabbath, invites us not to legalism or laziness—but to life.

What follows is an attempt to trace the biblical contours of that invitation. To lay out what Scripture says on both sides. To sit with the tension. To honor the mystery. And to find rest not only in the doctrine, but in the Person behind it.

For those who've struggled like I have, I hope you find light. For those who disagree, I hope you feel respected. And for all of us, I hope we come to see the Sabbath not as a burden—but as a blessing too beautiful to ignore.

Here is a fair strongman argument for both sides in this chapter and the next. Ten reasons we should honor the Sabbath, followed by ten reasons we should not. This is after countless hours of research, prayer, and seeking expert advice on this topic.

The Case That Christians Are Still Bound to the Sabbath

The argument that Christians are still bound to honor the Sabbath rests not on a single verse or cultural tradition, but on a rich, layered tapestry of biblical theology, covenant continuity, historical testimony, and pastoral wisdom. This section presents ten deeply developed arguments in favor of Sabbath observance, each rooted in Scripture, enriched by church history, and affirmed by many scholars, reformers, and pastors throughout the centuries.

1. The Sabbath Was Instituted at Creation, Not at Sinai

Genesis 2:2–3

"And on the seventh day God finished his work that he had done, and he rested . . . So God blessed the seventh day and made it holy."

Before there was a nation of Israel, before the covenant with Abraham, before Moses ever walked up Mount Sinai—God instituted the Sabbath. Genesis does not present the seventh day as an Israelite ritual, but as a divine rhythm embedded in the structure of creation itself. God did not rest because He was weary. He rested to bless and sanctify the seventh day as holy—a day of delight, fulfillment, and rest.

Old Testament scholar John Sailhamer argued that the sanctification of the seventh day is presented not as a Mosaic ordinance but as a creation pattern. Abraham Heschel, the great Jewish theologian, echoes this: "The Sabbath is the most precious present mankind has received from the treasure house of God." If the Sabbath is part of the fabric of creation, then it applies to all people, not just to the Mosaic covenant community.

God does not sanctify things randomly. His act of blessing the seventh day gives it enduring significance. Unlike every other day in the creation account, the seventh day is not closed with the phrase *"and there was evening and there was morning."* The implication, some theologians suggest, is that the Sabbath is timeless—an eternal rest into which creation is invited. Jesus' later invitation recorded in Matthew 11:28 to *"come . . . and I will give you rest"* may be a continuation of that unending seventh day.

2. The Sabbath Is Part of the Ten Commandments, Written in Stone by God

Exodus 20:8, 10

"Remember the Sabbath day, to keep it holy . . .
the seventh day is a Sabbath to the Lord your God.
On it you shall not do any work."

Deuteronomy 5:22

"These words the Lord spoke . . . and he added no more.
And he wrote them on two tablets of stone
and gave them to me."

The Ten Commandments are the moral core of the covenant between God and His people. Written by God's own hand on tablets of stone, they are distinct from the civil and ceremonial laws given to Israel. They were not suggestions, nor were they temporary legal statutes subject to cultural shifts.

Reformer John Calvin insisted that the Sabbath commandment retains its force because it belongs not to the ceremonies but to the moral law. Likewise, the Westminster Confession of Faith declares the Sabbath to be "a part of the moral law," binding on all people at all times.

Modern evangelical theologian John Frame views the Sabbath as not merely a shadow but as reflecting the moral order, the created pattern of work and rest—and that the Sabbath points to the ultimate rest in Christ. Ignoring the Sabbath thus becomes a moral failure—not merely a lapse in ritual observance.

3. The Sabbath Was Made for Humanity, Not Just for Israel

Mark 2:27–28

*"And he said to them, 'The Sabbath was made for man,
not man for the Sabbath. So the Son of Man
is lord even of the Sabbath.' "*

This oft-quoted statement by Jesus is more radical than it first appears. When He says the Sabbath was made "for man," He uses the Greek *anthrōpos*—meaning humankind in general, not Jews in particular. He is affirming that the Sabbath was created as a gift for all humanity, not a burden imposed on a single nation.

Jesus' point was not to abolish the Sabbath, but to restore its purpose. The Pharisees had buried it beneath a mountain of legalistic regulations. But Jesus, as "Lord of the Sabbath," was reclaiming it for what it was always intended to be: a day of mercy, restoration, joy, and worship.

The early church recognized this universality. Even church fathers who emphasized the resurrection did not treat the Sabbath lightly. Ignatius, writing in the early second century, cautioned believers not to treat the Sabbath as a cold tradition, but rather to understand it spiritually through the lens of Christ. Still, the principle of a sacred rest endured.

4. The Sabbath Is a Sign of Covenant Identity and Sanctification

Exodus 31:13

*"Above all you shall keep my Sabbaths, for this is a sign between
me and you . . . that you may know that I, the Lord, sanctify you."*

God calls the Sabbath "a sign" between Himself and His people. In covenantal terms, signs are outward, visible markers of belonging. Just as circumcision marked the Abrahamic covenant and baptism marks the new covenant, the Sabbath functioned as a distinguishing feature of those set apart by God.

This theme continues in Ezekiel 20:12:

"I gave them my Sabbaths, as a sign between me and them, that they might know that I am the Lord who sanctifies them."

The Sabbath was a weekly covenant renewal. It was a time to remember who you were, who God was, and the relationship between the two. If our identity is in Christ—and if He Himself is Lord of the Sabbath—then we must not discard the sign that proclaims our sanctification.

5. Jesus Practiced and Defended the Sabbath Without Nullifying It

Luke 4:16

"And as was his custom, he went to the synagogue on the Sabbath day."

Jesus' consistent Sabbath observance is recorded across all four Gospels. His disputes with religious leaders were never about whether to keep the Sabbath, but about how. The Pharisees had turned it into a crushing yoke. Jesus sought to return it to its life-giving purpose.

Found in Matthew 12:12, Jesus says, *"It is lawful to do good on the Sabbath."* This was not a weakening of the commandment—it was a restoration. In John 5, we read about Jesus healing a man and being accused of violating the Sabbath, but instead of denying the Sabbath's authority, He reorients it toward compassion and healing.

To argue that Jesus broke or annulled the Sabbath is to misread both the spirit and the text of the Gospels.

6. The Sabbath Appears in Eschatological Prophecy

Isaiah 66:22–23

" 'From Sabbath to Sabbath, all flesh shall come to worship before me,' declares the Lord."

In one of the clearest Old Testament glimpses of the new heavens and the new earth, Isaiah declares that the redeemed from "all flesh" will gather before God—from Sabbath to Sabbath. This is not a return to old covenant law, but a vision of new creation worship.

The presence of the Sabbath in this eschatological vision implies its continuity into eternity. If the Sabbath exists in Eden (Genesis 2) and again in the new creation (Isaiah 66), then it is difficult to argue it is obsolete in the present.

7. Hebrews Teaches There "Remains a Sabbath" for God's People

Hebrews 4:9

"So then, there remains a Sabbath rest for the people of God."

The Greek word used here—*sabbatismos*—is rare and precise. It does not mean generic rest (*katapausis*), but Sabbath observance. This passage is part of a broader theological argument that connects God's rest in creation with the believer's spiritual rest in Christ. But the conclusion is striking: The Sabbath is not gone. It *remains*.

Scholars like Andreas Köstenberger and Andrew Lincoln affirm that *sabbatismos* cannot be reduced to metaphor. It speaks to the enduring value of setting aside sacred time for communion with God.

Far from abrogating the Sabbath, the book of Hebrews elevates it—pointing both backward to creation and forward to final rest in Christ.

8. The Moral Law Still Applies Under the New Covenant

Matthew 5:17–18

"Do not think that I have come to abolish the Law or the Prophets . . . not an iota, not a dot, will pass from the Law until all is accomplished."

Jesus explicitly states that He did not come to abolish the law. While the ceremonial laws of Israel (e.g., sacrifices, festivals) were fulfilled and rendered obsolete in Christ, the moral law—including the Ten Commandments—remains.

Romans 3:31

"Do we then overthrow the law by this faith? By no means! On the contrary, we uphold the law."

The Sabbath belongs to the moral framework of God's covenant—not as a ladder to earn salvation, but as a mirror that reflects His holiness and order. John Wesley emphasized that every part of the moral law stands firm, and is to be observed. That includes the Sabbath.

9. Revelation Identifies God's People as Commandment Keepers

Revelation 14:12

"Here is a call for the endurance of the saints, those who keep the commandments of God and their faith in Jesus."

In the final book of Scripture, God's people are identified as those who hold two defining marks: They trust in Jesus, and they keep God's commandments. These are not two different camps, but one people—faithful to both covenant and Christ.

The Sabbath commandment is the longest, most detailed of the Ten, and the only one that explicitly identifies God as Creator. It makes sense, then, that in an apocalyptic age defined by spiritual deception and false worship, the Sabbath would reemerge as a sign of fidelity.

10. The Sabbath Is a Gift, Not a Burden

Exodus 23:12

"On the seventh day you shall rest; that your ox and your donkey may have rest, and the son of your servant woman, and the alien, may be refreshed."

The Sabbath is about more than worship. It's about justice, humility, rest, and remembering who we are. It is the antithesis of Pharaoh's endless labor. It declares, "I am not what I produce. I belong to the Lord." In an age of burnout, digital fatigue, and constant noise, the Sabbath is God's timeless solution. It is not legalism—it is liberation.

As Abraham Heschel said, "The Sabbath is not for the sake of the weekdays; the weekdays are for the sake of the Sabbath." And as Jesus reminds us: "*The Sabbath was made for man*" (Mark 2:27)—for his healing, his joy, and his soul.

Beyond these scriptural verses, I wanted to look back at some of the greatest theologians in history. What did the greatest minds who thought deeply about the Word of God say about whether Christians are bound to the Sabbath?

John Wesley and A. W. Pink: Two Giants Who Upheld the Sabbath

Throughout Christian history, a wide spectrum of views has emerged regarding the Sabbath's relevance under the new covenant. While many modern evangelicals lean toward liberty in this area, two of the most respected and widely read theologians—**John Wesley** and **Arthur W. Pink**—believed firmly that the Sabbath commandment remains morally binding. Though they came from different theological worlds—Wesley from the Arminian Methodist revival, and Pink from the Reformed Calvinist tradition—they each concluded, through careful exegesis and spiritual conviction, that the fourth commandment is not ceremonial or optional, but a necessary expression of obedience to God's enduring moral law.

John Wesley: The Sabbath as a Means of Grace and Moral Necessity

John Wesley (1703–1791), the founder of Methodism, was one of the most influential Christian voices of the eighteenth century. A deeply disciplined man of God, Wesley emphasized personal holiness, the necessity of sanctification, and the daily life of piety. While Wesley was crystal clear in his theology of salvation by grace through faith, he also taught that genuine faith must produce a transformed life, one rooted in obedience to God's moral law. For Wesley, this law was not abolished by Christ, but fulfilled in such a way that it remained the believer's path to joyful communion with God.

Wesley placed the Ten Commandments at the heart of Christian ethics. In his *Explanatory Notes Upon the Old Testament*, he affirmed that the fourth commandment concerning the Sabbath was not to be spiritualized away or dismissed. Though he recognized Sunday as the Christian Sabbath in acknowledgment of the resurrection, Wesley did not treat the shift from Saturday to Sunday as grounds for laxity. He saw the day as sacred and binding—"a day which God hath hallowed," as he described it. In a sermon titled "The Duty and Advantage of Early Rising," Wesley remarks, "Keep the Sabbath holy, not in the letter only, but in the spirit." He called Christians to observe it with sincerity and purpose—not just by abstaining from work, but by actively engaging in worship, acts of mercy, Scripture meditation, and rest.

In *The Works of John Wesley*, he explains his position in stronger terms: As a means of grace, the Sabbath is not to be trifled with, and he who breaks it persistently will soon find his soul leprous with pride, avarice, and rebellion. Wesley saw Sabbath observance as deeply connected to both spiritual vitality and societal well-being. He lamented the moral collapse of communities that neglected the Lord's Day, arguing that when Sabbath rest is cast aside, the foundation of the home, the church, and the soul begins to crumble.

His methodical journals reflect this seriousness. Wesley rose early, fasted regularly, and organized his entire week around the rhythm of preparation for and recovery from Sabbath worship. For him, the Sabbath was not about legalistic precision, but about divine invitation. He considered it an appointment with God—a day when heaven and earth met in praise, refreshment, and reflection.

A. W. Pink: The Sabbath as Creational, Moral, and Theological

Arthur W. Pink (1886–1952) was a reclusive but profound Reformed theologian whose influence has steadily grown posthumously. Best known for his classic work *The Sovereignty of God*, Pink was an unapologetically God-centered thinker who believed that reverence for Scripture was the bedrock of spiritual health. In his view, Christianity had grown far too casual, emotional, and permissive. One major symptom of this decline, in Pink's judgment, was the widespread neglect of the Lord's Day.

Pink saw the Sabbath not as a Jewish tradition, but as a creational ordinance and a moral necessity. Drawing from Genesis 2:2–3, he argued that the sanctification of the seventh day preceded both the fall and the Mosaic covenant. "The actual sanctification and appointment of the Sacred Day of rest in worship takes us back to Eden itself," he wrote, "synchronizing with the very creation of man. It has also been shown that there are quite a number of unmistakable traces of the Sabbath being actually observed by God's people in the very earliest days of human history." He believed the Sabbath was made for man in Eden—long before there was a Jew or a written law. For Pink, this meant that Sabbath observance was not temporary or ceremonial, but permanent and universal, rooted in the very design of the human person.

In his book *The Holy Sabbath*, Pink critiques those who claim that the moral law was abolished in Christ. He writes, "Are we to suppose that the commandment 'Thou shalt not kill' is moral, but 'Remember the Sabbath day' is ceremonial? The absurdity of such a position should be self-evident. The fourth commandment belongs to the same unchanging law of God." He viewed the Ten Commandments as a coherent moral unit. To break one was to undermine the whole.

Pink also tackled the spiritual implications of Sabbath neglect. He warned that continuous labor without pause breeds self-sufficiency, idolatry of work, and spiritual barrenness. The Sabbath was given, in Pink's eyes, to remind humanity that rest is not laziness, but worship. To cease from labor is not to indulge the flesh, but to renew the soul.

Interestingly, while Wesley emphasized the Sabbath as a *means of grace*, Pink framed it more as a *test of loyalty*. For Wesley, Sabbath rest kept the believer close to God; for Pink, it also revealed whether the believer was willing to submit to God's rule. Those who trample the Sabbath, he believed, may offer much praise with their lips, but their hearts are far from obedience.

Though he was often suspicious of emotionalism and anti-intellectual fervor in religious practice, Pink believed in the experiential richness of Sabbath observance. He saw it not as a cold duty, but as a fountain of spiritual vitality. "It is on the Sabbath," he once penned, "that the Christian re-learns who he is, who God is, and what eternity means."

While Wesley and Pink would not have agreed on predestination, sacramental theology, or ecclesiology, they found common ground in their reverence for the Sabbath. Both believed it was not merely a tradition to be preserved, but a divine command to be honored, rooted in creation and relevant for every age. Their writings serve as a rebuke to both the antinomian impulse to cast off the law and the secular impulse to treat time as our own.

In a culture obsessed with productivity and plagued by burnout, their insights are more relevant than ever. Wesley's warm appeal to the Sabbath as a gracious rhythm of renewal and Pink's stern defense of it as an unchanging ordinance both speak to our need for sacred time. They remind us that Sabbath observance is not about earning favor with God, but about living as if He alone rules time—and we are not our own.

Their witness also serves as a challenge to modern Christians who assume that Sabbath observance is an issue of mere personal preference. Both Wesley and Pink were well-read, rigorously theological, and deeply immersed in Scripture. They did not arrive at their conclusions through sentiment, but through study. In their view, the fourth commandment was not a cultural relic, but a moral compass—a gift that, when ignored, leaves us spiritually disoriented and relationally impoverished.

To read them today is to be reminded that the Sabbath is not first and foremost about what we *can't* do—it is about what we *get* to do. We get to stop. We get to rest. We get to worship without distraction. And in doing so, we remember that God is God—and we are not.

Now, as compelling as all that is, I would be remiss not to show the other side of the argument.

Chapter 10

JESUS DOESN'T OFFER A DAY—HE OFFERS HIMSELF

As I have stated previously and repeatedly throughout this book, the Sabbath is the most ignored commandment by modern Christians to our own detriment. Some bodies of theology reject all the prior claims and believe that the Sabbath is null and void and that we no longer need to make the seventh day holy. Here is my best attempt after years of thinking and research to articulate that school of thought:

The Case That Christians Are Not Bound to the Sabbath

The case that Christians are not bound to Sabbath observance under the new covenant is grounded in the life, death, and resurrection of Jesus Christ and the transformation He inaugurated. This position is not rooted in hostility toward the Sabbath, but in a careful reading of how the New Testament treats the law, the covenant, and sacred time. Below are ten robust arguments, each carefully developed.

1. Colossians Declares the Sabbath a Shadow Fulfilled in Christ

Colossians 2:16–17

"Therefore let no one pass judgment on you in questions of food and drink, or with regard to a festival or a new moon or a Sabbath. These are a shadow of the things to come, but the substance belongs to Christ."

Paul's message to the Colossians is bold: Don't let anyone judge you for not observing Sabbath days. He groups Sabbaths with other ritual observances—food laws and festivals—and calls them "shadows." In contrast, Christ is the substance. This implies that Sabbath observance was a temporary sign pointing to a greater reality.

The Sabbath pointed forward to the rest we would receive in Christ (Hebrews 4), but once the substance comes, the shadow no longer binds. This is not a dismissal of Sabbath as unimportant—but as fulfilled. The moral command to rest, trust, and worship continues, but the ceremonial yoke has been lifted.

2. Romans 14 Affirms Liberty Regarding Sacred Days

Romans 14:5–6

"One person esteems one day as better than another, while another esteems all days alike. Each one should be fully convinced in his own mind."

Here, Paul grants liberty of conscience about "esteeming" days. In context, this includes Sabbath days. He neither mandates Sabbath observance nor forbids it—but insists on grace and nonjudgment.

Paul is dealing with early Christian communities where some Jewish believers continued to observe the Sabbath, while Gentiles did not. Rather than enforce uniformity, Paul defends freedom.

In reading the Bible, I believe that Paul refrains from forcing his own opinion. He embraces variety within unity. This exemplifies mature grace. Under the new covenant, sacred time is transformed—not abolished—but no longer legislated.

3. Galatians Warns Against Returning to Calendar Observance

Galatians 4:10–11

"You observe days and months and seasons and years!
I am afraid I may have labored over you in vain."

Paul's words here are deeply concerned. He sees the Galatian Christians sliding back into Jewish calendar observances—not as cultural expressions, but as obligations. His alarm isn't over *when* they worship, but *why*.

According to Frank Turek, the thrust of Paul's letter to the Galatians is that Jesus plus NOTHING equals salvation. Whether it's special days, circumcision, or any other rite or ritual, adding that to the Gospel is "another gospel" that he warns about in Chapter 1. Relying on the law rather than grace is the heresy he's combating. So even if the Sabbath is a command, it is not necessary for justification.

Sabbath observance, when turned into law rather than a gift, becomes dangerous.

To be clear: Paul doesn't forbid voluntary rest. But when days become required—particularly for righteousness—they become a threat to the gospel of grace.

4. Jesus Offers a Deeper Rest Than the Sabbath Could

Matthew 11:28–29

"Come to me, all who labor and are heavy laden, and I will give you rest . . . and you will find rest for your souls."

This is the most important theological point in the New Testament discussion of Sabbath. Jesus doesn't say, "Come and keep the Sabbath." He says, "Come to Me." He doesn't offer a day—He offers Himself.

In Christ, the weary find a deeper, fuller, eternal rest that the Sabbath only foreshadowed. The law commanded physical rest one day a week. Jesus offers soul rest every day through grace.

Augustine said it best: "Our hearts are restless until they find their rest in Thee." Sabbath rest is fulfilled not on a calendar, but on a cross.

5. Hebrews Teaches Rest Is Spiritual, Not Ritual

Hebrews 4:9–10

"So then, there remains a Sabbath rest for the people of God, for whoever has entered God's rest has also rested from his works as God did from his."

Hebrews is not calling believers back to the Sabbath day. It is calling them forward into something greater. The "Sabbath rest" that remains is not a day—it's a state of faith in Christ. It is the "rest from works" that comes through justification by faith.

Scholar Andreas Köstenberger highlights that the rest offered in Hebrews is not merely a halt from labor, but an entrance into

God's eternal rest through faith in Jesus. The author uses Sabbath imagery but applies it spiritually—not ritually.

6. The Jerusalem Council Did Not Require Sabbath Observance

Acts 15:28–29

"For it has seemed good to the Holy Spirit and to us to lay on you no greater burden than these requirements."

At the Jerusalem Council, the apostles faced a massive question: Should Gentile converts obey the Mosaic law—including circumcision and Sabbath? Their answer is clear: *No*. They gave a few essentials related to idolatry and morality, but Sabbath observance was conspicuously absent.

If Sabbath-keeping were essential for salvation or spiritual maturity, it is inconceivable that the apostles would have omitted it in the church's first doctrinal council.

7. Christians Are Not Under Law but Under Grace

Romans 6:14

"For sin will have no dominion over you, since you are not under law but under grace."

This is one of Paul's foundational declarations. Believers are not under the Mosaic law. We are under the law of Christ (Galatians 6:2)—a law of love, led by the Spirit.

The Sabbath law belonged to the old covenant. With Christ's resurrection, that covenant is fulfilled and surpassed. Paul emphasizes in 2 Corinthians 3:6 that *"the letter kills, but the Spirit gives life."*

We are not antinomians. We do not discard the moral guidance of Scripture. But we are not under the Mosaic framework of law-keeping, including Sabbaths, feasts, and dietary codes.

8. Jesus' Resurrection Transformed the Church's Rhythm

Acts 20:7

"On the first day of the week,
when we were gathered together to break bread."

1 Corinthians 16:2

"On the first day of every week,
each of you is to put something aside."

The early church began to gather on Sunday—not to replace the Sabbath, but to celebrate the resurrection. Over time, this became the normative rhythm for worship and community.

Justin Martyr, in the second century, wrote, "Sunday is the day on which we all hold our common assembly, because it is the first day on which God, having wrought a change in the darkness and matter, made the world, and Jesus Christ our Savior on the same day rose from the dead." This shift was not law, but liberty. Sunday was never called "the Christian Sabbath" in Scripture. But it became the joyful heartbeat of the resurrection people.

9. The Sabbath Law Is Part of a Fulfilled Covenant

Ephesians 2:15

"[Christ abolished] the law of commandments expressed in ordinances."

The Sabbath law belonged to the old covenant—a system of shadows and symbols pointing to Christ. That covenant has been fulfilled.

Hebrews 8:13 says, *"In speaking of a new covenant, he makes the first one obsolete."*

Theologian John Piper believes that the core meaning of the Sabbath command is fulfilled through the spiritual rest that Christ offers. The sign has accomplished its purpose. When a contract is fulfilled, it doesn't mean the original terms were bad—it means they've been completed.

10. The Gospel Warns Against Legalism and Bondage

Galatians 5:1

"For freedom Christ has set us free; stand firm therefore, and do not submit again to a yoke of slavery."

Paul's warning is severe. When Christians return to the law as a basis for righteousness—even in seemingly good ways—they risk undermining grace. The Sabbath can become such a trap.

We are not saved by our calendar. We are not sanctified by external observances. We are saved and sustained by Christ alone.

Martin Luther is attributed with saying, "He [Christ] is the true fulfillment of the sabbath."

To insist that Sabbath observance is required under the gospel risks building a new legalism. And as Paul reminds us, *"Christ will be of no advantage to you"* if you seek justification by law (Galatians 5:2).

Similar to the above argument, I wanted to find two legendary theologians who believe we are NOT bound to the Sabbath. These two names you will likely recognize, Luther and Calvin, and here is their profound take on the adherence to the Sabbath:

Martin Luther: Freedom from the Sabbath as Law

Martin Luther (1483–1546), the German monk and reformer who ignited the Protestant Reformation in 1517, had a profound respect for the Scriptures and a radical commitment to the gospel of grace. His doctrine of justification by faith alone revolutionized Christianity and reframed the role of the law in Christian life. Luther believed that while the moral law still had value as a guide and mirror, the **ceremonial laws of the old covenant—including Sabbath observance—were abolished in Christ**.

Luther offers a striking interpretation of the Sabbath command in his belief that we Christians should also keep such a day for the sake of outward discipline and education of the young and the ignorant people, but the Sabbath, strictly speaking, is not binding upon us because it is an entirely external matter, like other ordinances of the Old Testament.

In his *Against the Heavenly Prophets*, he amplifies this:

> "It is not necessary to observe the sabbath or Sunday because of Moses' commandment. Nature also shows and

> teaches that one must now and then rest a day, so that man and beast may be refreshed."

Luther was adamant that the Sabbath was part of the Jewish ceremonial code, pointing toward Christ and therefore **fulfilled and no longer binding**. He opposed any doctrine that imposed Sabbath-keeping as a legal requirement on Christians, viewing such teachings as contrary to the gospel. For him, to insist on keeping the Sabbath as law was to fall back into "works-righteousness"—a mindset that he believed obscured the finished work of Christ.

That said, Luther did not dismiss the need for rest or worship. He advocated for a designated day when Christians could gather, hear the Word, teach the young, and refrain from unnecessary work. But he insisted this be seen not as a divine obligation, but as **a practical and pastoral arrangement**, one that served the church but did not bind the conscience.

Luther also rejected the common argument of his day that Sunday was a "Christian Sabbath." In fact, he believed it dangerous to refer to Sunday as a replacement of the Jewish Sabbath because it might lead people back into a legalistic observance of days. In his treatises against the Anabaptists and other legalistic sects, Luther often warned against Sabbatarianism as a subtle form of self-justification.

For Luther, every day was to be lived before God. The believer, justified by faith, was free from all ceremonial law—including the command to keep the Sabbath—because Christ had fulfilled it entirely.

John Calvin: The Sabbath Fulfilled Spiritually in Christ

John Calvin (1509–1564), the French reformer whose teachings became the theological bedrock of the Reformed and Presbyterian traditions, shared Luther's view that the Sabbath commandment was not **binding in its Mosaic, literal form**. Calvin, however, offered a more nuanced and systematized treatment of the Sabbath within his magisterial *Institutes of the Christian Religion*.

Calvin agreed that the moral law, as summarized in the Ten Commandments, continued to guide Christian conduct. But he distinguished between the **moral essence** of the Sabbath and its **ceremonial form**. According to Calvin, the fourth commandment included three components: (1) a shadowy, ceremonial part that pointed to Christ, (2) a civil order established for Israel's societal life, and (3) a moral element, which called all people to rest from sin and dedicate time to worship.

He wrote:

> "Spiritual rest is the mortification of the flesh; so that the sons of God should no longer live unto themselves, or indulge their own inclination."

And again:

> "Under the rest of the seventh day, the divine Lawgiver meant to furnish the people of Israel with a type of the spiritual rest by which believers were to cease from their own works, and allow God to work in them. . . . He [Christ] is, I say, the true fulfillment of the Sabbath."

For Calvin, the **literal observance of one day in seven was not binding** on Christians, though he affirmed the usefulness and benefit of a weekly rhythm of worship. The Lord's Day (Sunday) was founded by the apostles, not by divine mandate, and was meant to support the church in her worship and order—not as a revived Mosaic Sabbath, but as a new creation rhythm honoring the resurrection.

In *Institutes* II.8.34–35, Calvin explains that while it is useful for Christians to set aside a regular day for worship and rest, to enforce this as a divine law is to "Judaize" the gospel. He warned that many Christians, especially in the Roman Catholic Church, had fallen into the trap of treating Sunday as a rigid law, missing the gospel's liberating power.

Yet, Calvin also rejected the idea that Christians were now free to live without sacred time altogether. Stemming from his belief in the apostles' example, he wrote:

> "Although the Sabbath has been abrogated, there is still occasion for us . . . to assemble on stated days for hearing the Word, the breaking of the mystical bread, and for public prayers."

Thus, while Calvin denied that Sunday had replaced Saturday as a new law, he affirmed the principle of sacred rhythm. He viewed the moral substance of the Sabbath—devotion to God, rest from sin, and corporate worship—as still entirely relevant, though transformed under grace.

While Luther and Calvin diverged in many ways—particularly on the sacraments, predestination, and ecclesiology—they stood united in rejecting the idea that Christians are legally bound to observe the Sabbath commandment in its old covenant form. Both viewed such teachings as a regression into the law, a subtle undermining of the sufficiency of Christ's work on the cross.

Luther's theological concern was liberty. He feared any attempt to reimpose the law as binding would draw believers back under the yoke of works. Calvin's concern was typology. He believed the Sabbath had been a shadow of Christ, and once the reality had come, the sign no longer carried authority.

Both reformers upheld the **spiritual principle** of rest and worship but resisted the idea that one day—be it Saturday or Sunday—carried divine obligation for new covenant believers. And yet, neither dismissed the importance of public worship, sacred time, or weekly gathering. They saw these as matters of wisdom, not of law.

The views of Luther and Calvin continue to shape the theology of millions. Most Protestant traditions today—especially those from Lutheran and Reformed backgrounds—maintain a similar position. They honor Sunday as a day of worship, not because it is commanded, but because it is wise. They reject legalistic Sabbatarianism, insisting that Christ alone is our rest.

This view influenced major confessions, such as *The Augsburg Confession* and the *Second Helvetic Confession*, both of which emphasize Christian freedom from Mosaic ceremonial law. While Puritanism later revived strict Sabbatarianism, the mainstream Protestant tradition has remained with the Reformers.

Together, Luther and Calvin offered a vision of Sabbath that prioritized Christ over calendar, grace over regulation, and spiritual rest over external conformity. Their message endures: We are not bound to the Sabbath—but we are invited into the rest of God.

So—Are We Bound to the Sabbath?

Are we?

I'll be honest: I'm not a theologian, a professor, or a pastor. I don't have letters after my name, nor have I spent decades publishing academic papers on covenant theology or biblical law. My answer here will not carry the weight of someone with a PhD in biblical studies or systematic theology. But I've labored over this question with my Bible open, my conscience stirred, and my heart submitted to God. What follows is not an authoritative decree—but a faithful summary of how I've come to understand this sacred, complex question as a Christian, a father, and a man trying to walk in the truth.

The Sabbath is God ordained. It was blessed and sanctified at creation, written in stone at Sinai, honored by Christ during His earthly ministry, and—whether in principle or practice—respected by the early church. At its core, the Sabbath is a standing celebration of the world's beginning, a weekly reminder that creation has meaning, that rest is holy, and that we are not slaves to our labor, our devices, or our ambitions. Whether you believe it is legally binding or not, it remains a *divinely instituted rhythm*—and to ignore it entirely is to disregard something God declared good.

I do not believe Christians are in sin simply for not keeping the Sabbath in the traditional or Mosaic sense. We are saved by grace, not by keeping holy days. Christ is our righteousness—not our calendars. But I do believe something tragic happens when we treat the Sabbath as irrelevant. We lose a vital part of our witness. We lose access to one of God's most gracious provisions. We lose a countercultural rhythm that exposes the idolatry of productivity, self-sufficiency, and ceaseless busyness.

To live without Sabbath is not neutral—it's dangerous. Our

families suffer when we never rest. Our churches burn out when we never stop. Our bodies pay the price, our relationships dry up, and our souls become shallow. Why? Because we're ignoring something God wove into the very fabric of creation.

The truth is, you can live without Sabbath. But you won't live *well.* You can survive without it. But you cannot thrive in the full blessing of God's design while rejecting one of His most generous gifts.

And so, while I do not believe disobeying the Sabbath in a legal sense is a sin for Christians under grace, I am convinced that *living as though we have no need of rest, worship, recovery, and delight in God* is a path that leads us toward pride, exhaustion, and ultimately sin. Working for seven days a week without pause is not just unhealthy—it is an act of spiritual arrogance. It says, "I don't need the rhythm God created. I'll make my own."

But we are not our own. We are not machines. We are not slaves. We are sons and daughters of the Most High, created in His image, called to reflect His pattern of work and rest, labor and love, worship and wonder.

So whether you keep the Sabbath on Saturday, honor the Lord's Day on Sunday, or practice daily rhythms of intentional rest and worship—do not abandon the principle. Receive the gift. Let it humble you. Let it heal you. Let it set you apart.

The Sabbath is not a burden to bear—it's a grace to embrace.

And in a world that never stops, one of the holiest things you can do is stop.

Stop running. Stop working. Stop striving.

And remember—you are not God. But you are His.

So, rest. Not because you must.

But because He did.

Chapter 11

NOW IT'S YOUR TURN TO ACT

Throughout this book, I've endeavored to persuade you that embracing the Sabbath—truly setting aside one day a week for sacred rest—has the potential to transform your life. Now I want to challenge you directly: Take the bold and countercultural step to unplug, disconnect, power down, and *cease.*

I'm willing to bet that, somewhere along the way, you've felt the pull. You've read these pages and thought, *I wish I could do that. I don't have the time. I wish my life allowed for it.* But let's be honest—those are just wishes and excuses. And excuses and wishes, no matter how polished, will not lead you into rest.

I write this with as much humility as possible: If I can carve out a Sabbath, so can you.

Consider the demands placed on my time. I lead two major national organizations—Turning Point USA and Turning Point Action—with over one thousand team members. I'm responsible for raising over $100 million annually to keep the mission moving forward. I host a daily national radio program and podcast, produce a steady stream of digital content, and participate in over one hundred hours of open-air debate each school semester—debates that are grueling, combative, and travel intensive. Beyond those events, I deliver more than seventy-five public speeches per year. I'm also a husband to Erika, a father to two children under the age of two, and the author of this very book.

And yet—I *still* Sabbath.

Not because it's convenient. Not because it fits easily into my schedule. But because I've decided I *must*. Because I know that without it, everything else begins to unravel.

So, let me say this plainly: If I can do it, you can too.

In this final section, I want to walk you through some of the most common objections, hesitations, and logistical questions people raise when considering the Sabbath. My hope is that this will not only clarify misconceptions, but give you the final nudge to take *immediate action*.

The time to reflect is over. The time to *begin* is now.

"I don't have enough time!"

We touched on this earlier—but let's go deeper. Because yes, you *do* have time. You might be wondering how I manage to do all that I do. The answer isn't magic. It's mastery.

First, I don't pollute my body. I don't drink alcohol. I don't consume sugar. I don't willingly ingest things that cloud my judgment or slow me down. That alone unlocks a tremendous amount of productive energy throughout the day. Second, I am a relentless time manager—down to the half minute, at times. At my worst, I'm impatient. At my best, I'm lethally efficient with how I allocate each moment.

I schedule everything: calls, workouts, deep reading, Scripture study, playtime with my kids, date nights with my wife, even my sleep. As I argued in an earlier chapter (and may someday expand into an entire book), *sleep is a forgotten superpower in the West.* We neglect it at our peril. If you missed that chapter, I encourage you to revisit it—because reclaiming your sleep is one of the first steps to reclaiming your time.

Here's a quick exercise: Take out your phone and check your screen time. Go ahead—actually look. Unless you work in social media or customer engagement, odds are you don't need to be on your phone for more than ninety minutes a day. If you're over that, you're not "busy"—you're distracted. And that's a hard pill to swallow.

I challenge you: Try one week without any social media apps. Just one. Delete them from your phone, cold turkey. What you'll experience isn't withdrawal—it's awakening. Suddenly, you'll find balance again. You'll realize how much time you've been wasting scrolling endlessly, feeding an addiction to distraction. When the noise goes quiet, clarity arrives. You'll become exponentially more efficient—simply because you stopped chasing dopamine.

Time management is brutally honest work. It forces you to face what truly matters. And whether you admit it or not, how you manage your time is a direct mirror of your values. It is a living record of your priorities. Tragically, for many Americans, the most valued daily ritual is television. According to a 2023 Nielsen report, the average American adult watches nearly **3 hours of television per day**. That's over **1,000 hours a year**. A full month—gone.

Now, let me be clear: I love a good college football game. If the Oregon Ducks are playing, or if it's March Madness, or the Bears are on the field, I'll watch. But for the stage of life I'm in, entertainment is not the engine of my week. God is. Family is. Purpose is. And leisure—*real,* restorative leisure—comes after those.

If you share those values—and I suspect most of you reading this do—then the Sabbath isn't a burden. It's a *gift*. It allows you to honor God and bless your family in a sacred, protected way—shielded from the world's noise, nourished by peace.

Renowned time management expert Laura Vanderkam once said, "Time passes whether you acknowledge it or not. But how you spend your hours determines what your life becomes." That's it. That's the truth.

You're not too busy for the Sabbath. You're just busy with things that aren't the Sabbath. And the beautiful thing is—*you can choose differently*. You don't need a permission slip. You don't need perfect conditions. You just need conviction.

You *can* manage your time. You *can* rewire your week. You *can* live a life that honors what matters most.

So, start. Not next month. Not when your schedule "clears up." Now. Because time is not a tyrant. It is a tool. And the Sabbath is how you wield it well.

"It's too hard to unplug because of my work."

I want to speak to this with grace, but also with clarity: Respectfully, unless you're literally running a country, you're probably not too busy to rest. And if you *are* that busy, I'd sincerely like to meet you. I say that with love—not to diminish your responsibility, but to call out the truth we often avoid: **Work can become a form of servitude** when it consumes every hour and robs us of rest.

God addressed this dynamic head-on in the Ten Commandments—not once, but twice. I wrote about this in Chapter 4, but it bears repeating here.

The first mention is in **Exodus 20:8–11**, and the second in **Deuteronomy 5:12, 14–15**. These two passages are almost identical, yet they contain one profound difference.

Exodus 20:8–11

"Remember the Sabbath day, to keep it holy . . .
the seventh day is a Sabbath to the Lord your God.
On it you shall not do any work . . . For in six days the Lord
made the heavens and the earth . . . and rested on the seventh day.
Therefore the Lord blessed the Sabbath day and made it holy."

Deuteronomy 5:12, 14–15

"Observe the Sabbath day, to keep it holy . . .
On it you shall not do any work . . . You shall remember
that you were a slave in the land of Egypt, and the Lord
your God brought you out . . . Therefore the Lord your God
commanded you to keep the Sabbath day."

Did you catch the difference?

In *Exodus*, we're called to rest because God rested. In *Deuteronomy*, we're commanded to rest because only *slaves* work without stopping. God links Sabbath to freedom. To resist the Sabbath is, in essence, to flirt with slavery again—not the kind imposed by Pharaoh, but the kind we willingly chain ourselves to through unrelenting busyness, performance, and obligation.

Let that sink in: **Slaves don't rest. Free people do.**

Now, I understand that some of you reading this truly have demanding roles. Emergency responders, medical professionals, and others in crisis-based work—you may not have the luxury of a fully unplugged Sabbath. I get that. This is not about guilt, but about growth. And even for you, I believe there's *something* you can do to honor the principle of rest.

So rather than saying, "I can't," ask this:

- Can I set up an emergency-only phone line and silence all others?
- Can I check my phone twice instead of twenty times during the day?
- Can I front-load my workweek so my team knows I won't be responding on the Sabbath?
- Can I draw a boundary with my boss and ask for space that aligns with my values?

Don't make excuses. Make adjustments.

Don't give up. Get creative.

Rest is not about perfection—it's about intention. The goal isn't to follow a legalistic rule, but to cultivate a sacred rhythm of freedom and trust. Sabbath is not a burden. It's a *gift*. And like all good gifts, it requires humility to receive and courage to protect.

So, here's the challenge: Honor the Sabbath not because you've earned rest, but because you *belong* to a God who has already set you free.

"I'll rest when things calm down."

I hear this one all the time. People say their lives are too busy right now, but they'll rest later—maybe in a different season, when the kids are older, the business stabilizes, or the inbox is finally under control. First, let me say this: I get it. I really do. You're moving fast, spinning plates, and trying to hold everything together. Rest feels like a luxury you can't afford.

But here's the truth: This is procrastination dressed up as planning. The root of this excuse isn't timing—it's avoidance. It's not about being too busy to rest; it's about postponing the decision to trust that God's design for your life includes a rhythm of stillness.

One of my mentors, Tony Robbins, puts it this way:

"The path to success is to take massive, determined action."

Rest doesn't happen by accident. You don't drift into renewal. You choose it. You protect it. You build around it. Sabbath is not about having time; it's about making a decision to stop even when everything else tells you to keep going.

Let me be clear: You will never not be busy. Life doesn't calm down—it just shifts into different types of busyness. The work doesn't stop, but you can. And that's the real test: If I believe in God, do I love and trust Him enough to stop what I'm doing and rest in His presence?

We learn in Exodus 33:14 that God says this to Moses:

"My presence will go with you, and I will give you rest."

This is more than a promise—it's a posture. Rest is not just a physical pause; it's the fruit of God's presence. It's not something we earn at the end of a productive week, but something we receive because we're in relationship with the One who carries the weight of the world—so we don't have to. Sabbath isn't a reward for the disciplined; it's a gift for the dependent.

In America, procrastination is more than a habit—it's a lifestyle. A study published in *Psychological Science* found that 20 percent of US adults are chronic procrastinators. And according to the American Psychological Association, 94 percent of people admit to procrastinating in ways that negatively affect their healthiness, work, and relationships.

Dr. Joseph Ferrari, a professor of psychology at DePaul University and a leading expert on procrastination, says this:

> "Procrastination is not a time management issue. It's an emotion regulation issue. We delay because the task makes us feel uncomfortable."

That discomfort includes stopping. Many of us don't rest, not because we don't want to, but because the silence exposes things we'd rather avoid—fear, anxiety, a lack of trust. So, we keep moving, convincing ourselves that one day we'll slow down. But we rarely do.

In a culture where overwork is a badge of honor, procrastination around rest becomes a socially accepted addiction. The price we pay is exhaustion, disconnection, and shallow faith. The more we delay honoring the Sabbath, the more distant we feel from the God who offers us rest.

When we delay, we lie to ourselves. We believe that "future us" will have more willpower, more clarity, more bandwidth. But procrastination doesn't create space—it creates stress. The longer we delay making a decision that brings life, the more we suffocate under the weight of indecision.

Procrastination is not just a bad habit. It's a thief. It robs us of presence, progress, and peace. Rest requires courage. It means confronting our fear that the world will fall apart if we stop working. It means choosing trust over control. And it means recognizing that the things that matter most—our health, our relationships, our spiritual life—cannot thrive on leftovers.

Let's reject the myth that rest will happen "eventually." That day doesn't exist. There will always be laundry. Always be meetings. Always be a new crisis, a new deadline, a new reason to push Sabbath one more week down the road.

If you don't stop now, there's no guarantee you ever will. Rest doesn't wait for life to get easier—it shows up as resistance *within* the chaos. Sabbath is a declaration that God is in control, and that your worth is not measured by your output.

So the next time you catch yourself thinking, "I'll rest when things calm down," try saying this instead:

"I'll rest because God is with me—even when life isn't calm."

"My kids' sports take up the whole weekend."

I hear this one often—some variation of the idea that parents with children ages five through eighteen are in perpetual motion every weekend. Practices, games, tournaments, carpools—it can feel like an unending cycle of activity. But here's the thing: No inherent conflict exists between participating in your child's life and honoring the Sabbath. The commandment does not prohibit movement, joy, or community. It prohibits *melachah*—the kind of work associated with dominion, production, and control, as we discussed earlier in the book.

In fact, Sabbath is not just about ceasing from toil; it's about becoming fully present. It is a spiritual architecture that invites us back into the orbit of our families and into the awareness of God's gifts. It's no coincidence that Sabbath, rightly observed, helps reinforce other commandments—like honoring your father and mother or guarding against the slow erosion of intimacy that leads to adultery. Sabbath is a divine gift to re-center you within your household and restore the sacred rhythm of love and attention.

So the next time you're taking your thirteen-year-old to a basketball game, resist the temptation to kill time by scrolling endlessly through your phone. Be present. Watch your child warm up. Listen to the squeak of sneakers, the whistle blasts, the sideline chatter. Pray for a safe game, for your child's confidence, for their joy. Let the Sabbath moment baptize you in awareness.

No emails. No calls. No urgent Slack messages. For even two hours, step out of Egypt's digital chains. You may just discover that in honoring the Sabbath in this quiet, unseen way, you're becoming a better parent, a truer friend, and a more peaceful person.

Too many parents today are physically present but emotionally absent. They sit in the bleachers but never look up from their phones. They miss the clutch shot, the smile from the court, the nervous glance looking for their approval—because their attention is devoured by digital distractions. We are raising a generation starved for the presence of their parents. Not just the logistics of parenting, but the soul of it.

The Sabbath is God's rebellion against our inattentiveness. It demands that we stop moving long enough to actually *see* the people right in front of us—our children, our spouse, our aging parents. It reminds us that love cannot be automated or multitasked. Your child may not remember the score of that weekend's game, but they will remember whether you were watching.

And here's the deeper irony: In our rush to "support" our kids, we sometimes sacrifice what they need the most. What if your presence—your full, undistracted, joyful presence—was more important than the sport itself? What if honoring the Sabbath gave your child a deeper sense of security and identity than all the accolades on the field ever could?

Sabbath doesn't pull us away from our families. It pushes us closer. It says, "You don't need to do more—you need to be more." More attentive. More rooted. More present. And in doing so, you give your children a gift this world can't offer: your undivided attention, anchored in holy time.

"Resting makes me feel guilty."

If this is you, then it's time for a radical reevaluation of what truly matters. I don't say this to scorn or shame you—but to lovingly challenge you. If resting in God stirs up guilt rather than peace, then something is profoundly out of alignment in your soul. That guilt is not the voice of God—it's the voice of a taskmaster you've allowed to take His place.

I know this firsthand. For the first ten years of building Turning Point USA, I worked constantly—Easter, Christmas, Thanksgiving, New Year's Day, the Fourth of July. There wasn't a single idle square on the calendar. I wore exhaustion like a badge of honor. But it led to physical depletion, spiritual dryness, and mental exhaustion. Ironically, it wasn't until I began honoring the Sabbath—dedicating one day to the Lord—that everything truly began to flourish. My leadership, our mission, and my soul all experienced renewal. The guilt I used to feel for resting wasn't from the Holy Spirit. It was something darker—rooted in fear, pride, and misplaced identity.

If taking one day off makes you anxious or ashamed, then you must ask, *What am I really worshipping?* Because no idol condemns rest like the idol of productivity. This is the golden calf of the modern age. We bow to output, chase metrics, and sacrifice our joy on the altar of efficiency. Somewhere along the way, many Christians began living as if "hurry" were a fruit of the Spirit.

Rest feels like rebellion when you've built your worth on constant striving. But the Sabbath is that rebellion. It is God's weekly act of liberation. The same God who freed His people from Egyptian slavery now frees us from internal Pharaohs—those invisible tyrants that crack the whip and whisper, *You are only as valuable as what you produce.*

Our identity must be anchored in something far greater than toil. Work is good—it reflects God's creative nature. But rest is holy—it reflects His sufficiency. The same God who calls us to labor for six days also commands us to rest for one. That's not weakness; that's worship. It's a weekly declaration that God is God—and we are not.

When you choose Sabbath, you declare this to your calendar, your boss, your own ego: *I am not in charge.* You remember that the world keeps spinning even when your hands stop moving. That's not passivity—that's trust.

If your soul feels uneasy when you stop, it may be because you've built your worth on what you do, not who you are in Christ. Sabbath rest is not an interruption to your purpose—it's a restoration of it. It realigns your heart with the truth that you are not a machine, a brand, or a project. You are a child of God. And He is not glorified by burnout—He is glorified by obedience, delight, and trust.

We often think that more hustle will solve our problems. But many of our greatest breakthroughs—emotionally, spiritually, even vocationally—don't come from pushing harder. They come from surrender. From stillness. From letting God do what only He can do. Psalm 46:10 says, *"Be still, and know that I am God."* That's not a suggestion—it's a command. And it's a promise.

When you obey the Sabbath, you're not just resting—you're repenting. You're confessing that your time belongs to God, that your value isn't earned, and that your limits are not liabilities. In doing so, you step out of the chaos of a culture that never stops, and into the peace of a kingdom that was built on rest from the beginning.

So, lay down your guilt. Pick up grace. Rest isn't a reward for finishing the work. It's a command that reminds us the work is never ours to finish alone.

"There are many weekends a year where I simply can't take a Sabbath."

If this is your excuse, then I fully understand. In fact, I resonate with it. About five weekends out of the year—sometimes more—it becomes genuinely difficult for me to take a Sabbath. Events like AmericaFest or other major Turning Point USA gatherings can demand my full presence and attention. Occasionally, I'm asked to speak at conferences, churches, or public forums that fall squarely on weekends. And in those moments, I face the same tension many of you do: *How do I honor God when life won't slow down?*

Here's my answer: I do everything in my power to plan around it. I say no more often than I say yes. I try to protect my Saturdays. But when that's not possible, I get creative and deliberate. If I have to work on Saturday, I take Sunday as my Sabbath. If both days are booked and filled with travel or obligations, I plan ahead to block off the following weekend for extended rest—phone off, no emails, no output. I double down. I lean into it.

Nowhere in this book am I calling you to legalism. The goal isn't a rigid formula—it's a reordered life. I'm not trying to burden you with guilt; I'm trying to provoke you to hunger. As the apostle Paul wrote, *"I magnify my ministry in order somehow to make my fellow Jews jealous, and thus save some of them"* (Romans 11:13–14). I want you to become jealous for peace. Jealous for balance and freedom. Jealous for communion with God.

Jesus Himself said, *"The Sabbath was made for man, not man for the Sabbath"* (Mark 2:27). The Sabbath is a gift—a divine invitation, not a chain. It is not meant to shame you into rest, but to awaken you to how much you've been missing.

Just because you can't rest every weekend doesn't mean you abandon the pursuit altogether. The goal is not perfection, but pursuit. Think of Sabbath not as an all-or-nothing practice, but as a rhythm of renewal you fiercely prioritize. Even if you can only guard one weekend a month, or one evening a week, build your life around sacred pauses. Your soul and your family need that space more than you realize.

The point is this: Don't let what you *can't* do keep you from doing what you *can*. The modern world will take every minute you give it. But God gives something back—something infinitely more valuable: stillness, clarity, joy, perspective. That's what Sabbath holds in its hands. So even in your busiest seasons, fight for rest. Rearrange. Reclaim. Receive the gift.

And remember: Your Sabbath is not just about you. It is not a private act of self-care, but a public declaration of allegiance to a different kingdom. In a culture drunk on exhaustion, your refusal to live at a frantic pace is a form of protest. Your rest says, *God is my provider. I do not have to earn my worth. I am not owned by the clock or controlled by the crowd.*

You are also teaching your family something profound. Every time you pause your productivity and make room for stillness, you are discipling your children. You are showing them that faith isn't confined to church pews but is woven into time itself. You are offering them a theology of rhythm; a vision of life that includes both labor and rest, effort and peace.

One day, your children will tell their children how you lived. What will they say? That you were always busy, always stressed, always distracted? Or will they say, *"My father knew how to stop. My mother knew how to delight. They made time for joy. They protected space for God."*

That's the legacy Sabbath helps build—not just one of rest, but of witness. In a world that never stops, be the person who knows how to stop well. Not because you're lazy, but because you trust the Lord of time more than the tyranny of hustle. That's Sabbath. That's freedom. That's worship.

"There are just too many distractions, and I'm going to miss out. I can't be without my phone."

The first part of this objection I completely agree with—yes, there are *too many* distractions in the world. According to recent data from Asurion, the average American checks their phone **more than 350 times daily**—or once every 2 minutes and 43 seconds. So yes, you are living in a whirlwind of digital noise.

If you're young, single, or socially active, your options at any given moment are endless: going out, streaming the latest show, playing video games, scrolling on TikTok, swiping through dating apps, binging sports highlights, checking news alerts, shopping online, or jumping into the latest Twitter/X debate. But none of these distractions are neutral. Over time, they rewire our minds toward reaction, overstimulation, and instant gratification.

But here's the good news: The Sabbath was never meant to cancel your joy—it's meant to sanctify it. God didn't tell you to become somber and bored for twenty-four hours. He's not anti-laughter, anti-celebration, or anti-fun. He simply wants to reorient our joy to what lasts. The Sabbath is the space where delight is deepened, not dulled.

If the fear is, *"I'll miss out,"* ask yourself, "Miss out on what?" The group chat meme you'll forget tomorrow? The Instagram post that will be buried in twenty-four hours? The news alert that someone will summarize for you later anyway? FOMO—fear of missing out—is not a reason to stay tethered to a device. It's a modern form of spiritual anxiety. And Sabbath is its cure.

So, try something radical. When you host a Shabbat dinner, ask your friends to drop their phones into a basket at the door. Let them know: *This space is sacred—free from pings, scrolls, and distractions.* At Shabbat dinner, let conversation flow without interruption. You'll be astonished by the result. People open up. They linger longer. They laugh more. Eye contact returns. There's a warmth that screens simply can't manufacture. It feels like recovering a lost treasure.

Instead of constantly looking down and checking texts, alerts, and notifications, try creating sacred boundaries. Set the tone:

"For this meal, this night, we are going analog." If someone needs to check their phone, they can do it outside. Inside, the table is a sanctuary—a phone-free zone. What you will witness will surprise you: deeper eye contact, more laughter, vulnerability, even silence that isn't awkward, but sacred. Your friendships will feel richer. You'll enter a kind of time capsule—a restoration of what we once had before the tyranny of the glowing screen took over every idle second.

The truth is, your fear of missing out is not rooted in joy—it's rooted in anxiety. The group chat will survive without you for a night. The meme will still be there tomorrow. And whatever crisis Twitter/X is panicking over won't be solved by your attention. But what *won't* wait forever is the relationship you're in, the soul you're losing, the God you're ignoring.

We've been conditioned to believe that our worth is tied to our availability, our output, our visibility. But Sabbath teaches us that your value is not measured by your responsiveness or productivity. It's measured by your belonging—your rootedness in God's love.

When you power down your phone, you're not "missing out"—you're stepping in. You're entering a different kind of time, what the rabbis call *"sacred time."* Time that doesn't drain you, but restores you. Time that doesn't demand from you, but blesses you. You begin to see things more clearly—your thoughts settle, your heart slows, your conversations deepen. And most importantly, you remember who you are apart from the endless stream of noise.

Sabbath isn't anti-technology—it's just anti-tyranny. It's not a rejection of connection, but a reclamation of *real* connection. So don't be afraid to turn off your phone. You're not falling behind—

you're catching up to what matters most. The people in front of you. The presence of God. The peace you've been craving.

Let the Sabbath be your weekly rebellion. Let it be the time when the world's demands go silent, and the eternal voice becomes audible again.

Let me show you how.

Chapter 12

SABBATH MADE SIMPLE

So, these are some of the most popular excuses I receive, and now I want to prescribe ten immediate action items that you can take THIS WEEK to include the Sabbath into your life.

Honoring the Sabbath does not always require monumental lifestyle shifts or grand gestures. For many, it begins with small, intentional changes—conscious choices to pause, reflect, and reconnect with what truly matters. Each of these ten practices is simple, flexible, and rooted in the spirit of rest and renewal.

1. Create a "Sabbath Start" Ritual

Every sacred rhythm benefits from a clear beginning. One of the most powerful ways to mark the start of your Sabbath is through a consistent ritual. This could be as simple as lighting a candle, saying a short prayer, or playing a specific piece of music. The goal is not performance, but presence.

When you do something physical to welcome Sabbath, it signals to your heart and body that this time is set apart. In the Jewish tradition, lighting candles before sunset on Friday evening is a long-standing practice that transforms the ordinary into the sacred. You can adapt this in your own way—light a candle, breathe deeply, or say aloud, “This is my Sabbath, and it begins now.”

This moment becomes a threshold. Your mind may still race from the workweek, but your ritual invites your soul to slow down. Over time, your body will begin to recognize this signal as an entry point into rest, making it easier to release stress and lean into the stillness that Sabbath offers. Whether practiced alone or with others, this small act becomes a doorway into something eternal.

2. Turn Off Your Phone for Twenty-Four Hours (Start with Four to Six if Needed)

Few things destroy Sabbath more effectively than the constant ping of a smartphone. The modern world has trained us to react instantly, to respond immediately, and to be always available. But Sabbath dares us to disconnect—not as a rejection of others, but as a return to ourselves and to God.

The bold goal is to turn off your phone for the full twenty-four hours of your Sabbath. If that feels overwhelming, begin by choosing a four- to six-hour window where your phone is powered off and out of sight. Place it in a drawer, a closet, or a designated “Sabbath box.” Tell your friends or coworkers in advance if you’re concerned about urgent communication. Then, let it go.

In those first few hours, you may feel anxious. Your hand will reflexively reach for a device that isn’t there. But stay with it. What feels like withdrawal at first is actually detox. And soon, you’ll discover a stillness you didn’t know you needed.

In the absence of notifications, your thoughts become clearer. Your conversations deepen. You notice things: the sound of birds, the flicker of candlelight, the feel of a warm mug in your hands. This is presence—the foundation of rest. And this small digital fast may very well become your favorite part of the week.

3. Plan Screen-Free Meals with Friends or Family

Food is one of the great unifiers of humanity. And when shared in the spirit of Sabbath, a simple meal becomes a sacred gathering. One of the most transformative Sabbath practices you can begin is hosting a screen-free meal with family, friends, or neighbors.

Pick a time—Friday evening, Saturday brunch, Sunday lunch—and set the expectation clearly: No phones at the table. Create a physical boundary by placing a bowl or basket near the door. Invite guests to drop their devices inside before entering the dining space. You'll be amazed by the shift in atmosphere.

Without screens, people linger longer. Conversations stretch and deepen. Laughter becomes contagious. Eye-to-eye contact brings connection. The act of eating together becomes more than nourishment; it becomes communion.

You don't need fancy recipes or Pinterest-perfect decor. In fact, simplicity honors the spirit of Sabbath. The goal is not to impress, but to connect. Bless the food, give thanks for the people around the table, and savor each bite without distraction.

This meal can be a weekly anchor—a moment of joy that shapes the rhythm of your life. Over time, your guests will begin to associate your table with peace, presence, and the kind of rest that lingers in the soul.

4. Take a Slow Walk in Nature

God built creation before He built a cathedral. The first temple was a garden, and it still preaches. A slow walk in nature on the Sabbath—without earbuds or a destination—is one of the most powerful ways to reconnect to God's voice. This isn't exercise. This is worship through wonder.

Choose a trail, a quiet neighborhood, or even your backyard. Don't time it. Don't treat it like cardio. Just observe. Look at the patterns on leaves, the movement of clouds, the way light lands on water. Nature invites your soul to match its unhurried pace.

This is how you recalibrate. The modern world teaches you to rush, to push, to hustle. But trees don't hustle. Rivers don't rush. Birds don't multitask. When you walk slowly through creation, you're submitting to a deeper rhythm—the one God Himself embedded into the world.

You'll return from that walk with more clarity, more calm, and often, more gratitude. The world doesn't need another sprinting soul. It needs people rooted like trees beside still waters. Sabbath invites you to become one of them.

5. Curate a Sabbath Basket or Shelf

One of the most practical and joyful things you can do is create a physical "Sabbath basket" or shelf. Fill it with items that bring peace, beauty, and renewal: a favorite book, a well-loved Bible, a journal, a sketch pad, a poem, candles, herbal tea, or even a small instrument. The idea is simple: When Sabbath begins, you reach for this space—not your inbox.

This practice makes Sabbath tangible. It creates boundaries

without becoming rigid. It reminds you that this day is *different*, and that difference is good.

Let your children make their own Sabbath boxes, too. Fill them with quiet toys, crafts, picture books, or puzzles they only use on that day. Over time, these items take on special meaning. They become sacred objects—not because of their function, but because of the time they represent.

You can even add index cards with quotes or Scriptures that calm your spirit. What's important is not what's in the basket, but what it displaces. It's a preplanned act of joy. The Sabbath is meant to be remembered and delighted in. Having a set-apart basket says, "I've prepared for this rest. I'm ready for joy."

6. Write a Gratitude List at the End of the Day

The Sabbath is meant to end with as much intention as it begins. One of the most soul-shaping ways to close the day is by writing a short gratitude list. Take ten minutes before bed and reflect: What filled me with joy today? What moments stood out? Where did I sense God's peace?

Write down five things—big or small. A warm cup of tea. A surprising conversation. A deeper rest than usual. The more you do this, the more your eyes will open throughout the day to notice what you'll later write down.

Gratitude is not just a posture—it's a spiritual discipline. It reorients your mind away from scarcity and complaint, and toward abundance and contentment. Sabbath is about remembering what's true, and gratitude is how we anchor that truth into our memory.

Over time, your gratitude lists will become a record of God's faithfulness. A weekly chronicle of joy. A reminder that the Sabbath is not a passive day, but a treasure chest of moments that God has prepared in advance for you to receive.

7. Say No to One Nonessential Task Each Sabbath

The world constantly demands more from you—emails, errands, laundry, bills, projects. But on the Sabbath, you have divine permission to say no. Begin simply: Identify one nonessential task you normally do on your day off and choose to *not* do it. That act of refusal—of resistance—is sacred.

It might be responding to messages, scrolling the news, grocery shopping, or catching up on chores. These things can wait. The Sabbath is not about productivity—it's about peace. And that peace is impossible without boundaries.

Each no you say on Sabbath is a yes to something higher: rest, worship, connection, joy. You'll find that protecting space—just one task at a time—begins to create a buffer around your soul. It's not about laziness; it's about realignment.

Over time, saying no on Sabbath becomes easier. You'll start anticipating the relief it brings. And surprisingly, nothing falls apart when you stop for a day. The bills get paid. The emails wait. The world keeps spinning. And you? You breathe again.

8. Try a "Sabbath Soundtrack"

Music has a unique way of shaping atmosphere, settling the heart, and signaling a shift in pace. One beautiful way to usher in the Sabbath is by curating a specific playlist—a "Sabbath soundtrack" that plays only during your day of rest. Whether it's peaceful instrumental, sacred hymns, slow jazz, or ambient nature sounds, music can become a holy cue for your soul to slow down.

Start the playlist at the same time each week—maybe during your candle-lighting ritual or first cup of coffee. Let the first few notes signal that this day is different. That it's not for hustling, scrolling, or planning—but for receiving, listening, and delighting.

Play this music while you make breakfast, walk through your home, or lie in stillness. It transforms the environment. You'll find your breathing slows, your anxiety lifts, and your awareness sharpens.

Make it a tradition. Let your children or spouse contribute to the playlist. Soon, those melodies will become familiar and comforting—like the sound of Sabbath itself. In a noisy world, a Sabbath soundtrack is a gentle act of rebellion. You don't need to fill every moment with commentary—just beauty. And music is beauty that speaks even when we can't.

9. Read One Psalm Every Sabbath

The Psalms are the Bible's songbook, prayer book, and emotional journal—all in one. They give voice to joy, sorrow, anger, peace, and awe. Reading just one psalm each Sabbath can connect you to generations of believers who've poured their hearts out to God through these ancient words.

This is not a Bible study. You don't need to analyze or dissect. You're not reading for output—you're reading for encounter. Sit with the psalm slowly. Read it aloud. Read it twice. Let a word or phrase stand out and stay with you.

Ask yourself: What does this reveal about God? What does it stir in me? What do I need to hear today?

You might choose a psalm at random, follow a schedule, or return to the same one for a few weeks. Over time, you'll build a sacred rhythm—a gentle dialogue between your soul and the Word. You may find the psalms start echoing in your week, showing up in moments of joy or need.

This is what the Sabbath is for: Reconnecting with what's eternal. One psalm at a time, you quiet the static and tune your soul to God's voice. No pressure, just presence.

10. Establish a "Digital Sunset" Time Weekly

Instead of just turning off your phone on Sabbath morning, try establishing a "digital sunset"—a consistent time the night before where you shut down devices and begin to transition into rest. Much like the biblical pattern of days beginning at sundown *("and there was evening and there was morning"*), a digital sunset allows you to prepare your mind and body for Sabbath well before it starts.

Pick a time—6 p.m., 7 p.m., whenever makes sense—and stick to it. Put your phone in a drawer, log out of your laptop, turn off the TV. Light a candle, dim the lights, and let the digital world fade. You're not escaping reality—you're entering a better one.

This creates anticipation. It honors the Sabbath as something to be *entered into*, not stumbled into by accident.

Use this time for quiet preparation: Clean the kitchen, set out your Sabbath basket, pray with your spouse or children. The goal isn't perfection—it's transition. A digital sunset makes Sabbath feel like an arrival, not an interruption.

In a culture that never stops glowing, this one act can become a source of renewal for your entire week. Let the sun go down on your screens so the light of rest can rise.

Everything you've read in this chapter—every practice, every suggestion—is just a starting point. None of it truly matters unless you grasp the *why* behind the Sabbath. Without the heart, the habit is hollow. You can light the candles, turn off your phone, walk in nature, or read the Psalms—but if you miss the deeper meaning, you've only brushed the surface of something cosmic.

Let me be clear: The Sabbath is good for *everyone*. Even if you're not a believer, even if you're skeptical about God, even if you're just burned out and looking for peace—this rhythm of rest will begin to heal you. I've said this many times throughout this book: The Sabbath is not just for the religious, it is for the *human*. It is the original human rhythm. The world was made to breathe once every seven days—and so were you.

But rest, without reverence, eventually becomes routine. And routine without revelation becomes dull.

Sabbath is not just a day off. It is not self-care. It is not spiritualized leisure. It is a sacred act of resistance against the gods of busyness, performance, and distraction. When you keep Sabbath, you are aligning yourself with something eternal. You are participating in something your Creator did—not because He was tired, but because He was finished.

Think about that.

God created the heavens and the earth in six days—and then *He stopped*. Not because He ran out of energy, but because the work was complete, and it was *very good*. And then He blessed the seventh day—not the first, not the sixth—the seventh. He hallowed time itself. The Sabbath is not just something God told us to do—it's something He Himself *did*. Every time you observe it, you are joining Him in that rest.

What other practice gives you this kind of dignity? What other rhythm lets you imitate the Lord of the universe? It should bring you to your knees in awe. That the same God who knit galaxies into place invites you to stop working, stop producing, stop striving—and just *be* with Him, once every seven days.

It is in that stopping that we begin to see clearly. Our work is not our worth. Our screens are not our sanctuary. Our pace is not our purpose. The Sabbath recalibrates all of it. It breaks the illusion that the world depends on you, and reminds you who really holds it together.

So, yes—walk in the woods, unplug your phone, eat long meals, laugh with your kids, sing songs, sleep deeply, read slowly. But above all, do it with reverence. Do it with joy. Do it with the awareness that you are stepping into the same rhythm that shaped creation itself.

That alone—knowing that each seventh day echoes the very first one—should stop you in your tracks with wonder.

Honor the Sabbath, and you won't just find rest.

You'll find yourself.

And even more—you'll find God waiting for you there.

Shalom

How does one find peace in this ever-busy world?

We do not wake to silence anymore. We wake to buzzes, alarms, urgent banners, breaking news, and to-do lists that seem to multiply overnight. From the moment our feet touch the floor, we are pressed into motion, shoved into efficiency. The hum of artificial urgency surrounds us—emails to respond to, headlines to fear, errands to run, expectations to meet. Rest has become a rare and endangered rhythm.

Even our attempts at escape are noisy. We scroll instead of still. We binge instead of breathe. We flee to entertainment, to caffeine, to noise—anything but stillness. Our minds are restless, addicted to input. Our souls are like cities that never sleep; illuminated but weary, crowded but lonely.

And yet—hidden in the soil of Scripture, older than empire, and louder than static—is a word that pulses with another rhythm: **shalom**. Not just peace as modern minds define it—absence of war or momentary calm—but something weightier, richer, more ancient. It is wholeness. It is harmony. It is the sense that things are as they should be. Shalom is not escape; it is return. It is not a nap; it is restoration. It is not time off; it is sacred presence.

What if, instead of frantically chasing relief, we pursued what Scripture calls *peace*—a real, soul-deep, God-given peace that does not vanish with the closing of an app or the completion of a task?

"Shabbat shalom" is the traditional greeting exchanged by Jews on the Sabbath. It means "Sabbath peace," but its meaning runs deeper than a simple "have a nice day." It is a blessing. A reminder. A declaration. Shalom is not just the absence of conflict—it is the presence of wholeness, rest, harmony, and divine order. To wish someone Shabbat shalom is to say, *"May you enter into the fullness of God's rest."*

The roots of this peace reach back to the oldest parts of our sacred text. In the book of Numbers, the priestly blessing ends with a plea for peace: *"The Lord lift up his countenance upon you and give you peace*" (Numbers 6:26). This very passage was discovered inscribed on two tiny silver scrolls found in a burial cave near Jerusalem, dating to the seventh century BCE—making it the **oldest fragment of Scripture ever found**.

That discovery is not just archeologically remarkable—it is theologically profound. It proves the reliability of Scripture and confirms that the pursuit of shalom has always been central to the life God invites us into. Long before modern chaos, long before smartphones or schedules, the people of God were praying for and speaking peace. Not temporary relief—but enduring, divine stillness.

The priestly blessing in Numbers 6:24–26 is one of Scripture's most beautiful prayers:

> *"The Lord bless you and keep you; the Lord make his face to shine upon you and be gracious to you; the Lord lift up his countenance upon you and give you peace."*

This blessing does not call for mere ease or convenience—it invokes the radiance of God's face and the protective presence of His love. To receive God's shalom is to be held, shielded, illuminated, and delighted in.

If you want to know whether you've tasted Shabbat shalom, try this simple test: Can you sit on a park bench, without your phone, for one full hour, in joy—just soaking in the moment? Very few people I know can pass this test. It's difficult. We're addicted to stimulation, to scrolling, to tasks. But Shabbat shalom dares us to stop. To disconnect. To be still and know that He is God (Psalm 46:10).

Being still—and *knowing* God—is among the hardest spiritual disciplines in today's whirlwind of inputs and demands. And yet, ironically, this stillness is not inactivity—it is receptivity. It is posture. It is attentiveness to heaven. Yes, it risks sounding like something from the East. But maybe Christians should recover the ancient Hebrew practice of contemplative stillness before God—not as an escape, but as a return. A homecoming. A breath.

You don't need a worship band, a sermon, or even a Bible in hand. You need a quiet soul, a surrendered heart, and a willingness to let God love you. Breathe. Listen. Let His presence meet you like morning dew. I know, I know—I sound like a hippie. But this might be one of the highest levels of Christian ascent: stillness in the splendor of the Creator.

And we know it's biblical—because Jesus Himself lived this rhythm. He regularly withdrew to solitary places to pray. Consider these:

- **Matthew 14:23:** *"After he had dismissed the crowds, he went up on the mountain by himself to pray."*
- **Mark 1:35:** *"Rising very early in the morning, while it was still dark, he departed and went out to a desolate place, and there he prayed."*
- **Luke 5:16:** *"But he would withdraw to desolate places and pray."*
- **Luke 6:12:** *"In these days he went out to the mountain to pray, and all night he continued in prayer to God."*
- **Matthew 26:36–37:** *"Then Jesus went with them to a place called Gethsemane, and . . . began to be sorrowful and troubled."*

Jesus—our Lord—carved out space to be alone with the Father. Not because He needed to be productive, but because He needed *peace*.

The Gospels do not merely show Jesus as a teacher of peace; they reveal Him as its very embodiment. Isaiah 9:6 foretold His coming with the words: *"For to us a child is born, to us a son is given . . . and his name shall be called Wonderful Counselor, Mighty God, Everlasting Father, Prince of Peace."* The Hebrew phrase *Sar Shalom*—Prince of Peace—means He is the ruler and author of true shalom.

When the angels announced His birth, they proclaimed, *"Glory to God in the highest, and on earth peace among those with whom he is pleased!"* (Luke 2:14). His arrival marked not only divine intervention, but divine reconciliation—a heavenly peace offered to a fractured world.

Jesus' ministry was full of peacemaking moments. He healed not just bodies, but hearts. He calmed storms—externally on the Sea of Galilee, and internally in the lives of those tormented by fear. We read in Mark 5, when the woman with the issue of blood reached out and touched His garment, He did not just heal her physically. He said, *"Daughter, your faith has made you well; go in peace, and be healed of your disease"* (Mark 5:34). She walked away with more than health—she walked away with shalom.

In John 14:27, we see that Jesus comforts His disciples before His death: *"Peace I leave with you; my peace I give to you. Not as the world gives do I give to you. Let not your hearts be troubled, neither let them be afraid."* Notice the distinction—this is not circumstantial peace. It is not tied to politics, economy, or health. It is a Person's peace. It is Christ's own serenity, stability, and security handed directly to His followers.

And this is not abstract doctrine—it is deeply experiential. Romans 5:1 declares, *"Therefore, since we have been justified by faith, we have peace with God through our Lord Jesus Christ."* The deepest unrest in human history—the breach between God and man—has been mended by the blood of Christ. The veil was torn, the hostility slain, and now we stand in grace.

This is why Paul can say in Philippians 4:7, *"And the peace of God, which surpasses all understanding, will guard your hearts and your minds in Christ Jesus."* This peace is not a tranquilizer—it is a fortress. It is not a soft breeze—it is a shield.

And He doesn't just give peace in the abstract—He *brings* it personally. After His resurrection, the first words out of Jesus' mouth to His stunned, hiding disciples were not rebuke, but comfort: *"Peace be with you"* (John 20:19). He said it again just moments later, doubling the blessing: *"Peace be with you. As the Father has sent me, even so I am sending you"* (John 20:21).

Even now, Jesus intercedes for us (Romans 8:34; Hebrews 7:25), and His ongoing ministry is one of securing and applying peace to our lives—peace with God, peace within ourselves, peace among one another.

To be in Christ is to be in peace. And to follow Him is to walk the narrow road that leads to shalom. Jesus did not promise the absence of trouble—He promised His presence in it: *"I have said these things to you, that in me you may have peace. In the world you will have tribulation. But take heart; I have overcome the world"* (John 16:33).

So if we are in turmoil, we must look not for escape, but for Emmanuel. If we are restless, we do not need silence—we need the Shepherd who leads us beside still waters (Psalm 23:2). If we are broken, we do not need anesthesia—we need the Prince of Peace who comes bearing healing in His wings (Malachi 4:2).

This peace is offered freely. It is not earned. It is not merited. It is received by faith. As Colossians 3:15 urges, *"And let the peace of*

Christ rule in your hearts, to which indeed you were called in one body." His peace is not a guest—it wants to reign. It wants to govern. It wants to hold sway over every anxiety and every competing voice.

To truly experience Shabbat shalom is to come into contact not just with an idea, but with a Person. It is to rest in Christ, to delight in His sufficiency, and to welcome His nearness like the cool shade of a tree on a blazing day. He is the source, the center, and the substance of our peace.

This **shalom** that we speak of is fundamentally different from the peace promised by Buddhism or Eastern meditation. Eastern philosophy often centers on detachment: emptying the mind, suppressing desire, dissolving the ego. The goal is often nirvana, a state beyond pain, beyond self, beyond the world. To achieve this, practitioners are taught to empty their thoughts and embrace nothingness.

But biblical shalom is not about detachment—it is about **connection**. It is not the loss of self, but the healing and restoration of self. God does not ask us to disappear into a void, but to be **known**, **loved**, and **transformed** in His presence.

Where Eastern meditation invites you to silence your longings, Scripture invites you to **bring them to God**:

> "*Cast all your anxiety on him because he cares for you*" (1 Peter 5:7 NIV).

Where the East tells you to let go of your identity, the gospel tells you this:

> "*See what kind of love the Father has given to us, that we should be called children of God; and so we are*" (1 John 3:1).

Eastern practice says, "Empty." The Bible says, ***"Be filled with the Spirit"*** (Ephesians 5:18).

We are not trying to reach a blank state; we are being filled with the radiant glory of God. We meditate not to escape the world, but to see it clearly through God's eyes. We do not erase suffering—we bring it to the Healer. We do not seek peace by numbing ourselves—we find it by surrendering ourselves.

This is why Psalm 131 is so powerful:

> *"But I have calmed and quieted my soul, like a weaned child with its mother; like a weaned child is my soul within me."*

Shalom is not empty. It's safe. It's still. It's full of love.

So on the Sabbath, set aside just twenty minutes to be with God. Let the world wait. Let the inbox pile up. Go outside and dwell. Feel the air. Hear the birdsong. Watch a squirrel chase a leaf. Sit under a tree and notice its stillness. Watch a child's face at play. Gaze at a sunset, not to post it—but to praise it. See the world not as a utility, but as a *gift*.

You are celebrating the creation of the world on Shabbat—so go delight in it.

Watch the clouds drift in silent procession like angels marching. Smell the fragrance of the breeze as it stirs through pine. Touch the grass and remember that man was formed from earth. Taste the sweetness of Sabbath bread and recall the manna. Let the hush of twilight remind you that time is holy.

And when you do, you may find that peace has a name. That shalom is not a concept, but a Person. That rest is not a technique, but a promise.

He Is Our Peace

He doesn't just *offer* peace. He is peace.

In Ephesians 2:14, Paul writes, *"For he himself is our peace."* Not our productivity. Not our circumstances. Not even our quiet time. Christ Himself.

He is the one who speaks, *"Peace! Be still!"* to the storm (Mark 4:39). He is the one who enters locked rooms and says, *"Peace be with you"* (John 20:19). He is the one who says, *"Come to me, all who labor and are heavy laden, and I will give you rest"* (Matthew 11:28).

We live in a world of fractured minds, anxious hearts, and endless motion. But Sabbath is our rebellion. Our resistance. Our return. It is the declaration that *we are not slaves*, not to Egypt, not to Pharaoh, not to modernity. We are free people. And free people rest.

So as the sun sets, light a candle. Breathe. Turn off your phone. Speak a blessing over your home. Smile without agenda. And say the words the people of God have said for generations:

Shabbat shalom.

Not just a greeting. A way of life.

Chapter 13

CONCLUSION

Throughout this book, we have laid out a robust case for why the Sabbath can truly transform your life—not as a burdensome rule, but as a lifeline of renewal. In a culture addicted to motion and noise, turning off your phone, quitting the scrolling, silencing Netflix, and stepping away from the endless stream of notifications is nothing short of radical. The Sabbath is not passive; it is a form of resistance. It is a rebellion against the idol of productivity and the tyranny of busyness. To keep the Sabbath is to declare, boldly and counterculturally, "I am not a machine. I am not defined by what I produce. I am a soul, created by God, made for rest, worship, and communion." In a world that rewards exhaustion, the Sabbath invites us back to Eden—to simplicity, to stillness, and to sacred time set apart.

Now, imagine if America began to honor the Sabbath again—not merely as a personal spiritual practice, but as a national cultural rhythm.

Picture Saturday (or Sundays) once again becoming a time of collective pause, when commerce slows, screens dim, and the frenetic pace of life yields to presence, prayer, and family. Children would grow up with memories of meals shared, not just moments scrolled. Future generations would know that, for one day a week, you prioritize rest, family, friends, and God. Marriages would regain time for conversation and connection. Churches would be filled, not because of cultural obligation, but because of spiritual hunger. Rates of depression and anxiety would decline—not magically, but meaningfully—because the soul needs rest to thrive. Loneliness, that silent epidemic of our age, would finally be confronted, not with more digital "friends," but with real-life fellowship and shared sacred space. Our frayed, fractured society would begin to knit itself back together, not through government programs or corporate initiatives, but through God's design: one day in seven, set apart for healing, remembering, and being human again.

The entire week would once again be centered around the holy, the divine, the beautiful, and the sacred. Our nation would regain a core—a moral and spiritual center—that anchors it against the relentless pull of the digital age and the constant erosion of meaning.

Imagine a culture where everything flowed outward from one sacred day—a day not of consumption, but of contemplation; not of distraction, but of devotion. The rhythms of our work, our education, our politics, and even our entertainment would all be shaped by a higher order. Families would orient their schedules around togetherness. Communities would rediscover their churches not as optional gatherings, but as essential lifelines. Even the most secular among us would feel the gravitational force of reverence returning to the center of our lives. The Sabbath would become not just a private act of worship, but a public act of restoration—a weekly declaration that there is something higher than productivity, more beautiful than efficiency, more worthy than the algorithm. And slowly, the soul of our nation—tired, frayed, and divided—could begin to heal. Not through politics. Not through noise. But through stillness and sacred time.

When I was growing up, I used to sprain my ankle frequently. Sometimes it would prevent me from playing basketball, which drove me crazy. The doctor would always tell me, "Only time will solve it—you need to let it heal." Our adherence to the Sabbath is not so different. We can throw money, therapists, cold plunges, saunas, red light therapy, supplements, IV drips, and meditation apps at our problems—but fundamentally, what we need to do is stop and allow our wounds to heal.

We are not designed to operate at the pace we're currently going—and let me be very clear: It's only going to get worse. The screens are getting closer. The noise is getting louder. The technology is becoming smarter, faster, and more addictive. We are stepping into a future where artificial intelligence will know you better than you know yourself. It will finish your sentences, anticipate your cravings, tell you when to sleep, and even suggest what to believe. It will organize your calendar, manage your inbox, write your papers, select your music, and eventually even raise your children—unless you push back. The days of you being able to think for yourself are coming to an end. Your capacity to be a sovereign, conscious being will fade—unless you mightily resist the pull by forcibly unplugging.

AI is not coming—it's here. And with it comes a strange paradox: We have never been more "connected," yet never more detached from what matters. With every technological "leap," we grow more efficient but less human. More informed, but less wise. We scroll past sunsets. We forget our neighbors' names. We ignore the sound of silence because we've trained our minds to fear boredom and our hearts to fear stillness. And now, we're being told the next frontier is to merge with the machine—to upload, enhance, and accelerate.

But here's the question no one seems to be asking: *At what cost?*

We are quickly approaching a moment when attention will be the rarest commodity on earth. Not oil. Not gold. Not even data. Pure, uninterrupted human attention. The ability to be fully present—to look someone in the eyes without glancing down at a screen, to hear God's voice without a notification dinging in your pocket, to play with your kids without the tug of an email or algorithm whispering your name—that will be the new luxury. And unless we build a discipline around guarding it, we will lose it entirely.

Enter the Sabbath.

The Sabbath is not just a nice idea. It's not just a rest day for the religious or the nostalgic. The Sabbath is God's answer to a culture spinning out of control. It is His ancient rhythm of sanity, planted like an anchor in a world swept away by currents of chaos. Six days we work, build, create, engage. On the seventh day, we stop—but not because we're weak. We stop because we're human. We don't rest because we're lazy. We rest because we're obedient.

The Sabbath is God's resistance against the machine. It is His weekly reminder that your worth is not in your productivity, that your soul cannot be sustained by screens, and that your body was made not just for motion—but for stillness, reflection, and worship. You weren't made to go 24/7. You weren't created to be reachable at all hours, flooded by headlines, marketing emails, and the endless scroll of digital noise.

The coming age will promise "freedom" through technology, but what it will actually deliver is exhaustion and enslavement. Everything will be on demand. Everything will be customizable.

But you will be so busy, so overstimulated, so mentally fragmented that you won't even remember what silence sounds like. You won't know what it's like to sit with your own thoughts without outsourcing them to an app, or to read Scripture without checking your phone halfway through.

The Sabbath cuts through that fog. It calls us back. It rehumanizes us.

In a world that relentlessly blurs the line between man and machine—where you're valued for how fast you respond, how much you produce, and how constantly you engage—the Sabbath stands as a divine interruption. It slices through the mental clutter and soul-numbing routine with a clear and holy command: *Stop.* The fog of modern life—saturated with headlines, pings, algorithms, and artificial urgency—dulls our senses and fractures our attention. But the Sabbath clears the air. It gives us back our sight. It reminds us that we are not gears in an economic machine or data points in a tech ecosystem. We are image-bearers of God, called not just to labor, but to rest, reflect, worship, and *be.*

Rehumanization begins with recovery—of time, of purpose, of presence. On the Sabbath, we put away the tools of the world and return to what makes us fully alive: conversation, prayer, laughter, stillness, song. We recover our capacity to listen without distraction, to observe beauty without rushing, to touch heaven without needing a screen. The Sabbath doesn't just give us time off; it restores our true identity. It takes us out of the fog of performance and back into the light of grace. It tells us again, week after week, that we are more than what we do—we are beloved children of God, made to delight in Him, and to be fully human once more.

For one day a week, we unplug so we can reconnect. We say no to the tyranny of the urgent so we can say yes to what's eternal. We eat slowly. We speak face to face. We listen—*really* listen. We sing. We pray. We remember. We become rooted again. And here's the crazy part—it's all free. The Sabbath doesn't cost you a dime. But it might just save your life.

Because if we don't draw the line now, where does it end? Do we wait until we're wearing goggles to church? Until our children only know their grandparents through a screen? Until human relationships are seen as inefficient, unpredictable, and optional?

What happens when presence becomes outdated? When algorithms manage our friendships, AI filters our sermons, and our homes are filled with machines that respond faster than our spouses? We are already outsourcing the sacred—outsourcing conversation to text, connection to apps, reflection to curated content. The more we digitize our lives, the more we desensitize our souls. And slowly, almost imperceptibly, we trade communion for convenience, intimacy for automation, the holy for the high tech. If we do not fight now for sacred space and real presence, we will wake up one day and discover we have lost what made us human—and worse, that we surrendered it willingly.

The Sabbath is the line. It is the place where we say, *"Enough."* We will not sacrifice wonder on the altar of efficiency. We will not hand over our families to screens or let technology parent our children. We will not allow worship to become another background task. The Sabbath reclaims one day from the machine and gives it back to God. It teaches our children that there is something better than constant entertainment, something more meaningful than digital connection. If we do not draw that line boldly and consistently, we are not just compromising our future—we are forfeiting it. The Sabbath is our chance to say, "This far, no farther."

We need boundaries. Sacred space. Sacred time. God gave us

both. He didn't just give us rules to restrict us—He gave us rhythms to *restore* us. The Sabbath is not a prison—it's a gift. In a world trying to make you more like a machine, the Sabbath reminds you that you are made in the image of God.

So while the world keeps sprinting, downloading, upgrading, and merging, let the people of God be the ones who pause. Who breathe. Who say, "This day belongs to the Lord." Let us be the ones who shut it all down—not out of fear, but out of faith. Not because we reject progress, but because we know that without margin, progress becomes a god—and gods without grace always destroy.

None of this is an abstraction. You can make the definitive choice to follow the mold of how God designed you. Failing to honor the Sabbath is, quietly, to wage war on your own design—and the consequences of that are all around us.

I personally have been transformed by adhering to this ancient practice—this gift from God. Knowing about the Sabbath is helpful, but limited, if you don't apply it in your life. The gift of the Sabbath is right in front of you. Embrace it. Seize it. And my call to action for you is very clear:

Stop, in God's name.

ACKNOWLEDGMENTS

A big thanks to Winning Team Publishing, especially its founders Donald Trump Jr. and Sergio Gor, for your support with this book and my previous books.

My deep appreciation to all those who have supported me, Turning Point USA, and Turning Point Action. These organizations have become cultural and political juggernauts because of you.

I thank the staff at Turning Point USA and Turning Point Action for their relentless spirit and hard work. I appreciate every member of these teams and their contributions to these organizations.

I also want to thank the boards of directors of the Turning Point organizations. Their service and mentorship have been instrumental in my personal growth and our organizational success.

I thank Pastor Rob McCoy for his years of spiritual direction. Your guidance has helped shape who I am. And thank you Pastor David Engelhart for helping open my eyes to what it means to honor the Sabbath.

I thank my wife, Erika, for her unending love. She is an inspiration to me daily.

Finally, I thank God for blessing me in ways I never imagined. Everything I do is pointed toward Heaven and expressing gratitude for the salvation given to me by His only Son, Jesus Christ.